Critical Essays on Doris Lessing

Claire Sprague
and
Virginia Tiger

G. K. Hall & Co. • Boston, Massachusetts

The research for this book was supported in part by a grant from the City University of New York PSC/CUNY Research Award Program and the Rutgers University Graduate School at Newark. The authors also wish to thank Ingrid Mundari for her spirited tracking down of arcane bibliographical items.

Library of Congress Cataloging-in-Publication Data

Sprague, Claire.
   Critical essays on Doris Lessing.

   Bibliography: p. 225
   Includes index.
   1. Lessing, Doris May, 1919-   —Criticism and
interpretation—Addresses, essays, lectures. I. Tiger,
Virginia.   II. Title.
PR6023.E833Z896 1986   823'.914   85-27097

ISBN 0-8161-8756-8

This publication is printed on permanent durable acid-free paper
MANUFACTURED IN THE UNITED STATES OF AMERICA

CRITICAL ESSAYS ON MODERN BRITISH LITERATURE

This anthology breaks ground in a number of ways. The first collection of critical essays about Doris Lessing, with a historical overview of Lessing criticism, it has an innovative organizational design.

In their comprehensive introduction Claire Sprague, and Virginia Tiger, have given us a remarkably complete and lucid account of the more than thirty works that comprise the Lessing corpus. They begin with a brief assessment of Lessing's position in the literary world and a revealing discussion of Lessing's literary hoax in writing her last two novels under the pseudonym Jane Somers. They then present a chronological tour de force of Lessing's major works, pulling together the diverse strands of her novels into a concise and perceptive map of her evolving concerns.

Sprague and Tiger offer no mere encomium to Doris Lessing, but a balanced analysis, critical of Lessing's shortcomings and respectful of her triumphs. They then combine an analysis of the major Lessing scholarship with an explanation of the design of their book, which is divided into four rubrics. The first, "Politics and Patterns," counterpoints formal and thematic approaches to a prolific writer whose concerns have ranged from left-wing politics, feminism, race relations, and radical psychiatry to mysticism, science fiction, aging and dying, and terrorism. "Female (Other) Space" assembles essays illustrating an important critical controversy. Lessing "was early expropriated as a political symbol for what would become the feminist critique of literature, a critique whose historical development this section records." "Inner and Outer Space" is especially original in the application of the term "outer space" to non-galactic environments, to rooms, houses, and cities in Lessing's fiction.

The fourth and final section, "Reception and Reputation," demonstrates the range and perception of reviewers of Lessing's works and concludes with responses to her public appearances that speak eloquently to her uncompromising independence and her deserved place in the modern literary canon. The introduction and the articles that follow are timely and articulate, providing the first critical retrospective of Lessing and the critical issues she has generated as well as her place in modern literature. Sprague and Tiger have used the best of published criticism and include five major new critical pieces, principally papers delivered at Lessing sections of the Modern Language Association in the last several years, in this truly remarkable and comprehensive volume.

Zack Bowen, GENERAL EDITOR

University of Delaware

For our sons
Jesse Sprague and Sebastian Tiger

CONTENTS

INTRODUCTION   1
     Claire Sprague and Virginia Tiger

CHRONOLOGY   27
     Mona Knapp

POLITICS AND PATTERNS
     The Doom of Empire: *Memoirs of a Survivor*   31
         Martin Green
     Memory and Desire on Going Home:
         The Deconstruction of a Colonial Radical   37
         Jenny Taylor
     Doubles Talk in *The Golden Notebook*   44
         Claire Sprague
     The Marriages between Zones Three, Four,
         and Five: Doris Lessing's Alchemical Allegory   60
         Roberta Rubenstein

FEMALE (OTHER) SPACE
     Lessing and Lawrence: The Battle of the Sexes   69
         Mark Spilka
     "Woman of Many Summers":
         The Summer before the Dark   86
         Virginia Tiger
     Martha Quest and "The Anguish of
         Feminine Fragmentation"   94
         Jean Pickering
     The Golden Notebook: "Female Writing" and
         "The Great Tradition"   101
         Elizabeth Abel
     The Woman Writer as Exile: Gender and Possession in
         the African Stories of Doris Lessing   107
         Clare Hanson

INNER AND OUTER SPACE

"Disorderly Company": From *The Golden Notebook*
to *The Four-Gated City*   115
Dagmar Barnouw
Doris Lessing and R. D. Laing:
Psychopolitics and Prophecy   126
Marion Vlastos
Doris Lessing's *Città Felice*   141
Ellen Cronan Rose
Competing Codes in *Shikasta*   153
Betsy Draine

RECEPTION AND REPUTATION

The Grass Is Singing

Some Recent Fiction   171
Ernest Jones
The Grass Is Singing   171
Klad.

Children of Violence

Frustration on the Veldt   173
C. P. Snow
New Novels   174
Kingsley Amis
Last Children of Violence   174
Joyce Carol Oates

The Golden Notebook

Neither Compromise nor Happiness   177
Irving Howe
"An Interview with Adrienne Rich"   181
Elly Bulkin

On Several Novels

Doris Lessing: Cassandra in a
World under Siege   183
Margaret Drabble
And They All Lived Unhappily Ever After   191
Rebecca West
Briefing for a Descent into Hell   192
Joan Didion

The Summer before the Dark

Everywoman out of Love?   197
Erica Jong

Canopus in Argos: Archives

    Paradise Regained   200
        Gore Vidal
    The Spacing Out of Doris Lessing   204
        John Leonard
    Galactic Orthodoxies   209
        Claire Sprague

The Diaries of Jane Somers

    The Doris Lessing Hoax   213
        Ellen Goodman
    Lessing Is More: An "Unknown" Author
        and the Success Syndrome   215
        Jonathan Yardley

Doris Lessing in New York: 1969 and 1984

    "Best Battles Are Fought by
        Men and Women Together"   218
        Susan Brownmiller
    Candid Shot: Lessing in New York City,
        April 1 and 2, 1984   221
        Virginia Tiger

SELECTED BIBLIOGRAPHY   225

INDEX   231

INTRODUCTION

I

When a literary reputation is once established, people quickly forget
how long it was in growing.
— T. S. Eliot on Virginia Woolf (1941)

Prolific, prolix, in formal terms sometimes displaying an aesthetic
clubfoot, yet always as imaginatively sensitive as a barometer to the
twentieth century's complex climate, Doris Lessing has — for the past
thirty-five years — spoken directly to a whole generation's experience,
teaching it about private pain, public chauvinism, the divisiveness inherent in even the most radical causes. Her over thirty books — many copious
disheveled novels, a regiment of short stories, plays, poetry, essays,
memoirs, and apocalyptic fables — display a spacious panoply of themes,
ranging from left-wing politics, feminism, and sexual license to the
generation gap, religious zealotry, and schizophrenia.[1] Many of these
coalesced in the encyclopedic study of women in *The Golden Notebook*
(1962), which at the time of its publication seemed as prescient as Simone
de Beauvoir's *The Second Sex* (1949, trans. 1953). As one reader looking
back some twenty years later at these two now canonical books observed:
"In the strange cultural landscape of 1960 [de Beauvoir and Lessing]
loomed up, Cassandras of women's experience, an experience that was
everywhere silenced, concealed and denied."[2]

Despite the passionate sense of identification that Lessing's female
characters inspired in her women readers, the greatness of *The Golden
Notebook* was no simple result of a particular historical and political
moment. It stands as the paradigmatic example of Lessing's ability to
appeal to increasing numbers of scholars as well as millions of readers.
Since its publication, over 900,000 hardback copies alone of *The Golden
Notebook* have been sold.

From the beginning Lessing's subjects have been ponderous and
public; her moral earnestness like that of the great realists Balzac, Tolstoy,
and Turgenev; her hunger for enlightenment like that of the great
symbolists, Lawrence and Yeats. She shares her major theme — the

1

fragmentation of civilization and consciousness — with a great many modern writers: Faulkner, Joyce, Woolf, Golding. Possessing what is still too often rare for women writers, a rich fund of experience, she writes from some central longing for religious coherence. It is a quest that has taken her through various belief systems: the diagnosis of racial animosities, communism, feminism, Laingian psychopolitics, and now the mysticism of Sufism. (That she has turned to mystic themes of madness as spiritual release is no minor abberation: she herself converted to Sufism under Idries Shah.) But like other mystics before her — Boehme, Swedenborg, Sir Isaac Newton, who practically abandoned mathematics for mysticism after he was thirty — Lessing remains highly rational. In Margaret Drabble's words, "she is prophetic, but not in a vague, exhortatory, passionate mode."[3]

Like Hemingway, Lessing has attracted an enormous general as well as specialized readership, and her literary reputation has coexisted with her presence as a formidable public persona. In recent years she has become an international figure, traveling and speaking all over the world — in Spain, France, Germany, Africa, Japan, Canada, the United States. She gives radio and television interviews, accepts prizes (the French Prix Medicis is one example) and is regularly mentioned as a Nobel Prize candidate. Again, like Hemingway, she has come to stand for things outside her fiction. Furthermore, in her public appearances she seems to have accepted the writer's function as part of the promotional process. Despite her claim that "this lecture giving is all very jolly, but it has nothing to do with my writing,"[4] she continues to travel and lecture, showing both discomfort with and submission to the promotional process.

That dimension of her career can no longer be ignored. Before our introduction examines the major works and the criticism and the selections in this anthology, it will focus on the controversy recently provoked by the revelation in 1984 that Lessing had published two novels under the pseudonym Jane Somers. A media explosion ensued.

For the first time in her career, Lessing could be accused of manipulating the media. Newspapers, radio, and television all responded to her revelation and to her claim that her pseudonymous novels were written to dramatize the plight of first novelists. Very few media responses questioned her claim to altruism or pointed out that her "literary mischief" vastly increased her sales.[5] Her revelation was better news than a new novel. The major newspapers devoted a great deal of space to her caper, far more than they give to her novels. (The *New York Times*, for example, took two weeks to report her sellout talks in New York in April 1984 by contrast with next-day reports of Saul Bellow's talk in the same series.) In other words, Doris Lessing, at the height of her reputation as a major novelist, had consciously decided to give newspapers what she knew they wanted. (Incidentally, the Jane Somers novels received the kind of favorable review in major U.S. newspapers like the *New York Times*, the

Washington Post, and the *Los Angeles Times* that an unknown novelist would have been delighted to receive.)

Lessing's introduction to the Jane Somers novels, now available under her own name, suggests a more complicated motivation and function, displaying Lessing's ambivalent reclusive and participatory selves. For example, Lessing claims unconcern with critical response yet describes one of her motives, the desire to get back at critics who have not liked her current Canopus in Argos space fiction series as "faintly malicious." On a profounder level, one Lessing is perhaps less willing to confront, she is projecting a long-standing exploration of self-division in women and in herself.

In fact, Lessing's doubling and multiplication of her female characters is a consistent feature of her work.[6] Her duplications and reflections are like halls of mirrors. In *The Golden Notebook*, for example, Lessing projects a writer, Anna Wulf, who is writing a novel about another writer, Ella, who is in turn writing another novel. In the diaries of Jane Somers, Lessing projects as a writer, Jane Somers, who, like Ella, is a journalist for a women's magazine. Jane writes for *Lilith*; Ella for *Hearth and Home*. (These magazines titles suggest the different outlooks of women in 1982 and 1962.) The authentic writing life of Ella and Jane is not in news and feature writing but in novel writing. Jane writes two kinds of novels, romantic and realistic. Also, like both Anna and Ella, Jane keeps a diary. The self-conscious diarist and novelist, Anna Wulf says, "I, Anna, see Ella, who is of course Anna." She is describing the interaction between art and autobiography, an interaction the public Lessing denies. Although Lessing could never say, "I, Doris, see Anna, who is of course Doris," the parallels between Lessing's life and that of her heroines are self-evident.

What Lessing doesn't say about her own life as a writer is that she reached an impasse in her Canopus space fiction series, the series she had so emphatically described as a liberation from the cage of realistic writing. Earlier in her career, she had escaped from what she called the cage of the Children of Violence series by writing *The Golden Notebook*. Her way out of the current cage of the Canopus series was convoluted in the extreme. Unable to admit the constrictions of Canopus, she turned to pseudonymous realistic novels, works clearly in her earlier style. Liberation now apparently consists in returning to a type of fiction Lessing has berated as conventional and to a time and place — the here and now — she has called petty. Thus, her compulsion to write realistic novels again clearly cannot be explained simply in terms of a game to expose the publishing industry. It has to do with deep private and artistic needs. The Somers novels, for example, intersect dramatically and compellingly with the fourth Canopus novel, *The Making of the Representative from Planet 8* (1982), a novel about dying and annihilation. They confront aging and dying from an individual rather than a species point of view. It is indeed likely that the Jane Somers and *Making* novels overlapped in compositional time as did the Martha Quest and Anna Wulf novels. Together they offer an unusual double perspective on aging and dying.

II

When she was herself a Jane Somers, that is, an unknown fledgling, Lessing's first novel, *The Grass Is Singing* (the book she carried with her to England, her permanent residence since her emigration from Southern Rhodesia / Zimbabwe in 1949), received over twenty reviews in such major newspapers as the *Times Literary Supplement*, the *Nation*, the *New Yorker*, the *New Statesman and Nation* and the *Saturday Review*. "No impartial critic can fail to overlook the depth and maturity of this remarkable psychological study," commented John Barkham in the *New York Times Book Review* and concluded, "It is seldom that a first novel, one so sensitive and so powerful, comes to hand."[7] What first engaged reviewers was the immediacy of the African theme and the social relations of apartheid, a view that did much to establish Lessing as an anticolonial colonial. But the novel introduced in minor key many of her major concerns, in particular the centrality of the female lens.

Since that initial generous reception, critics have paid little attention to *The Grass Is Singing*; recently, however, it has been read as more than a sociological study of racism fused to a psychological study of breakdown. Remarking upon the ambivalence of early reviewers, Jenny Taylor places *The Grass Is Singing* within the category of "the 'black peril' story structured around the transgression of racial and sexual taboos."[8] She reminds us that *Grass* is the only novel Lessing wrote in Africa; all her other books have been written in England, looking back on the colonial experience through the eyes of the mother country.

Hindsight now permits us to detect connections between *The Grass Is Singing* and Lessing's later novels, especially *The Golden Notebook*. Betsy Draine examines the ways in which *Grass* resembles *Frontiers of War*, the first novel written by the protagonist of *The Golden Notebook*.[9] Anna's *Frontiers of War* is set in Africa, its atmosphere redolent with lying nostalgia, its critical reception reflective of what Taylor would call "racist voyeurism."

One remembers rather ironically Anna bristling at agents who want to make *Frontiers of War* into a television play now that one knows Lessing gave permission for *The Grass Is Singing* to be turned into a movie. Anna's parodies of media exploitation in "The Black Notebook" ("Oh Africa! for soon the banana leaves will be senile with dark red, the red dust will be redder yet, redder than the new-lipsticked lips of my dark love, store-betrayed to the commerce-lust of the white trader")[10] appear larger than life in the recent movie version of *The Grass Is Singing*, whose American title, "Killing Heat," outparodies Anna's parody. (Readers, however, remain devoted; in yet another tribute to Lessing's literary renown, one faithful fan annotated a 42d Street subway poster advertising the movie by scrawling across the depiction of a white woman almost molesting a supine male of indeterminate color: "Doris Lessing didn't mean this!")

Lessing's first decade in England, the decade of the 1950s, is *the* critical period in her career, for the first three books in the five-volume Martha Quest series known as the Children of Violence were published at that time. The 1950s as subject matter consumes half of *The Four-Gated City* and all of *The Golden Notebook*, whose fictional present time is 1957 and whose retrospective time is largely in the fifties. (That the fifties reappear compulsively in Lessing's second series, Canopus in Argos, further testifies to how crucial those years were in her artistic development.) Life lived and life imagined coalesced, for during these years Lessing joined and left the British Communist party, underwent psychoanalysis, experienced explosive private relationships, and wrote prodigiously.

The decade fed many other works: the political novel *Retreat to Innocence* (1956), which Lessing continues to repudiate; and two reportorial works, *Going Home* (1957), an account of her first visit back to Southern Rhodesia, and *In Pursuit of the English* (1960), an acerbic but affectionate take on the English character from a colonial's observant eye. In addition, plays, poems, essays, reviews (in such magazines as the *New Statesman* and *New Left Review*), and short stories all poured forth during the decade. The stories are a major part of Lessing's work. They date back to the very beginning of her career (the first was published in an African magazine) and are considered by many to be her best work. Writing them may have functioned as diversion or relief from novel writing, much as diary, review, and essay writing did for Virginia Woolf. The stories also have a relation to the novels; sometimes they are interpolated into them — as is especially true in *The Golden Notebook*. Sometimes they are germs or données to a later novel. For example, *The Temptation of Jack Orkney* is recast in *Briefing*, "A Room" in *Memoirs*, "Report on the Threatened City" in Canopus, and "An Old Woman and a Cat" in *The Diary of a Good Neighbor*, while "To Room Nineteen" is positively reimagined in *The Summer before the Dark*.

The first three volumes of the Children of Violence series trace the development of Martha Quest through what Ellen Rose calls "various collectively imposed identities — dutiful daughter, good time party girl, suburban wife and mother, dedicated Communist."[11] Lessing accomplished something quite new here; she wrote the first bildungsroman whose central consciousness is a female and whose reportorial mapping brought into legitimate fictional focus such exclusively female phases and activities as menstruation, childbirth, childrearing, and the community of women. Its heroine is a complex character, "an intelligent woman capable of great feats of self-deception, subject to suffocating passivity."[12]

Martha Quest has become, as Catharine Stimpson notes, "a character whom readers mentally lift from the page and incorporate into their own lives as a reference point."[13] *Martha Quest* (1952) opens with the resentful fifteen-year-old heroine pitted against two mother figures, fearful that she will be doomed to repeat the "dull staple" of their lives despite her ostentatiously displayed copy of Havelock Ellis's *Psychology of Sex*, which "lay like an irritant, on the top steps with title well in view" (2).

Indeed, from the start, Martha the individual is conscious of her place in various collectivities: "She was adolescent and therefore bound to be unhappy; British, and therefore uneasy and defensive; in the fourth decade of the twentieth century, and therefore inescapably beset with problems of race and class; female, and obliged to repudiate the shackled women of the past. She was tormented with guilt and responsibility and self-consciousness" (8). Drawn here is an adolescent heroine not besotted by plots of romance, marriage, and motherhood; in fact, so repelled is she by marriage and babies that her sense of responsibility takes on a public dimension more characteristically male than female. She *has* to save the world.

Neither life nor literature offers Martha, this heir to Maggie Tulliver and other nineteenth-century heroines, a viable female model. Motherless Jane Eyre receives comfort from surrogate mothers and intellectual companionship with sympathetic teachers. Martha, dominated by and fearful of becoming like her own mother, rejects the living community of women. Nor can she be helped by women in books. But then, she asks, "who was she to be like? Her mind turned towards the heroines she had been offered, and discarded them. There seemed to be a gap between herself and the past" (10). Her solution is to refashion "the unused country" of her actual life — Southern Rhodesia — to "the scale of her imagination" (11), to a four-gated city that is spacious and noble and ennobling. Here for the first time a female appropriates that beckoning image of freedom, the city. Indeed, she can be likened to male questers, young provincials like Paul Morel or Stephen Dedalus, who escape familial homes and parochial confines by striding forward to the city of promise.

Our questing heroine begins with a dream of freedom; Martha Quest does journey to a city — Salisbury — but the novel painfully and paradoxically concludes with Martha's "proper" marriage: "In this manner, therefore, was Martha Quest married on a warm Thursday afternoon in the month of March, 1939, in the capital city of a British colony in the centre of the great African continent" (246). Here where Jane Eyre's triumphant, "Reader, I married him," might have been given contemporary voice, Lessing chooses to subvert the marriage plot by having the repository of patriarchal culture, the magistrate who married Martha, cynically predict her divorce. Indeed, the four weddings he will have to get through will mean four divorces for him to deal with: "Five counting the one he had just finished" (247). This proliferation of marriage, described as "the first infection from that brutal sentimentality which poisons us all in time of war" (247), is precipitated not so much by private choices as by the wedding of these choices to larger political events. For it is "the individual conscience in its relations with the collective"[14] that Lessing — as she once explained — intended the Children of Violence series to dramatize.

The magistrate's anticipation of divorces merely foreshadows the total eradication of the marriage plot in the second volume, ironically titled *A Proper Marriage*. Once more a prescient Lessing initiated what has become a common counterplot to the nineteenth-century pattern: the female need to dissolve a marriage. If the new condition of Martha's freedom is her ability to leave hearth and husband, what is the new plot for her as a liberated heroine? Martha goes very far indeed for she "frees" (some would say abandons) her daughter Caroline by leaving the child with her father on the grounds that doing so might break the cycle of a female repetition, daughter becoming like mother. Martha immerses herself in a collectivity rather different from that of the family, a communist group, an immersion that will lead to another improper marriage. This marriage, theoretically a political act to prevent the German alien Anton Hesse from being expelled, represents one of the many ways that the third volume, *A Ripple from the Storm* (1958), intertwines the political and the personal. By the end of the novel Martha finds herself saddened and desperate, once more trapped by marriage and a sexually inadequate husband, one more intellectually and emotionally authoritarian than the first who — despite his communist orthodoxy — is totally bourgeois and patriarchal. Fighting against the final collapse of her conception of him, Martha knows that if she is conventionally feminine, "capricious, charming, filial: to this compliant little girl Anton would be kind — and patronizing." Her final painful conclusion is, "why, he's not a man at all — in anything" (255). Her remark, of course, exposes her own complicity in sexual stereotypes.

Of all the volumes in the sequence that is the Children of Violence, *A Ripple from the Storm* can best be described as a novel of negative education. The twentieth-century bildungsroman heroine who had reached toward emancipation and vindication by rejecting the twin comforts of marriage and the family now seeks in political radicalism ways to connect her private life with the public world. Yet Martha finds herself more profoundly landlocked than Stephen Dedalus was before he freed himself by flying over seas far beyond fatherland, family, and church. Feeling "overwhelmed with futility," Martha observes dispassionately near the end of the novel, "the fact is, I'm not a person at all, I'm nothing yet — perhaps I never will be" (260).

Apprenticeship novels conventionally show protagonists developing chronologically from childhood to maturity and Children of Violence is no exception. Central to acquiring what might be called "a philosophy of life and art of living"[15] is the education of the heart as well as the head. In striking contrast to traditional fictional heroines who are perhaps natural inhabitants of that territory known as sensibility, Martha's heart remains untutored. Although by her twenties she has lived far more than Jane Austen's Emma, Charlotte Brontë's Lucy Snowe, or George Eliot's Dorothea, the lessons of *eros* and *thanatos* — of love and loss — await their absorption in the fourth volume. In it, for the first time, Martha will be unified.

In *Landlocked* (1965), so somber and tight a title, Martha is allowed the sea-swept currents of sensuality; love instructs and heals. The Martha who "had complained that her life had consisted of a dozen rooms, each self-contained," discovers that "adding a new room to her house had ended the division. From this centre she now lived"(99). She is a woman in love, her flesh tongue-ready for embrace, her being brought into being by one man, her soul saturated with the person of that beloved. Her lover, Thomas Stern, is a gardener, a Polish Jew, a survivor of the holocaust, the quintessential child of our time's violence. Their love is passionate, short-lived, painful. He dies; we suspect as readers that it is an almost willed suicide and we place that death beside Martha's other losses: her father, throughout his life a casualty of the Great War, and Athen, the archetypally "incorruptible" Communist, who will become the first casualty of the Cold War. Martha has lost to violence the three most important men in her life. And forever her ability to commit herself to political parties. And with her arrival in England in the final volume of her quintet, Martha has also (and forever) lost her homeland.

The Martha of *Landlocked* has become the kind of inner register she never was in her first three fictional appearances. No wonder. Seven years separate this Martha from the Martha of *Ripple*. The "gaps," to use Nicole Ward Jouve's word, between these two Marthas are, nevertheless, not too difficult to paper over.[16] *The Four-Gated City* (1969), however, erupts into so considerable and so different a space of its own that it demands equal time with *The Golden Notebook* (1962) rather than with its Martha Quest predecessors. Between *Ripple* and the last two novels of the Children of Violence series falls the great shadow of *The Golden Notebook* (1962). It must be considered before *The Four-Gated City*.

Anna Freeman Wulf, the protagonist of *The Golden Notebook* (1962), is the only major protagonist in Lessing's considerable oeuvre who is given a vocation. Her writing career distinguishes her from Lessing's other heroines. Unlike Martha Quest, Anna is already divorced when we meet her, already a single parent, already a Communist. Anna's apparently "free" life is, however, coming apart sexually, politically, artistically, psychologically. She keeps four notebooks, she explains, to keep chaos at bay. As Anna's first spoken words announce, "The point is . . . everything is cracking up"(3).

The paradoxical other point is that in a novel about cracking up, Lessing takes the symptoms of personal, gender, and societal malaise and develops them through carefully patterned innovative formal strategies.

Lessing described the shape of the novel nearly ten years after its publication as consisting of a "skeleton, or frame, called *Free Women* . . . which could stand by itself. But it is divided into five sections and separated by stages of the four Notebooks, Black, Red, Yellow, and Blue. [Anna] keeps four and not one, because, as she recognizes, she has to separate things off from each other, out of fear of chaos, of formlessness — of breakdown" (vii). The counterpoint between the conventional *Free Women* sections and the Notebook entries provides the primary narrative dialectic. Together they comprise what Elizabeth Abel calls a "composite novel."[17] *Free Women* can be described, Lessing suggests, as "an absolutely whole conventional novel, and the rest of the book is the material that went into making it."[18] Thus, the Notebooks are the rich raw material to the finished work that is *Free Women*. Moreover, *Free Women* raises questions about the limits of the finished public work. What the straightforward narrative of *Free Women* lacks, the Notebook sections have in abundance — interest, complexity, and contradiction. Anna might have been speaking of *Free Women* when she says, "How can this small neat thing be truth when what I have experienced was so rough and so apparently formless and unshaped?" (17).

The theme of fragmentation is so strong it is easy to overlook what Lessing describes as the "triumph of the second theme, which is that of unity" (vii). Lessing overstates that "triumph" in the fifth, the Golden Notebook, for in it Anna is still mad, still in breakdown, although able to rerun all her selves in one film. "Unity" is accurate only if we do not think of it as golden or glorious. It is an approximation of wholeness, not wholeness itself. The different endings of the novel should caution us against assuming total healing is possible or even desirable.

One of the most delicious ironies in the novel is that a writer described as suffering from writer's block keeps voluminous journals. These journals freely play with the various prose forms: parody, film script, book review, diary, short story, letter, headline, news clipping, synopsis. These forms are another way in which the novel raises questions about fictive form and its relation to experience.

On the surface, the novel is not radical in language or form in the way of early twentieth-century modernists like Joyce or Woolf or Faulkner. Time, so wonderfully dislocated by these writers, is barely wrenched out of straight chronology in *The Golden Notebook*. If movement in time is limited, movement in space is virtually eliminated, existing only in the Black Notebook when Anna remembers her African past. Indeed, the primary space of *The Golden Notebook* is the isolated, often claustrophobic, private room. The outside world of London erupts only as menace, during a subway ride when Anna feels assaulted by a strange man, or at a pavement happening when a pigeon is violently killed. The outside political world only impinges through newspaper headlines.

The language of *The Golden Notebook* is even more straightforward than its use of time and space. The novel talks about disorder in a very orderly way — in an accessible style, and a determinedly everyday vocabulary, one usually nonallusive, even pedestrian. The language of madness is lucid and generally syntactically normal; "These last three days I have been inside madness," says Anna of herself (Blue 4, 590). Her representation of chaos is quite unchaotic. Anna may recall Leopold Bloom in the Circe section of Joyce's *Ulysses*, in that, like him, she plays out various roles and sex changes in a long night of dreams. But Anna is always in control. Lessing's mode is reportorial rather than dramatic.

> Then I was conscious of danger, for Paul came in, who was dead. . . . Then he dissolved into [Anna], and I, screaming with fear . . . fought to reenter her.
>
> And I was not Anna, but a soldier. (Blue 4, 600)

Anna becomes Saul, mad Charlie Themba, and other men in her set of continuing nightmares in the Blue 4 Notebook. As Lessing puts this process in her introduction, her characters " 'break down' into each other, into other people" (viii). But these shifting and interchanging selves are asserted rather than shown.

We have then a radical novel that wasn't put together very radically. How do we account for its power? Its duplications, repetitions with variations of character and plot elements grow and intensify so that the novel rather resembles the experience of seeing all at once the three hundred or so works Van Gogh created in that one year at Arles. Anna's breakdown is mirrored differently and in different intensities in Tommy, Ella, De Silva, Paul Blackenhurst, Saul Green, Charlie Themba, and others. The incremental power of the novel is therefore exceptional as are the effects of the shifts in narrative mode and chronological time. The Notebooks are first person narrations, for example, while *Free Women* is third person. The slight wrenching of chronology into a present and several recent pasts combines with the interleaved Notebooks to become deliberately disorienting strategies. Is Tommy dead, we wonder, at the end of one *Free Women* section? The reader must wait in suspense while the four Notebooks interrupt his story. Furthermore, the reader believes in the truth of the *Free Women* sections (and other sections as well) before its fictional nature is revealed near the end of the novel. The separation between fiction and fact is finally and intentionally precarious.

The portrayal of women's lives in *The Golden Notebook* is also radical. Lessing was probably the first novelist to shift away from the traditional focus that a woman must satisfy a man's expectations. In *The Golden Notebook* women make demands of men and dare to evaluate their excellence in bed, in conversation, in political morality, in professional ethics. The metaphor of breakdown is powerfully and newly integrated with private lives and public events. As Irving Howe points out in his by now classic review of the novel, Lessing is almost the only major novelist in our time to grasp "the connection between Anna Wulf's neuroses and the public disorders of the day."[19] In fact, in *The Golden Notebook*, Lessing comes close to realizing her dream, so evident in her introduction to the novel, of being the English Tolstoy. The novel has even been called "one of the sacred texts of our time."[20] Its greatness, while related to its formal and thematic strengths, cannot finally be fully explained by them.

Frederick Karl describes Lessing's two great works of the 1960s, *The Golden Notebook* and *The Four-Gated City*, as approaching each other "like asymptotes . . . without touching, all the while utilizing common images and symbols: the gate, the door, the house or room, the descent into hell, the quest."[21] The asymptotic image is apt. The differences between the two novels are equally instructive. The personal intensity of Anna's inner world is, for example, quite lacking in the later novel. Or, the collective, barely visible in *The Golden Notebook*, nearly overwhelms Martha in *The Four-Gated City*. Indeed critics have argued that in Martha-Mark-Lynda the novel has a collective protagonist.[22]

As housekeeper for the Coldridge home — that so British and Bloomsbury establishment on Radlett Street — Martha Quest seems a literary revision of earlier housekeepers who, like Esther Summerson, the heroine of Dickens's *Bleak House*, symbolically possess the keys to England's moral and spiritual health. *The Four-Gated City* can be placed in the tradition of "The Condition of England Novel" where works apparently as diverse as *Bleak House, Tono-Bungay, Howards End*, and *Mrs. Dalloway* share a common subject — the diagnosis of English society.

The documentation of postwar Britain is impressive. The promised land across the sea that a landlocked Martha longed for is in decay. The empire is finished. Food, housing, clothes are shabby, dreary, and in short supply. The Cold War decade of the fifties with its hysterical anticommunism turns the Coldridge house that Martha manages into a house under seige by ravenous reporters and cameramen, a bleak house. One member defects to Russia; his wife, a holocaust survivor, commits suicide; a mad wife lives in the basement. Hungary and Suez become code words for the inner meaning of that "bad time." Save for peace marches, Martha has left politics and will, in the 1960s, undertake her last and longest journey, one that takes her telepathic powers out of hiding.

Like Howards End and other houses in earlier Condition of England novels, the Coldridge household serves as a sociopolitical-cultural microcosm of Britain — this time of the Cold War 1950s, and the swinging sixties.[23] The poisoned and dying London of the 1950s, "not one tree; therefore, no roots, Martha had never seen soil that was so dead, that had no roots" (8), has another look in the next decade: "For already in the early sixties London had begun that extraordinary whirling dance" (44), which was to cloak rootlessness in consumerism. (In the United States the decade had another name and a darker quality, suffused as it was with the drug culture and anti-Vietnam protests.)

Compared to the male hero of the bildungsroman, Martha's growth is interior and private and from the feminist point of view filled with ironies. Martha is not, after all, so different from the ideal nineteenth-century heroine, the angel in the house. She may no longer be married; the children she mothers may not be biologically hers; the men she succors may not be patriarchal — functionally, however, she becomes "that person who once she hated and feared more than any other — the matron" (343) — before she becomes an inner immigrant. Until her death on a contaminated island off the coast of Scotland, Martha is and remains the wise, maternal woman, not the new woman. Or, in Mark's last apt judgment, Martha is the woman "who brought up the children and kept my house and was reliable and good" (653).

Her last child, a grandchild really and the newest child of violence, the black Joseph Batts, is a communal charge who has survived the Catastrophe of the 1970s, perhaps mutated to acquire special powers. He seems "superlatively ordinary," but isn't — like Martha. Ordinariness shields the two from exploitation or destruction in the post-Catastrophe world, which is as far away as ever from the four-gated city of Martha's adolescent dream. Perhaps this is because the ideal city is "not so much . . . a Utopian dream . . . as a state of mind."[24]

One so-called female gift is the talent for manipulating appearance. In her lifetime Martha has tried on any number of physical disguises, testing the falsehood of appearances and the utility of manipulating them. Consider the virginal white dress the adolescent Martha makes and remakes later to reflect sexual experience. Or the costumes that permit her sexual anonymity — the oversized black coat she wears in order to wander the streets of London freely; or the housedress that transforms her into a shabby charwoman able to get by reporters. By the 1960s Martha is fashionable, freaky, wearing vintage clothing, able to treat herself as an art form. But in manipulating her own appearance, Martha is actually developing major political strategies that will ensure personal and species survival. By contrast, women who choose public power and its set of disguises are savagely depicted — Phoebe Coldridge, Labour party minister; Margaret Patten, Tory hostess. The novel gives inner immigrants like Martha Quest and her spiritual mentor, Lynda Coldridge, the madwoman in the basement, great social and political powers. It vindicates so-called female gifts.

No other work in Lessing's career so looks both backward and forward. As Mona Knapp put it, *The Four-Gated City* "stands in a direct line of descent" from Martha's earliest visionary experience and also "anticipates the new dimensions of Lessing's fiction in the 1970s and 1980s. It is both a second zenith (following *The Golden Notebook*) and a turning point."[25] The Appendix section, whose archives span the years

1968 to 1997, represents Lessing's first attempt at future fiction; its graft on the realism of the novel proper creates a new kind of disjunction and another kind of plural text. This "powerful, prophetic, mysterious work" successfully fuses naturalism and fantasy in Joyce Carol Oates's view[26] — somehow overcoming its "dragging, waiting quality" and its compulsion to record everything.[27]

In retrospect, *Briefing for a Descent into Hell* (1971), *The Summer before the Dark* (1973), and *Memoirs of a Survivor* (1974) can be seen to mark an enriching interlude between the major series, Children of Violence and Canopus in Argos, allowing Lessing to fiddle innovatively with themes that will inform the galactic voyages of the space fantasies that follow. Forming a kind of secular triptych, each novel concerns itself with its protagonist's midlife crisis, though the middle panel, *The Summer before the Dark*, represents the novel most connected to Lessing's earlier concerns. Its heroine, one so typical as to be almost a flattened Martha Quest, is the 45-year-old Kate Brown, who finds herself bereft of domestic obligations and comforts one late July afternoon. Lessing appears to be testing what might happen in the new feminist era to a woman of the old dispensation who has fully accepted her role as housemaker, mother, and — too often a part of the territory — betrayed wife. Another Lessing heroine without volition, Kate slides into what will become the summer's adventure only because her husband forces her into it: "she saw that that had been the characteristic of her life — passivity, adaptability to others" (22).

Working as a translator in Global Foods, Kate discovers that her administrative skills in the corporate world are simply household managerial skills transferred. She is as she was: "provider of invisible manna, consolation, warmth and 'sympathy' " (52). The perpetual mother who dispenses food becomes the administrative mother who manages seating arrangements, hotel food, the care and feeding of convention delegates. Even in her obligatory love affair with the younger man, Kate finds herself feeding and mothering a sick child.

When the novel first appeared, Kate was read as "a kind of twentieth century Everywoman" although some reviewers saw that Kate spoke to issues larger than her personal predicament.[28] Not least among the devastating portrayals of the collectivity in this novel is the bold-stroke sketch of the ways in which international organizations feed not the hungry but one another. The hunger in Spain's interior, the starvation in the underdeveloped countries, the soup kitchens in London — each is an aspect of a collective breakdown that goes with the power cuts with which the novel opens. Feminist critics were dismayed by Kate's "unemancipated" return to home and hearth, claiming she had capitulated to conventionality; the success of her journey, however, has to be answered by considering the title's ambiguity. Juxtaposed as it is to the promise of "summer," the word "dark" suggests either the unknown into which the changed Kate will leap, her defeat and her oncoming death or — more painfully still — the death of the planet itself.

Briefing for a Descent Into Hell explores another middle-aged breakdown; that the protagonist is male and a Classics professor permits the allusive, multilayered incorporation of quest myths pertinent to male voyagers: Jason, Sinbad the Sailor, Odysseus. An additional reason for the choice of a male protagonist might well be that it subverts the traditional association of women with madness, which trivializes both.

As Herbert Marder points out, *Briefing* occupies a zone of hybrid narrative he defines as "borderline fantasy."[29] The collage technique of the novel — diary, letter, news report, science fiction speculation, medical dialogue, poetry, stream of consciousness, popular songs, interpolated short story and afterword — is complex; its theme is, however, anything but complicated. Lessing's attack on the bankruptcy of the psychiatric medical establishment is relentlessly single-minded. The epic briefing Charles Watkins receives from the gods is forgotten when he descends — with the all too available help of shock treatment — to the hell that is the here and now.

Watkins may be defeated by the medical world; *Memoirs's* unnamed narrator successfully negotiates between the known and the unknown. For *Briefing's* inner space voyage becomes the world behind the wall in *Memoirs*. A novel of retrospective reminiscence, its opening line — "we all remember that time" — forecasts the voice of the Chronicler in Canopus. *Memoirs* is the first novel in which Lessing adopts the sage persona. Although she documents the anarchic pavements of a dying city, she disentangles herself, as Martin Green has so effectively argued, from the merely social and political.[30] The formal originality of this novel — which the director of the film version found difficult to represent — can be seen in the life of Emily, the prepubescent who is left (because of a bureaucratic error?) to the custodianship of an elderly weary woman.

Juxtaposed to the plausible world of the city is an imagined world behind the wall of the narrator's apartment. If public life is being chronicled on the city side of the wall, private history proceeds simultaneously on the other side. Emily's rapid chronological development from infancy to adolescence does not match her psychological development, for at fourteen she has become a fatigued middle-aged woman much like the narrator — and, of course, like the very figure Martha Quest hated and never wanted to become: the middle-aged matron, burdened with responsibilities, children, the deployment of food, and the management of household tasks. When Emily behind the wall is the same age as Emily in front of the wall the novel comes to a close.

But Emily is also a daughter, a role she plays out on both sides of the wall. In the foreground the narrator is the good mother. Indeed, the intense mother-daughter rivalry initiated in the Martha Quest novels is here exorcised in their nonbiological relationship as it also is in the Kate-

Maureen relationship of *Summer*. In the background world the bad mother is delineated. The family constellation of the distracted soldierly father, the buxom harassed mother, the older ignored daughter, and the younger favored brother, is that of the Quest family, itself a duplicate of Doris Lessing's family: Alfred Michael, Emily Maude, Doris May, and Harry Tayler.

Lessing has in her public remarks admonished critics that they were inattentive to the autobiography that she intended *Memoirs* to be. Surely naming the daughter Emily Mary after her own mother, Emily Maude, amounts to classic Freudian revenge against the mother. For the narrator dominates the daughter as Lessing could not do in life and in her more conventional autobiographical fiction. Furthermore, the unnamed narrator is Emily as much as she is Emily's mother and the past that is repeated and exorcised behind the wall belongs to both women, perhaps to Everywoman.

One reviewer describes *Shikasta* (1979) as "at once a brief history of the world, a tract against human destructiveness, an ode to the natural beauties of this earth and a hymn to the music of the spheres."[31] His description begins to suggest Lessing's large canvas in this first of her now five Canopus in Argos: Archives series. Even those who have blasted *Shikasta*, and many have, often simultaneously praise it. Gore Vidal, for example, doesn't find "much music in Lessing's spheres," yet calls the novel "a work of formidable imagination."[32] These contradictory remarks seem to mirror the "competing codes" in the series as a whole. In Betsy Draine's words, the series promises to be "a work at odds with itself philosophically, stylistically, generically" (143).

The labored preface to *Shikasta* is probably the best introduction to the plot patterns of the series. In the galactic new world, "the petty fate of planets, let alone individuals, are only aspects of cosmic evolution expressed in the rivalries and interactions of great galactic Empires: Canopus, Sirius, and their enemy, the Empire Puttiora, with its criminal planet, Shammat" (ix). In these "rivalries and interactions," Canopus, "benevolent and mysterious," tries to convert "technological Sirius" to an understanding of the "Necessity" that rules the universe. In eternal battle with "vampiric Shammat," the principle of evil, Canopus pursues its complex machinations over passive populations.[33] It is almost as though Lessing has recast the British Empire in an idealized galactic incarnation. In the name of goodness and "the long run," Canopus eradicates whole planets, relocates whole cultures, eugenically manipulates whole populations. The passivity of these new colonials is appalling; their subjection to "a small tic in the cosmos" even more so.[34] Compared with Canopean Necessity, Marxist economic determinism seems laissez-faire. History no longer depends on human actions; it is a "byproduct of cosmography."[35]

Once Lessing's protagonists looked toward a utopian future; now progress is a return to an Edenic golden age. The fall from grace, that most universal of mythic explanations — is reworked in *Shikasta*. In fact, some of its most haunting passages, those relating to the First Time of the Giants or to the geometric cities, for example, occur within this prelapsarian pattern.

We watch our suffering through the cool, sometimes compassionate eye of Johor, a Canopean agent who takes on human form. His reports back to headquarters, the primary "Archives" of this novel, make him as close to a central character as the donnée of the novel permits. The various documents, passages from Canopean history books, official communiqués, sociological reports, diaries, letters, distance the authorial voice. That authorial voice, given the context of Lessing's lifework, is surprising, for it is atypically male though Canopean agents appear to be androgynous and matriarchal cultures like Adalantaland or Al·Ith's kingdom of Zone Three are presented positively.

The fable form of the second and fourth volumes, *The Marriages between Zones Three, Four, and Five* (1980) and *The Making of the Representative from Planet 8* (1982) break through the limits of Lessing's new didacticism. In them, simple chronology acquires unexpected density and resonance. Their imaginative reach and their unity of conception is exceptional. The fable form seems to have provided Lessing with a way to subvert the conventional novel without going the way of modernism.

Marriages is only technically connected to the space fiction series in that the Canopean Providers order the marriage of Al·Ith, the queen of Zone Three, to Ben Ata, the ruler of Zone Four. Both realms, Three and Four, have become stagnant, complacent. Their boundaries are too rigid, infertility is becoming a problem. Interchange between the feminist agrarian nonhierarchal Zone Three and the patriarchal, military, hierarchal Zone Four is the condition of revival and growth. Four into Three must go. And so it does. In what has been called a "fable of communication,"[36] the barbarian king changes; the gentle queen changes. Their relationship becomes an anatomy of a marriage as erotic as it is allegorical, political, and psychological. Dualities and boundaries break down; sameness and difference intersect. What Rubenstein calls the alchemical representation of male and female as "equal and opposite powers" is accomplished.[37] When the Providers separate the lovers and order Ben Ata to marry Vahshi, the queen of Zone Five, a nomadic, anarchic realm that combines elements of the other two, their action dramatizes the law of the novel — that history is not static. As Ben Ata and Vahshi now instruct one another, Al·Ith moves toward the blue of Zone Two.

Al·Ith comments about Zone Four: "It is a place of compulsion . . . They have no inner listening to the law" (56). The inhabitants of Planet 8 in *Making* listen well inwardly and outwardly to the Law of Canopus, once again communicated through the agent Johor. Some misalignment of the stars dooms their planet to extinction; Canopus backs down on its promise to airlift the inhabitants to safety. Thus, the novel becomes a fable about learning to die (and "an ecological thriller," in John Leonard's words) (11). Although Sufi teachings about suffering and transcendence all too plainly motivate the ethos of the novel, Lessing remains the consummate artist, for she shrewdly grounds her fable in childhood memories of tales about the Scott expedition to Antartica. The moving wall of ice, vast as the African veld, is oppressively communicated, recalling all the other walls in Lessing's fiction that her characters try to break through. Breakthrough in this novel becomes mystical transcendence; the collective dissolution into atoms of the survivors the precondition to new creation.

If the success of the third Canopus novel, *The Sirian Experiments* (1981) is questionable, the failure of the fifth, *The Sentimental Agents* (1983) seems unambiguous. In *The Sirian Experiments*, for the first time in the series, Lessing depicts a female administrator and a single central consciousness. The first-person narrative of *Sirian* proceeds through the mind of Ambien II, a high level Sirian bureaucrat in the colonial service, as she travels through galaxies and millennia. It is another novel of education, for it "documents her conversion to Canopean values" under the tutelage of the male Canopean agent Klorathy.[38] Under him, Ambien will learn a wise rather than a merely technological approach to colonialism. Ambien is dry, scrupulous, dull. Moreover, although her name suggests the possibility of androgyny, a possibility reinforced by the existence of a male Ambien I, the novel casts Ambien II's education in the direction of maleness. Ellen Rose wonders why Lessing internalizes "the war between the sexes, so that Ambien must repress her skepticism, suspect her sexuality, and accept uncritically the precepts of a godlike male in order to achieve transcendence."[39]

The Sentimental Agents is also cast in the novel of education mold as Incent, a Canopean novice, must unlearn the vacuity, distortion, and danger of political rhetoric. Once again, as in *Shikasta*, there are multiple archival documents and a wise teacher, this time Klorathy. Incent's education proceeds through the kind of social-political satire Lessing has done much better in earlier novels. Krolgul as the evil Shammatan seems like a Star Wars caricature. The novel as a whole suggests the series is running down. It was therefore no surprise to learn that Lessing was bogged down in the sixth novel and had turned for a change of pace to a novel about a contemporary female terrorist, one suggested by the assassination of Lord Mountbatten (*The Good Terrorist*, 1985). What Lessing did not say when she spoke in the United States in 1984 was that she had already left outer space and returned to inner (female) space in two novels under the pseudonym of Jane Somers.

These novels, *The Diary of a Good Neighbor* and *If the Old Could . . .* , demonstrate Lessing's continuing need for a complex distancing strategy that is also paradoxically a more immediate mirror of where she is in her own life. Lessing in her sixties watches Jane / Janna in her fifties watching women in their nineties to find out what life at that age will be like. Lessing's mirror is public as well as personal — as always — for the care of the dying and the elderly ill has become a major social concern in industrial nations.[40] Jane's aggressive cultivation of Maudie Fowler, whose death concludes *Diary*, is not altogether altruistic. Jane, the glossy, the perfectly groomed, the overbathed, enters the malodorous world of incontinence, dirt, illness in order to exorcise her guilt over her inability to feel, to tend, or to grieve for her mother and her husband when they were dying. Washing Maudie becomes a ritual act allowing disgust to turn to love. In the world of Home Help, Meals on Wheels, and Good Neighbors, Jane is an old-fashioned good neighbor. Meanwhile Jane / Janna keeps on writing romances — *The Gracious Lady*, *The Milliners of Marylebone* — as well as her "serious book, *Fashion Changes*," and the sociological *Real and Apparent Structures*. Her productivity and range suggest Doris Lessing's; the titles of her books the only bit of parody in this somber novel. The names Janna and Maudie echo those of two fictional predecessors, Anna and Molly.

If the Old Could . . ., the sequel to *The Diary of a Good Neighbour*, is an almost unmitigated failure. Jane, still professional and glossy, falls in love — a metaphor taken so literally that Lessing has her tumble into the arms of an unknown dark stranger, the "beau" with whom she will have a gushing, cloying, mooning, skittish *romantic entente*. They commingle platonically from spring to fall in wine bars, Italian cafés, pubs, parks, and London streets. Aquiver, she waits for telephone calls at work, at home. Oddly counterpointed to their *affaire de coeur* is the developing relationship with her niece Kate, an adolescent punker who drifts into Jane's flat one afternoon to stay. It's as though a sluggish Martha Quest — ears drugged by Walkman plugs — had determined to make *The Golden Notebook* Ella into a den mother and her apartment a flophouse. The reworking of earlier characters and themes borders on self-parody. But, as suggested at the beginning of our introduction, the Jane Somers novels also mark a series of provocative returns — to realism, to the female voice, and an expansion of Lessing's recent preoccupation with aging and dying.

III

Lessing is, finally, a rather demanding figure. Certainly she has written what the French call the *roman idéologique*, never hesitating in the midst of a conventional realistic novel to interrupt the dinner party to give detailed descriptions of a course's ingredients. She instructs; she berates. But critical attempts to fit her complexity into a prescriptive ideological system inevitably fall short, damage the wonderful fictiveness of her imagined world. To approach her achievement successfully demands an explicitly formulated theory of literature, one that will locate her world in its historical or literary context, one that will engage in textual analyses that release rather than impose meanings. Or an innovative critical methodology capable of moving through disciplinary barriers.

Earlier studies of Lessing by Dorothy Brewster (*Doris Lessing*, 1965) and Paul Schlueter (*The Novels of Doris Lessing*, 1973) were helpful, if limited, introductory guides, necessary groundwork for more elaborate examinations of the edifice. Two more recent considerations explored major symbols, images, and motifs. Mary Singleton (*The City and the Veld*, 1977) outlined the sources for Lessing's vision: alchemy, Carl Jung, Idries Shah, R. D. Laing; and Ellen Cronan Rose (*The Tree Outside the Window*, 1976) analyzed the Children of Violence bildungsroman, employing Erik Erikson's psychoanalytical theories on the "eight ages of man."

Roberta Rubenstein's *The Novelistic Vision of Doris Lessing* (1979) is far more ambitious. Eschewing biographical, formal, feminist, and Marxist schema as too reductive, Rubenstein is committed to a fresh critical method. She adopts an interdisciplinary psycho-literary approach, identifying the ideological furniture of Lessing's creative house. (Instructive in this regard is the eclectic bibliography, which includes Mircea Eliade, William James, Carl Jung, Jalaluddin Rumi, and Northrop Frye.) Her central thesis is that the common denominator in Lessing's fictional world is the concept of mind: "the mind discovering, interpreting and ultimately shaping its own reality."(7)

Taking its title from the preface to *Shikasta*, which speaks of joy as "the song of substance under pressure forced into new songs and shapes," Betsy Draine's *Substance Under Pressure* (1983) boldly reverses the usual emphasis on content in Lessing criticism and centers its analysis on "the evolution of form as an imperative in itself and as a pressure on context" (xii). The study, the first to treat the Canopus series, charts Lessing's journey through such narrative forms as tragedy (*The Grass Is Singing*), socialist realism (*Retreat To Innocence*), bildungsroman (Children of Violence), "modernist perspectivism" (*The Golden Notebook*), parody, allegory, quest romance, parable, legend, and science fiction saga. Draine's approach is particularly successful for Lessing's more demanding nonrealistic forms such as the apologue in *Briefing*, the changing frames in *Memoirs*, the competing scriptural and science fiction codes in *Shikasta*. Perhaps one of her more original cross-disciplinary forays is the use of Erving Goffman's frame analysis in her chapter on *Memoirs*.

The profusion of critical commentary in America about Lessing contrasts sharply with the British reception. Michael Thorpe's *Doris Lessing's Africa* (1978), containing a useful chapter on the short stories, is the only book to precede Jenny Taylor's *Notebooks / Memoirs / Archives* (1982) and Lorna Sage's *Doris Lessing* (1983). Taylor's work contains eight essays by women who are both inside and outside the academy. Its intention is to show how controversial Lessing's fiction remains, "how it is culturally active in different historical and discursive contexts" (12). For example, Nicole Ward Jouve's essay "Of Mud and Other Matters: The Children of Violence" forces us to reread the series without the assumption that it all hangs together; her essay is the first to develop in some detail the proposition that Lessing's conception of Martha changed over the years.[41] Sage's monograph has related emphases. It questions continuities, respects context, recovers work generally neglected in the United States, for example, *In Pursuit of the English.* As its three categories, Africa, England, and New Worlds, indicate, displacement is its organizing metaphor.

Like Sage's work, Mona Knapp's more recent *Doris Lessing* (1984) is intended as an overview for the general reader. It goes beyond serviceability, however, to provide some trenchant readings of Lessing's many and heterogeneous texts. Knapp notices, for example, that the depersonalized protagonist of *Memoirs* ("She has no name, no age, no personal background, no profession") "already speaks comfortably in the 'We' " that governs the Canopean archivists (129). Her study, the first to treat the complete Lessing corpus — essays, plays, poems, occasional journalism as well as fiction — also contains the most comprehensive biographical treatment to date.

Eve Bertelsen's "Casebook on Doris Lessing" (at this writing soon to be published in Capetown) focuses on Lessing's African origins and her reception in Southern Rhodesia and South Africa, presenting material hitherto unavailable to British and American scholars. In the long and remarkable Bertelsen-Lessing interview (taped in London in January 1984), Lessing drops her public persona and stock responses to by now worn-out questions. Instead, she is refreshingly candid, particularly about her African youth and African politics then and now.

These book-length studies about Lessing's work represent only one strand in the accumulated critical corpus, which includes bibliographies, dissertations, critical reviews, articles, interviews, special issues of journals, and Modern Language Association seminars. A *Doris Lessing Newsletter* has been published since 1976; a Doris Lessing Society was founded in 1979.

IV

Lessing has written too much, too quickly, and in too many different forms for an anthology of this size to adequately summarize, indeed even represent, critical assessment of her work. Our three major rubrics, "Politics and Patterns," "Female (Other) Space," and "Inner and Outer Space," are meant to suggest the variety of approaches, the richness of response, the competing interpretations as well as the historical directions in Lessing criticism. In the first section, "Politics and Patterns," for example, Martin Green and Jenny Taylor place Lessing in the British literary and political tradition; Green makes witty leaps of association, drawing parallels between *Memoirs of a Survivor* and other novels of empire, while Taylor looks anew at Lessing's doubly exilic status (from both Africa and England) by reconsidering a hitherto generally dismissed minor work, *Going Home.* "Politics and Patterns" brings together formal as well as thematic strategies, shape as well as ideology. Claire Sprague suggests a formal patterning in *The Golden Notebook* based on the doubling and multiplication of character. In this view Anna must internalize the destructive principle, which she typically construes as male. Roberta Rubinstein reads *Marriages* as a contemporary parallel to an alchemical text, a reading that is one way of exploring the acknowledged allegorical implications of the novel.

Our second rubric, "Female (Other) Space," shows how dense, how complex the approach to that other space which is female space can be. For one thing men can enter it — as is shown by Mark Spilka's essay on *Women in Love* and *The Golden Notebook*, which elaborates the similarities between sexist Lawrence and feminocentric Lessing. A favorite figure of feminist critics despite her repeated assertions that she is not a feminist, Lessing was early expropriated as a political symbol for what would become the feminist critique of literature, a critique whose historical development this section records. Virginia Tiger's essay on *The Summer before the Dark*, representing feminist literary criticism in its pioneering stages, examines character and structure from a gender perspective. The three essays by Jean Pickering, Elizabeth Abel, and Claire Hanson represent developing directions in feminist poetics. Pickering's essay contains a succinct summary of American feminist poetic. Strongly influenced by Sandra Gilbert and Susan Gubar's *The Madwoman in the Attic*, Pickering excavates covert plots and subtexts in the Children of Violence. If Pickering's critical links are to Gilbert and Gubar, then Abel's and Hanson's are to French feminist theory. Abel argues that in *The Golden Notebook* "Anna's ironic recitation of the oppositions that shape our experience . . . sketches the deconstructive impulse underlying her composite work of fiction" and develops the view that the novel "implies a theory of gendered writing." In what amounts to a unique contribution to the Lessing critical canon, Hanson applies sophisticated feminist analyses to the short stories that everyone admires but few write about. She makes a strong case for including "these fissured, disjointed, problematic texts" in any consideration of Lessing's work.

Like the two preceding categories, our "Inner and Outer Space," suggests both traditional and radical conceptions of inner and outer space. Dagmar Barnouw and Marion Vlastos treat inner space in its more traditional sense: the realm of the psyche. Although Barnouw's essay, like many in this collection, could fit under more than one rubric, its position here suggests its relation to that inner space defined in the bildungsroman tradition. Barnouw argues that the first four volumes of the Children of Violence are not bildungsromane "in the strict sense of the word." She is also unorthodox in preferring the more open narrative form, the "disorderly company," of *The Four-Gated City* to the orderly *The Golden Notebook*. Vlastos, on the other hand, documents Lessing's debt to the controversial theorist R. D. Laing, arguing that Lessing's *Briefing* explores the Laingian proposition that madness can provide salvation and prophetic insight.

Ellen Cronan Rose takes the architectural metaphor that gave its name to the final volume of the Children of Violence series and unearths its relationship to classical and Renaissance utopias, especially to Campanella's *City of the Sun*. Our identification of the city as outer space is more original in this context than the usual association of that dimension with galactic other worlds. But, of course, the city *is* outer space just as much as the room is, a point Lessing forces us to acknowledge. Her move from the city to cosmological space in *Shikasta* simply extends that spatial metaphor. Dealing with what is more conventionally known as outer space, Draine traces "what Roland Barthes calls the 'braid of codes,' the stereophony, of the rich text" that is *Shikasta*. The novel, in her view, establishes a new creation myth, one indebted to the sacred literatures of the world. Ironically, therefore, outer space is no black hole; it is rooted firmly in earthly traditions.

Of the four sections that compose this collection, "Reception and Reputation" was the most intriguing to assemble, partly because Lessing has had the good fortune to attract lively, acute, outspoken reviewers who have been anything but pedestrian or sycophantic. The criticism reflected in these reviews in no way corresponds to Lessing's generally dismissive attitude to what she considers the parasitic role of reviewers. It is striking that so many of them are novelists themselves. Gore Vidal, Joyce Carol Oates, Joan Didion, Rebecca West, and Kingsley Amis were able to scissor through an established reputation and meet Lessing's strengths and weaknesses head-on. Two of the other novelist-reviewers, Margaret Drabble and Erica Jong, acknowledge their indebtedness to Lessing. Indeed, a whole essay could be devoted to tracing Lessing's influence on younger women writers, those who came of age in the women's movement of the sixties and seventies. Even the poet Adrienne Rich, although she quarrels with Lessing, testifies to her exemplary role.

As our small sample in this section indicates, Lessing's work has received sustained attention in both mainstream and what was once known as counterculture publications. *Ramparts*, the *Village Voice*, and the *New Republic* were as likely to consider a new Lessing publication as the *New York Times*, the *London Times* and the *New York Review of Books*. But the "cage of association and labels that every established writer has to learn to live inside"[42] became increasingly oppressive to Lessing and one of her stated reasons for engineering an escape into the pseudonymous novel. The Ellen Goodman and Jonathan Yardley newspaper accounts, although they differ in interpretation, are samples of the extravagant media response to Lessing's disguise as Jane Somers.

Associations and labels affixed to writers, however, are as much products of historical time as they are of promotional hype. The place was the same, but the Lessing who addressed a 92d Street Y audience in 1984 was not the same as in 1969. Nor was her audience. As Susan Brownmiller's report shows, the feminist issue was paramount for the critical-activist audience of 1969 while Virginia Tiger's report describes a 1984 audience at best apolitical and certainly adulatory.

This kind of adulation and reputation should not obscure the paradoxical fact that Lessing's place in academia is still securing itself. A generation of young scholars has done much to revise curricula so that her work can be absorbed. Her significant following does not yet have the institutional power to change the scholarly canon. There are exceptions. Mark Spilka's essay on Lessing and Lawrence, reprinted here, is an example of the legitimitizing of Lessing in the academy and the literary canon. It seems especially fitting to remember that D. H. Lawrence, an immensely popular novelist, was similarly not accepted by academicians as a suitable figure for study until the iconoclast F. R. Leavis announced in Cambridge—the pages of *Scrutiny* buttressing his claim—that the author of *The Rainbow* was indeed part of the Great Tradition of English literature.

What directions in Lessing criticism can be anticipated? The question must be asked; the answer must be partial and provisional. For one thing, Lessing is still writing and the creative body of any writer's life shifts with the publication of each new novel. In Lessing's case, the last two shifts have been fairly radical, to Canopus and to Jane Somers and *The Good Terrorist*. Her future shifts may well be equally radical. Certainly she has demonstrated the ability to unsettle our fondest notions of her. The early flush of intense identification with her feminocentric work—to the exclusion of other critical approaches—has all but spent itself. Women still see themselves in her work, but feminist theory is more richly informed by developing critical theory and cross-disciplinary insights as our "Female (Other) Space" section documents. Psychoanalytic theory, that inexhaustible ally of Lessing's concerns, has generally and only rudimentarily surfaced in influence studies. The Jungian archetypal approach, so balefully dominant in American criticism, is less likely to govern future critical approaches. The Marxist approach, more characteristic of British criticism, has, like feminist theory, become less prescriptive and more influenced by other disciplines and approaches like structuralism and semiotics These transformations suit the Lessing canon, which is too various to be served by one critical method, one critical focus, one form of scholarly archaeology.

Our anthology, the very first collection of critical essays about Doris

Lessing and the first to provide a historical overview of her work, has been structured to include essays that by their juxtaposition in each section suggest the various discourses available to critics and readers.

"Grandfathers Freud and Marx," still the dubious and inescapable patriarchs of our intellectual lives, will surely preside over future biographies of Lessing. Currently no biography exists. But Lessing is already looking over her shoulder at the first one, functioning as a wry matriarch for her future biographers by providing teasing hints about her life and its appearance in her literature. She herself has labeled as autobiographical essays her *Going Home* and *Particularly Cats*; incidentally, the cloying title of the latter obscures what is an utterly unsentimental account of Lessing's family life in Africa and her later single life in London. A third volume, *Memoirs of a Survivor*, she has called, maddeningly, "an attempt at autobiography," while she disclaims any biographical parallels in novels so patently autobiographical as *The Golden Notebook* and the Martha Quest series.

Such mixed signals are typical of Lessing even in her lesser hoaxes. Scholars about to deconstruct the encoded strands that constitute Lessing's life and her texts might focus on the title of Jane Somers's serious work, *Real and Apparent Structures*, a title that is both a "faintly malicious" parody of current critical jargon and an apt though unintended description of Lessing's own life-long endeavor to demystify and defamiliarize.

Lessing may always elude and confound her readers as any writer of her "narrative immensities"[42] is likely to do. But she has remained true to the goal announced so early on in "The Small Personal Voice." For her, the notion of the novel as a radical representational form fed by social urgencies has remained imperative. In her Preface to *The Golden Notebook* she noted "that it was not possible to find a novel which described the intellectual and moral climate of a hundred years ago, in the middle of the last century, in Britian, in the way Tolstoy did it for Russia, Stendhal for France" (xiv). Her statement implies her overriding ambition to become that kind of register for our time — indeed this ambition has been *the* profound constant in her writing career. Whether that ambition has been realized or not it is too early to say. It can be said that Doris Lessing has created more than "an encyclopedia of a psyche,"[44] to use Mary Ellmann's felicitous definition of the bildungsroman. She is in fact creating an encyclopedia of our century.

Notes

1. These opening paragraphs are indebted to Virginia Tiger's "Doris Lessing," *Contemporary Literature* 21(Spring 1980):286–90.

2. Elizabeth Wilson, "Yesterday's Heroines: On Rereading Lessing and de Beauvoir," in Jenny Taylor, ed., *Notebooks/Memoirs/Archives* (London: Routledge & Kegan Paul, 1982), 57.

3. "Cassandra in a World under Siege," *Ramparts* 10 (1972):54.

4. Virginia Tiger, "Candid Shot," *Doris Lessing Newsletter* 8(1984):5.

5. See, for example, Claire Tomalin, "Mischief: Why a Famous Novelist Played a Trick on the Literary World," *London Sunday Times*, 23 September 1984, p. 15; Claire Tomalin and John Witherow, "Doris Fails as Plain Jane," *London Sunday Times*, 23 September 1984, p. 1; Edwin McDowell, "Doris Lessing Says She Used Pen Name to Show New Writer's Difficulties," *New York Times*, 23 September 1984, p. 45. See also the Ellen Goodman and Jonathan Yardley responses in this volume.

6. See, for example, Claire Sprague's essay in this collection and " 'Without Contraries is no Progression': Lessing's *The Four-Gated City*," *Modern Fiction Studies* 26 (1980): 96–116.

7. John Barkham, *New York Times Book Review*, 10 September 1950, p. 4.

8. Jenny Taylor, "Introduction: Situating Reading," in Taylor, *Notebooks/Memoirs/Archives*, p. 21.

9. *Substance Under Pressure* (Madison: University of Wisconsin, 1983). See chapter 1.

10. *The Golden Notebook*, p. 440. All subsequent page references to Lessing's books refer to paperback reprints listed in the bibliography.

11. "Doris Lessing's *Città Felice*," *Massachusetts Review* 24(1983):38.

12. M. Mark, "Reports from the Front," *Village Voice*, 2 October 1978, p. 128.

13. Catharine R. Stimpson, "Doris Lessing and the Parables of Growth," in *The Voyage In: Fictions of Female Development*, ed. Elizabeth Abel, Marianne Hirsch, and Elizabeth Langland (Hanover and London: University Press of New England, 1983), 186.

14. Doris Lessing, "The Small Personal Voice," in *A Small Personal Voice: Essays, Reviews, Interviews*, ed. Paul Schlueter (New York: Alfred A. Knopf, 1974), 14.

15. See C. Hugh Holman, *A Handbook to Literature* (New York: Odyssey Press, 1960), 31.

16. Nicole Ward Jouve, "Of Mud and Other Matter: *The Children of Violence*," in Taylor, *Notebooks*, 75–134. See also Dagmar Barnouw, " 'Disorderly Company:' From *The Golden Notebook* to *The Four-Gated City*," *Contemporary Literature* 14 (1973):491–514, see also Drabble and Rose.

17. Elizabeth Abel, "*The Golden Notebook*: 'Female Writing' and 'The Great Tradition,' " Unpublished MLA paper, 1981. Reprinted in this volume.

18. "A Talk with Florence Howe," *A Small Personal Voice*, 81.

19. Irving Howe, "Neither Compromise nor Happiness," *New Republic* 147 (15 December 1962):17. Reprinted in this volume.

20. John Leonard, "The Spacing Out of Doris Lessing," *New York Times Book Review*, 7 February 1982, p. 35. Reprinted in this volume.

21. Frederick Karl, *The Contemporary English Novel* (New York: Farrar, Straus & Giroux, 1972), 293.

22. See Barnouw's article in this volume and Sprague, "Without Contraries."

23. See Carey Kaplan's discussion of the "pervasive and organic symbolic continuities of the Radlett house." "A Womb with a View: The House on Radlett Street in *The Four Gated City*," *Doris Lessing Newsletter* 7 (Summer 1983):3.

24. Mary Ann Singleton, *The City and the Veld: The Fiction of Doris Lessing* (Lewisburg, Penn.: Bucknell, 1977), 199.

25. Mona Knapp, *Doris Lessing* (New York: Frederick Ungar, 1984), 87.

26. Joyce Carol Oates, "Last Children of Violence," *Saturday Review* 57(17 May 1969):48. Reprinted in this volume.

27. Mary Ellmann, "*The Four-Gated City*," *New York Times Book Review*, 18 May 1969, p. 4.

28. See Erica Jong, "Everywoman Out of Love?" *Partisan Review* 40 (1973):501. Reprinted in this volume.

29. Herbert Marder, "Borderline Fantasies: The Two Worlds of *Briefing for a Descent into Hell*," *Papers on Language and Literature* 19 (1983):427–48.

30. Martin Green, "The Doom of Empire: *Memoirs of a Survivor*," *Doris Lessing Newsletter* 6(1982):6–7, 10. Reprinted in this volume.

31. Paul Gray, "Visit to a Small Planet," *Time*, 22 October 1979, p. 101.

32. Gore Vidal, "Paradise Regained," *New York Review of Books*, 30 December 1979, p. 3. Reprinted in this volume.

33. Lorna Sage, *Doris Lessing* (London: Methuen, 1983), 79.

34. Gray, "Small Planet," p. 102.

35. Sage, *Doris Lessing*, p. 79.

36. Ellen Peel, "Communicating Differently: Doris Lessing's *Marriages Between Zones Three, Four and Five*," *Doris Lessing Newsletter* 6(Winter 1982):11–13.

37. Roberta Rubenstein, "*The Marriages Between Zones Three, Four, and Five*: Doris Lessing's Alchemical Allegory," *Extrapolation* 24(1983):205. Reprinted in this volume.

38. Ellen Cronan Rose, "Let's Take Doris Lessing's Space Fiction Seriously," unpublished paper.

39. Ibid.

40. Simone de Beauvoir shares this concern. See *La Veillesse* (Paris: Gallimard, 1970), translated as *The Coming of Age* (New York: Putnam's 1972).

41. See also D. J. Enright, "Shivery Graves," *New York Review of Books* 13 (31 July 1969):22–24.

42. Preface to *The Diaries of Jane Somers* (New York: Knopf, 1984), vii.

43. Stimpson, "Doris Lessing and the Parables of Growth," 189.

44. Mary Ellmann, "*The Four-Gated City*," *New York Times Book Review*, 18 May 1969, p. 4.

CHRONOLOGY

Mona Knapp*

1919   Doris May Tayler is born on October 22 in Kermanshah, Persia (today Iran), the first child of Emily Maud (née McVeagh) Tayler and Alfred Cook (called Michael) Tayler, British citizens. Tayler is a bank official with the Imperial Bank of Persia.

1921   Doris's brother Harry, the Tayler's second child, born.

1924   The Tayler family emigrates to Southern Rhodesia.

1926–1932   Doris attends school at the Roman Catholic Convent in Salisbury.

1932–1933   She spends one year at the Girl's High School in Salisbury, which concludes her formal schooling.
Her education thereafter consists of extensive independent reading.

1934–1936   Doris Tayler does household work as an *au pair* girl with two families in Salisbury.

1936–1937   First efforts to write prose and poetry result in two novels and several novel fragments (unpublished).

1938   She takes final departure from her parents' farm to seek work in Salisbury. Her first job is with the telephone company as an operator.

1939   Marriage at age nineteen to Frank Charles Wisdom, a civil servant.

1942   Doris Wisdom becomes involved in local Marxist group.

1943   Divorce from Frank Wisdom, who retains custody of their son (John) and daughter (Jean). First poems and short fiction are published in local journals.

1945   Marriage to Gottfried Anton Lessing, a German refugee and fellow-member of the Marxist group in which she is active. Lessing works as a typist for two legal offices, then for

*From *Doris Lessing*, (New York: Frederick Ungar Co., 1984), xiii–xviii.

government commissions and Hansard, the official Parliament Record.

1947   Birth of Lessing's third child, Peter.

1947–1948   Lessing works on *The Grass Is Singing* and forms plans to emigrate to England.

1949   Divorce from Gottfried Lessing, who returns to Germany. Doris Lessing sails with her son Peter to London.

1950   Her first novel, *The Grass Is Singing*, is published.

1951   *This Was the Old Chief's Country*, short stories, is published.

1952   *Martha Quest*, Lessing's second novel and the initial volume of the *Children of Violence* series. Lessing is a participant in a delegation of the Authors' World Peace Appeal to the Soviet Union.

1953   *Five: Short Novels*. Lessing's first play, *Before the Deluge* (also known under the title *Mr. Dolinger*) is produced in London.

1954   *A Proper Marriage*, Lessing's third novel (volume two of *Children of Violence*) is published. Lessing receives the Somerset Maugham Award of the Society of Authors for *Five*.

1956   Lessing returns to Africa after seven years' absence. She has in the meantime been declared a "prohibited immigrant" because of her political views, but is admitted by mistake. On her return to England, she formally leaves the Communist Party in protest against Stalinist atrocities and the invasion of Hungary. *Retreat to Innocence*, her fourth novel, is published.

1957   *Going Home*, an autobiographical reportage describing her trip to Africa; *The Habit of Loving* (short stories).

1958   Her fifth novel, *A Ripple From the Storm* (volume three of *Children of Violence*). A second play, *Each His Own Wilderness*, is performed by the English Stage Society at the Royal Court Theatre, London, on 23 March. *Mr. Dolinger* produced in Oxford. [Dramatic criticism, briefly, for the *Observer*.]

1959   *Fourteen Poems* and *Each His Own Wilderness* published.

1960   Publication of *In Pursuit of the English*, Lessing's second major autobiographical essay. Third play, *The Truth About Billy Newton*, produced in Salisbury, Wiltshire.

1962   Publication of *The Golden Notebook*, Lessing's sixth novel, brings her overnight fame. Fourth drama, *Play With a Tiger*, produced in London. *The Grass Is Singing* is adapted as a television play.

1963   *A Man and Two Women* (short stories).

1964   *African Stories* published. *Play With a Tiger* produced in New York. Lessing begins her studies of the mystical Islam religion known as Sufism through the teachings of Idries Shah.

1964   *Landlocked*, seventh novel and volume four of *Children of Violence*.

1966   Lessing's literal translation of *The Storm*, a play by Alexander Ostrovsky, is produced unsuccessfully by the National Theatre in London. Production of two original television plays, *Please Do Not Disturb* and *Care and Protection*. Lessing collaborates on further television scripts based on works by Maupassant.

1967   *Particularly Cats* (autobiographical essay); *Between Men*, a fourth television play adapted from the short story of the same title.

1969   *The Four-Gated City*: Lessing's eighth novel completes her first novel sequence *Children of Violence*. Tour to United States includes visits to college campuses, among them SUNY Buffalo and Stony Brook, and Berkeley.

1971   *Briefing For a Descent Into Hell*, ninth novel.

1972   *The Story of a Non-Marrying Man and Other Stories*.

1973   *The Summer Before the Dark*, tenth novel. Publication of a sixth drama, *The Singing Door*, a one-act play written for a textbook anthology. *The Sun Between Their Feet* and *This Was the Old Chief's Country* (complete African stories).

1974   Second trip to the United States. *The Memoirs of a Survivor*, Lessing's eleventh novel. *A Small Personal Voice* (collected essays).

1976   Lessing is awarded the Prix Medicis for Foreigners (France).

1978   Publication of *To Room Nineteen* and *The Temptation of Jack Orkney* (complete British stories).

1971   *Shikasta*, Lessing's twelfth novel, is the first volume of a new series, *Canopus in Argos: Archives*.

1980   *The Marriages Between Zones Three, Four and Five*, volume two of *Canopus in Argos* and Lessing's thirteenth novel.

1981   *The Sirian Experiments*, the author's fourteenth novel and volume three of the new series.

1982   *The Making of the Representative for Planet 8*, volume four of *Canopus* and Lessing's fifteenth novel.

1982   Lessing receives the Shakespeare Prize of the West German Hamburger Stiftung. She is also awarded the Austrian State Prize for European Literature, given yearly to a literary figure of international significance. Trip to Spain in April. Second trip to Africa from July to September. Two week tour of Japan in November.

1983   Publication of *the Sentimental Agents*, fifth volume of *Canopus* and Lessing's sixteenth novel.

[1984   Visit to Canada. Third trip to the United States, April 1984. Publication of *The Diaries of Jane Somers*, containing two previously published novels under the pseudonym of Jane Somers: *The Diary of a Good Neighbor* and *If the Old Could.* . . .

1985   Talk for Afghan Relief, March 19, San Francisco. *The Good Terrorist*, Lessing's nineteenth novel.]

POLITICS AND PATTERNS

The Doom of Empire: *Memoirs of a Survivor*

Martin Green*

The Memoirs of a Survivor is in many ways a different sort of fiction from Lessing's early work. It is non-political and non-erotic. It is assertively non-autobiographical, non-personal, and describes the future, not the past. It employs the techniques of fantasy and rejects those of realism (nothing is named, not even London or the narrator). Its values are in some sense symbolic and mystical. Thus it is not a novel at all. Is Lessing's development then following Waugh's and Amis's, towards Kipling? Not entirely; because though she discards the role of revolutionary, she does not assume reactionary views; and though she turns away from the novelist's responsibilities, she does not accept the role of entertainer of the ruling class.

But even the book's most novelistic moments — when the writer persuades us to grieve over other people's grief — are very different from parallel moments in the early work. Thus the moment which impresses me most is when the narrator hears crying from the room beyond the wall of her apartment:

> I heard the sobbing of a child, a child alone, disliked, repudiated; and at the same time, beside it, I could hear the complaint of the mother, the woman's plaint, and the two sounds went on side by side, theme and descant.
>
> I sat listening. I sat by myself and listened. It was warm, over-warm; it was that final hot summer. (148)[1]

The crying is that of the child whom Emily had been. Emily is now nearly fifteen.

*From the *Doris Lessing Newsletter* 6 (Winter 1982):6–7, 10. This article is part of *The Doom of Empire* (1984), a critical study of three novelists of imperial Britain — Kipling, Lawrence, and Joyce — and three of ex-imperial Britain — Waugh, Amis, and Lessing. Reprinted with permission of the *Doris Lessing Newsletter*.

31

> One morning Emily came in, all brisk and lively, and, seeing me at work setting plums on trays to dry, she joined me. She was wearing that morning a striped cotton shirt, and jeans. The shirt lacked a button at breast level, and gaped, showing her already strong breasts. She looked tired, as well as full of energy; she had not yet bathed, and a smell of sex came from her. She was fulfilled and easy, a bit sad, but humorously so. She was, in short, a woman, and she sat wiping plums with slow easy movements, all the hungers, drives, and the needs pounded and hunted out of her, exorcised in the recent lovemaking. And all the time that child was crying. . . .(148) "Can't you hear someone crying?" I asked, as casual as could be, while I was twisting and turning inwardly not to hear that miserable sound.
> "No, can you?" And off she went to stand at the window, Hugo beside her. (149)

Such writing is on the far side of the novel, verging on the mythic and the legendary.

> I let my palms move over to the wall, slowly, inch by inch, but I did not find a way in that day, nor the next; I never did find that weeping child, who remained there, sobbing hopelessly alone and disowned, and with long years in front of her to live through before time could put strength into her and set her free. (151)

What she did find, she says, was something inevitable, even banal:

> Who else could it possibly be but Emily's mother, the large cart-horse woman, her tormentor, the world's image? . . . Up went the little arms, desperate for comfort, but they would be one day those great arms that had never been taught tenderness. . . .(151)

One of the elements in that structure of sensibility is a positive disinclination for personal relations and their analysis and everything else that characterizes novelistic experience. When she begins to tell us it was the mother who was crying, she breaks off in a boredom that has some element of revulsion.

> I never found Emily. But I did find . . . the thing is, what I did find was inevitable. I could have foreseen it. The finding had about it, had in it as its quintessence, the banality, the tedium, the smallness, the restriction, of that "personal" dimension.(151)

The narrator has talked before of the personal dimension and how she dislikes it. She finds behind the wall both the history that explains Emily, and the impersonal, a series of empty spaces; she hates the first and loves the second:

> One, the "personal," was instantly to be recognized by the air that was its prison, by the emotions that were its creatures. The impersonal scenes might bring discouragement of problems that had to be solved — like the rehabilitation of walls or furniture, cleaning, putting order into chaos —

but in that realm there was a lightness, a freedom, a feeling of possibility. Yes, that was it, the space and the knowledge of alternative action. One could refuse to clean that room, clear that patch of earth; one could walk into another room altogether, choose another scene. But to enter the "personal" was to enter a prison, where nothing could happen but what one saw happening, where the air was tight and limited, and above all where time was a strict unalterable law and long. . . .(42)

That note of weariness is sustained, though blended with other notes, of responsibility, of engagement, and together they make a new voice for fiction — the voice of the old woman.

What this book has to tell the student of Doris Lessing is perhaps primarily that she has revised her image of herself. Of course she does not appear in the novel — that freedom from the personal is largely a matter of the absence of Martha Quest, Anna Wulf, et al. But still the childhood and family situation which the narrator fantasizes about Emily, to explain her, is strikingly like the family and childhood of Martha Quest and Doris Lessing. The jolly but anxious mother, the silent resigned father, the girl who feels guilty and rejected, the younger brother who seems to be preferred — all these are familiar. But the typology assigned to the girl who is the product of this upbringing is now English middle-class, even upper middle-class. Emily is not, as Martha was, primarily a rebel, a victim, a passionate truth-seeker or "final heir to the long tradition of love"; she is primarily an anxious controller of others, a servant of the community, the person who takes responsibility and authority. At four she had "intensely serious, already defensive eyes" (43). And we see her thus.

> Emily came into view, her frowning face bent over a task. She wore a soft blue smock-like garment, like an old-fashioned child from a nursery, and she held a broom made of twigs. . . . But as she swept, as she made her piles, the leaves gathered again round her feet. She swept faster, faster, her face scarlet, desperate.(137)

This image of Emily is of course the narrator's diagnostic vision of her as a child. As an adolescent, she takes responsibility for the other children.

> I understood now what I had half noticed before — the way the children reacted when they saw Emily. This was how people respond to Authority (131). A child of about seven quite openly grimaced at June — it was that face which is made to say, *What does she think she is, bossing us?* — that absolutely routine reaction, to be observed in one form or another anywhere there are groups, hierarchies, institutions.(134)

The narrator's sympathies are with those in charge, those cut off by responsibility from full membership in the group. It is striking that she portrays Gerald, the gang leader, in the same terms that is, with sympathy for the man in authority: "From near by, this young chieftain was not so formidable; he seemed harassed, he was even forlorn . . . one saw a very young man, overburdened and overresponsible and unsure, asking for support, even tenderness (108)."

Doris Lessing's heroines always showed a sympathy for the man who took on responsibility (Martha Quest married Anton; Anna Wulf, Willi), and that sympathy always overflowed into erotic feeling; but in the earlier books the author always attacked that eroticism as inauthentic and self-destructive.

There is, moreover, a great gulf set in the book between Emily-and-Gerald and the Ryans, a slum family whose life-pattern is discussed at length as totally feckless. This is the categorization the novel observes, opposing the responsible to the irresponsible — the administrator's categories. Something like the opposite was true of Lessing's earlier books. Of course, I remember that Lessing's early heroines are often said to do welfare work; that is what Anna turns to at the end of *The Golden Notebook*. But in such cases the work was subsumed in the larger category of politics and radicalism; social distress was presented as somebody's fault, as the fault of "them." In this book, as the narrator says, "they" have been replaced by "it," the enemy by the catastrophe, anger by patience. Here that suggestion of original sin, made as a horizon to the analysis in *The Golden Notebook*, is the center or starting point of the myth.

If one accepts this suggestion, that Lessing is here identifying herself as someone implicated in the privileged and ruling class, then one finds a further poignancy in the Edwardian (or Imperial period) furniture and clothes fantasized for Emily; and in the Edwardian style of the fantasy itself — the style of Edwardian books about and for children — there is an echo of Barrie or the Kipling of "They" about the transparent wall, the world beyond it, and the children there. Changing the African farm for the Edwardian nursery, she changes innocence for guilt.

Moreover, the natural symbolism of painting walls, cleaning house, gardening, and cooking, so widespread in Lessing's earlier books, is here replayed in a more powerful and concentrated but self-diagnostic form. The book makes a symbolic antithesis between white paint (and white curtains, white baby-clothes, white bedspreads) and the brown, the dirt, of the feces with which the baby smears herself. House-painting is the role of Martha Quest and Anna Wulf, it is hinted; Doris Lessing had been acting out the anxiety of cleanliness, driven by the fear of dirt, a fear derived, via her family, from her class, with its duty to maintain standards and represent the social ideal.

What the book shows us, if we take the view of the history of the novel, is Lessing saying goodbye to the novel form. At the end, she, Emily, Gerald, their attendant animal, and the Presence behind the wall, move away from us into a legendary and emblematic land, away from people, cities, and actuality. Her imagery here seems to owe something to T.S. Eliot in "Ash-Wednesday," and it would be appropriate that this late Lessing should make some alliance with that poet in her withdrawal. The earlier Lessing, the Martha Quest and Anna Wulf (who lived in the same London of the fifties with Eliot) cannot be conjoined with him in the imagination. What could Anna have said of "The Cocktail Party" or "The Confidential Clerk"? But in fact since *Memoirs of a Survivor*, Lessing has not turned back to the novel form or to realism or to "life" as she would have defined it. She has stayed in the world of fantasy, in its characteristic modern form, future fiction. She too, like Kipling's heirs, had to turn away from the novel to fiction.

What *Memoirs* shows us, if we take the point of view of the history of England and the empire, is Lessing saying goodbye to the whole "wasp" enterprise. This may sound like less of a change from the early Lessing than the other features of *Memoirs of a Survivor*, but it is a goodbye this time, not a denunciation or a repudiation. There is no anger expressed, and no self-dissociation from those responsible — if anything, as we have seen, there is a self-association. Above all, there is a lingering, in a sense a loving, last recapitulation of the themes of the "wasp" myth, of that adventure story which was the energizing myth of the British empire.

We can see this recapitulation in terms of *Robinson Crusoe*, the archetype of the modern adventure, which is evoked in many passages of *Memoirs of a Survivor*. Gerald and Emily are both presented to us wearing skins, like illustrations to Defoe's story, for instance. Gerald,

> swaggered there with the knives in his belt, his whiskers, his strong brown arms. Good Lord, how many centuries had we overturned, how many long slow steps of man's upclimbing did Emily undo when she crossed from my flat to the life on the pavement! And what promise, what possibilities, what experiments, what variations on the human theme had been cancelled out! (150)

Then the do-it-yourself enthusiasm so strong in *Robinson Crusoe* is replayed in *Memoirs*:

> [There] were these houses which were as if the technological revolution had never occurred at all. The big house fifteen minutes' walk away had been an old people's home. It had large grounds. Shrubs and flowerbeds had been created and now there were only vegetables. There was even a little shed in which a few fowls were kept. . . . But they were about to get a hive of bees (104). The place was a conglomeration of little workshops; they made soap and candles and wove materials and dyed them; they cured leather; they dried and preserved food; they reconstructed and made furniture. (105)

In this passage Lessing shares Defoe's enthusiasm, or at least her differences from him are not dialectical or satirical. Briefly, she expresses a joy, quite like his, in the making of things. In other places she clearly expresses the melancholy of seeing so much destroyed:

> I cannot begin to give an idea of the mess in those rooms . . . heaped with cracking and splintering furniture. . . . Once I saw in the centre of

a formal and rich room — French, Second Empire, as lifeless as if it had
been arranged for a museum — the remains of a fire built on a piece of
old iron, some sleeping bags left anyhow, a big pot full of cold boiled
potatoes near the wall in line with a dozen pairs of boots. I knew the
soldiers would come back suddenly, and if I wanted to keep my life I
should leave. Already there was a corpse, with dried blood staining the
carpet around it. (159)

Thus *Memoirs of a Survivor* can be seen as an inverted and reverted
form of *Robinson Crusoe* and of Defoe's fiction in general. Instead of a
man alone on an island, we have a woman not alone in a city; instead of
an entrepreneur, a survivor; instead of a sense of a beginning, a sense of
ending; instead of a young narrator an old one; instead of a technology
and economy being built up before our eyes, we have them being broken
down; instead of the London of *Moll Flanders*, the new Rome, a great
growing labyrinth of excitements and extremes, we have a broken social
machinery, half-empty, about to become a ruin; instead of the beginnings
of the British Empire, and the modern world system, and the new
technology, we have their endings.

That is why it is an appropriate book to form the last in the series I
consider in *The Doom of Empire*, which begins with Kipling and looks
back to Defoe and that long tradition of adventures which constitutes in
some sense the main line of English fiction. (Leavis's Great Tradition can
be seen as a reaction against that line.) And that is also why the old
woman's voice is so appropriate to it. When the question of feminism is
raised, it is put by, wearily:

> And now I suppose it must be asked and answered why Emily did not
> choose to be a chieftainess, a leader on her own account? Well, why not?
> Yes, I did ask myself this, of course. The attitudes of women towards
> themselves and to men, the standards of women had set up for
> themselves, the gallantry of their fight for equality, the decades-long
> and very painful questioning of their roles, their functions — all this
> makes it very difficult to say, simply, that Emily was in love. . . . There
> was nothing to stop her. No law, written or unwritten, said she should
> not, and her capacities and talents were every bit as varied as Gerald's or
> anybody else's. But she did not. I don't think it occurred to her. (109)

There is even an explicit, though unstressed, wish for death. When Emily
for the first time takes a shirt of the narrator's without permission, the
latter is delighted and feels it is a liberation.

> *This is more mine than yours*, says the act of the theft; *more mine
> because I need it more; it fits my stage of life better than it does yours;
> you have outgrown it.* . . . And perhaps the exhilaration it releases is
> even a hint of an event still in the future, that moment when the person
> sees in the eyes of people the statement — still unconscious, perhaps: *You
> can hand over your life now; you don't need it any longer; we will live it
> for you; please go.* (59)

Lessing's protagonist speaks for all those who bore the "white man's burden," whether in the colonies or at home, including those who rebelled against their class. We can hear in her voice the echo of T.S. Eliot's. We can hear the weariness of the responsible class. Above all we can hear the end of empire.

Note

1. All page references are to the Bantam edition of *The Memoirs of a Survivor* (1975).

Memory and Desire on Going Home: The Deconstruction of a Colonial Radical

Jenny Taylor*

To begin with, three fragments. The first from Antonio Gramsci's *Prison Notebooks*:

> When one's conception of the world is not critical and coherent but disjointed and episodic, one belongs simultaneously to a multiplicity of human groups. . . . The starting-point of critical elaboration is the consciousness of what one really is, and is "knowing thyself" as a product of the historical process to date, which has left one in an infinity of traces, without leaving an inventory. . . .

The second, from Michel Foucault:

> The purpose of history is not to discover the roots of our identity, but to commit ourselves to its dissolution. . . .

The third from Doris Lessing, "The Small Personal Voice":

> But to imagine free man, leisured man, is to step outside of what we are. There is no one on this earth who is not twisted by insecurity and by the compromises of thinking made inevitable by want and fear. Those who say: you can't give man leisure, he won't know how to use it, are as much victims of a temporary phase of economic development as the coupon fillers and the screen dreamers. Their imaginations are in bond to their own necessities. Slaves can envy the free; slaves can fight to free their children; but slaves suddenly set free are marked by habits of submission and slaves imagining freedom see it through the eyes of slaves. . . .

Here I want to contribute to an analysis of Lessing's African writing

*This essay was presented at a Modern Language Association meeting sponsored by the Doris Lessing Society in 1983 and is published here for the first time with the permission of the author.

by exploring the relation between text and history at a particular moment — 1956 — and regarding a particular text — *Going Home* — a text that raises a second set of issues connected to the first: the relationship between fictional, documentary, and autobiographical discourse. *Going Home* is a problematic piece of writing, one which stubbornly refuses to be neatly pigeonholed within Lessing's oeuvre. At the most simple level, one might say that this is because *Going Home* is not a fiction, but rather some loosely defined "factual" work — often dipped into to produce a second order of meaning to underwrite and corroborate the fictional texts in some way. Yet Lessing's other nonfiction work, *In Pursuit of the English*, published in 1961, and also used for this purpose, does not pose the same problems of definition and interpretation as *Going Home* does. *In Pursuit of the English* has a greater formal and ideological coherence; it fits easily into the autobiographical genre. By contrast, *Going Home* is no such unified text. It employs different discursive conventions and transgresses a range of generic boundaries: autobiography, political analysis and commentary, journalistic reportage, travelogue. Narrative time is broken up and narrative perspective fractured; the authorial persona is now dreamer, now historical authority, now political analyst, now poet, now object of surveillance, now witness. It was this apparent lack of both literary and political coherence that was noted by the critical establishment when the piece first appeared. Yet this also enables the text to be sanitized.

Going Home, then, *can* be read as a rather confused piece of documentary writing. But here I want to offer a different interpretation — a symptomatic reading of the book as speaking the unspoken that lies beneath Lessing's official fictional project. By this I don't primarily mean that many of the thematic political concerns — particularly the dissection of racist ideologies — explored in *The Grass Is Singing*, the African stories, the first four volumes of *The Children of Violence* sequence, and the African sections of *The Golden Notebook*, are discussed in detail here, though that is obviously true. I mean rather that in a more complex way, and through its very interstitial and marginal status, *Going Home* articulates many of the simultaneously formal and ideological tensions which are reworked in the fiction itself.

To examine this process one needs to hold several — often contradictory — movements together simultaneously. Above all, it requires breaking with the conception of Lessing the author progressing smoothly from one stage of development to another, or as simply drawing on Africa as some sort of neutral inspiration or primal source for her writing. The process, rather, describes a double movement which is in certain respects the underside of that simultaneously Utopian and critical impulse which many critics have noted as characteristic of Lessing's fiction. Here the movement is also at once deconstructive and reconstructive.

Going Home does not simply reflect Lessing's political and historical situation; it is the stage on which the dilemmas of authorial identity, committed writing, and political stance are most sharply acted out. The text enacts a political and cultural crisis not least in its inability to produce either a stable narrative voice or a fixed implied reader.

Lessing must be resituated within a nexus of historical determinant. Africa and England; the past and the shifting present. Africa as representing England's colonial past; England as shaping while destroying Africa's history. In *Going Home*, Africa, more specifically "Rhodesia" (I am using the historical name Rhodesia here rather than the contemporary Zimbabwe) is not a geographical location so much as a political construction. It cannot be comprehended as one place, but as a cluster of dominant and oppositional myths. The past, moreover, does not lead in an inevitable teleological progression into the present, but is constantly interpreted and reinterpreted. We now read *Going Home* as a historical text, in the light of subsequent events — the Smith regime and UDI, the growth of black nationalism, the birth of Zimbabwe. And Lessing, the perceiver and writer, is herself a moving target; not going home, for the force of the title partly lies in its irony, but recalling a collection of pasts from the standpoint of an unstable present, and a collection of displaced identities. *Going* Home addresses and constructs an alien reader, looking at Africa from outside, whom the writer is leaving in order to inform. Going *Home* implies arriving somewhere familiar, seeing it through a pentimento of memories, overlapping biographical and historical time, but as an alien who cannot be assimilated, either by the dominant white or subordinate black culture. The process of perception/discovery that this engenders is close to Jacques Derrida's notion of the production of meaning as *différence*: meaning can never be seized as a presence, it is always deferred, displaced onto the next element in a chain of signification that has no end — no trancendental signified.

Going

The first thread to unravel, then, is *going*; the political and cultural tensions that contributed to Lessing's own position as a white Communist woman African writer, living in England, by 1956. I qualify "African writer" in this way deliberately. By 1956 Lessing had been living an expatriate existence in England for seven years, and though she was still being received and read primarily as an African writer, this was through a process of reconstruction that could only take place from England. Lessing *is* an "African" writer, but this is mediated by a chain of qualifying factors whereby marginality and difference, the formation of the writer through *absent* cultural and political traditions, are a source of strength and a point of impasse. On the one hand, and in terms of cultural tradition, the identity that she is able to hold as a white anticolonial colonial is crucial for negotiating a valid space as a woman writer — it helps defuse her gender (though without making it invisible) within the literary establishment. Her position here is of exotic exile rather than woman; and this isn't purely an ideological construction—it is a real advantage. On the other hand, Lessing's position as socialist humanist white Rhodesian *within* the political discourse surrounding colonialism in England in the mid-1950s enabled her to maintain the stance of communist intellectual—until the moment of *Going Home*—and at the same time to defuse it.

Both the status of colonial writing in the British cultural formation and the debates on the Left concerning the committed intellectual and realist writing are crucial here; and here too historical and geographical displacements overlie one another. Lessing's anticolonial colonial writing was able to find a place within the absent center of the English national culture and yet at the same time maintain a critical distance from it in several respects. Firstly there was the longer tradition, going back to the mid-nineteenth century; the tendency of the dominant culture to draw on exiles and émigres—be they from America, Ireland, or Yorkshire— Charlotte Brontë, Henry James, Joyce, for example. The motif of the marginal observer is a familiar feature of literary history. But this interstitial position is given a more specific twist in colonial writing of the 1950s. Africa overlaid with "Rhodesia" signifies both the strange and the familiar. The romantic construction of Africa as England's pastoral "Other" has been perceived by Lessing and others as the inverse side of colonial racism.[1] The political situation in Southern Rhodesia in the 1950s was in many ways too close, *too* home. In the postwar period, a moment of national reconstruction when a reformed concept of "Britishness" was a lynchpin in establishing a national consensus within the rhetoric of Tory Government and Labour opposition alike, Britain's colonial policy was in itself in disarray. This was most clearly visible in the Suez crisis of 1956, focussing as it did on the loss of control and contested territory. But the relationship between Britain and Rhodesia was more complex and, in many respects, more problematic. The problem of Rhodesia for England was precisely *not* of colonial lands being seized by an alien force, but of the legacy of nineteenth century imperialism growing in Rhodesian white settler culture itself, fed by waves of British immigrants. *Going Home* exposes both the inadequacy and hypocrisy of "Partnership," that legacy of nineteenth century British paternalism, and the inevitable assimilation of immigrant British trade unionists into a racist culture. . .

Nineteen fifty-six has been mythologized as a moment of crisis for the British Left—not least by *The Golden Notebook* and *The Four-Gated City*. The Suez crisis, the Soviet invasion of Hungary, Khrushchev's Twentieth Party Congress speech, the split in the British Communist Party, and the birth of the New Left, have become almost over-familiar. The main body of the text of *Going Home* was written *at* this moment, and therefore *before* it was constructed as historically significant. It reworks that moment in both the 1957 and 1968 postscripts almost in the tone of the retraction of a confession. The position *within* which Lessing wrote

Going Home was an excolonial on the British Left, in the context of the
need to reclaim an essentially English socialist humanist tradition formulated in the 1930s and traced through the writing of Blake, Shelley,
Morris; a tradition on the one hand romantic and utopian, on the other,
nostalgic, even little-Englandish. As a colonial radical Lessing at once
criticized this tradition and contributed to it; in the same year she wrote of
England in "The Small Personal Voice":

> It is a country so profoundly parochial that people like myself
> coming in from outside never cease to marvel. Do the British people
> know that all over what is politely referred to as the Commonwealth,
> millions of people continually discuss and speculate about their reac-
> tions to this or that event? No, and if they did they would not care. . . .[2]

Yet just as she was able to revitalize a waning tradition within the
dominant culture — a tradition also valorized by the Left — so her direct
experience of the extreme racism, even quasifascism, of Southern Rhodesia
meant that she "skipped a decade" and recalled the antifascist struggles of
the 1930s. Again, the negotiation of difference and familiarity.

Home

In 1956, Lessing returns to Africa as a successful novelist writing in
England, though Africa is the structuring absence. Her motives on
returning are at once personal and political. She was indirectly sponsored
by Tass, the Soviet news agency, to make the trip, which was both a return
to scenes of early childhood and to report on the contemporary political
situation in Southern Rhodesia. The early 1950s, between Lessing's
departure and her return visit, saw continued economic growth, but not
its cultural counterpart. Its main features were the expansion of multina-
tional capital, a wave of immigration of white English skilled workers,
escaping not from the depression of the thirties but from the austerity, red
tape, and welfare socialism of the postwar Labour government, and a
growing black industrial labor force. It is a moment, too, of the transformation of displaced national identities and mythologies. There is the myth
of Englishness itself, as Lessing discusses in *Going Home* and returns to in
In Pursuit of the English which is an essentially polysemic construction:
"While the word 'English' is tricky enough in England, this is nothing to
the variety of meanings it might bear in a Colony, self-governing or
otherwise."[3] Not only is "English" ambiguous; "England" itself is mythi-
cally constructed in different ways. There is the England of ordered
tradition, the mother's dream, mixing and combining different elements:
"A combination of the best parts of Blackheath, or Richmond, merged, or
mingled with a really large ranch, let's say about fifty thousand acres, in
the Kenyan highlands. This would have to be pervaded by a pre-1914
atmosphere, or ambiance, like an Edwardian afterglow."[4] There is the

dream of England as cultural metropolis and citadel of radical liberalism. But in the 1950s that concept of Englishness, so central to the construction of the colonial subject, seems to have been becoming increasing differentiated from the white settler culture and the growth of white Rhodesian nationalism that was to culminate a few years later in UDI. Here Englishness, or rather "Britishness," feeds into the white settler ideology of conquest and racial superiority. Here Rhodesia represents the culmination, rather than the negation, of Britishness. Ian Smith, the first Rhodesian prime minister to be born in Rhodesia, was to comment a few years later, "If Churchill were alive today, I believe he'd probably emigrate to Rhodesia — because I believe that all those admirable qualities and characteristics of the British we believed in, loved and preached to our children, no longer exist in Britain."[5] But if these attitudes sound disturbingly familiar in contemporary Thatcherite Britain, they were not so manifestly acceptable in the Macmillan-Butler "wind of change" era. In the 1950s Rhodesia is also the unacceptable face of that legacy of Empire.

The Text

The interaction of difference, assimilation, and exile emerges in various interacting forms in *Going Home*. Just as the title implies a double movement of leaving and arriving, so the narrative discourse does not so much shift from one level to another as articulate tensions through assuming different perspectives. This involves, too, sliding between one authorial position and another: "it would be good for me to be a journalist for a time, a person collecting facts and information after being a novelist who has to go inwards to probe out the truth." But it is precisely this division between "inner" and "outer" truth that is broken down in the text; fractured by the problematic position of the observer looking at herself looking at her reflection:

> Once a painter said to me that when his picture went wrong and he didn't know what was wrong with it, he used to creep out of bed in the middle of the night, go to his studio and very quickly and suddenly turn on the lights — *so that he could catch sight of his picture before it could see him..*
>
> Well, I wish I could switch on a new light so that I could see me before I saw myself.
>
> I am bored with my own contradictions. . . .
>   If only, just for half an hour, I could be fitted into a black skin, to see what the world looked like from there. Quite different. Everything different? Lord, how many centuries before all this colour nonsense dies away. . . .[6]

"Never to know, from the inside, the life of the people of one's own country." This explicit dilemma is linked to another, implied but never fully articulated: how to see Africa at all without reproducing the structures of perception of an inverted colonialism and its legacies. Here language, writing itself in the very struggle to free itself from a racist framework, reconstructs a Europocentric perspective:

> I have notebooks which are full of stories, plots, anecdotes, which at one time or another I felt compelled to write. But the impulse dies in a yawn. Even if I wrote them well, what then? It is always the colour bar; one cannot write truthfully about Africa without describing it. . . .

> When I am asked to recommend novels which describe white settler Africa most accurately, I always suggest a rereading of those parts of *Anna Karenina* about landowners and peasants. . . . In the person of Lenin one finds the decent worried white liberal who is drawn by the reserves of strength, the deep humanity of the African, but does not trust him to govern himself. . . . For the novelist based in Africa it is disconcerting that so much of what happens there is a repetition of the nineteenth century . . . trying to isolate what is specifically African, what is true of Africa at this time, one comes up against that complex of emotions, the colour bar. . . .[7]

Here, in the very escape from racism, Africa is described through the codes of nineteenth-century realism, from within a cultural tradition that imposes its own framework of reference that is in itself a form of domination.

I have done no more than briefly indicate the complexity of *Going Home* as a piece of colonial writing. It is a text that, far from simply "telling it like it is" about Southern Rhodesia, articulates a set of interacting political, cultural, and ontological crises that both contributed to Lessing's extraordinary strength as an "African" writer, yet also lays bare the ways in which that position is itself a construction, disintegrating at the very moment of its formation. It has become a commonplace, even a truism, of Lessing criticism to point to the forcefulness of that process of disintegration *as* the first stage of reconstruction, and to trace this back to the archetypal collapse of the house on the veldt — that tenuous citadel of white settlerdom. But ironically in *Going Home* that scene (too easy to use as the biographical confirmation of a fictional construction) is once more not so much *absent* as invented and reinvented through the willed transformation of the dream; through the overlapping replacement of memory and desire:

> One of the reasons I wanted to go home was to drive through the bush to the kopje and see where the house had been. But I could not bring myself to do it.
> Supposing, having driven seven miles through the bush to the place where the road opens into the big mealy land, supposing then I had

lifted my eyes expecting to see the kopje sloping up, a slope of empty green bush — supposing then that the house was still there after all?

For a long time I used to dream of the collapse and decay of that house and of the fire sweeping over it; and then I set myself to dream another way. It was urgently necessary to recover every detail of that house. . . . When I was working to regain that house from its collapse I used to set myself to sleep, saying, "Now you will dream of that room, or that tree, or that turn in the road." And most often I did. Over months I recovered the memory of it all. And so what was lost and buried in my mind I recovered from my mind; so *I suppose there is no need to go back and see what exists clearly, as long as I live.* (my emphasis).[8]

Notes

1. See Doris Lessing, "Desert Child," *New Statesman*, 15 November 1958, p. 700.

2. Doris Lessing, "The Small Personal Voice," in Tom Maschler, ed. *Declaration* (London: McGibbon and Kee, 1956), 24.

3. Doris Lessing, *In Pursuit of the English* (London: McGibbon and Kee, 1960), 6.

4. Ibid., 6.

5. Quoted in David Caute, *Under the Skin: The Death of White Rhodesia* (Harmondworth; Penguin, 1983) 90.

6. Doris Lessing, *Going Home* (London: Panther, 1968) 161.

7. Ibid., 164.

8. Ibid., 55–56.

Doubles Talk in *The Golden Notebook*

Claire Sprague*

Who am I, then? Tell me that first, and then, if I like being that person, I'll come up; if not, I'll stay down here till I'm somebody else.
— Lewis Carroll, *The Annotated Alice*

He used to wonder at the shallow psychology of those who conceive the ego in a man as a thing simple, permanent, reliable, and of one essence.
— Oscar Wilde, *The Portrait of Dorian Gray*

Lying there I remember the Anna who can dream at will, control time, move easily and is at home in the underworld of sleep. But I was not that Anna.
— Doris Lessing, *The Golden Notebook*

Critical response to *The Golden Notebook*'s intricate structure became substantial only some ten years after its publication. Its "shifting

*This essay has been revised from its original publication as "Doubletalk and Doubles Talk in *The Golden Notebook*," *Papers on Language and Literature* 17 (Spring 1982): 181–97. Reprinted with permission of *Papers on Language and Literature*.

narrator, unstable or merging characters and . . . non-chronological arrangement of events" were deliberately disorienting strategies.[1] It took a while to recognize Anna Wulf's role as Anna-editor or Anna-writer or Anna-script writer, or to accept Free Women as fiction or to question the "truth" of the notebooks. The novel, tied together by juxtaposition and contradiction, achieves its at best momentary stasis only with the very last line when one of the many fictive Annas walks away from a fictive Molly in belated acknowledgement of Anna's in fact earlier separation from Molly.

In a 1971 essay now regularly used as a preface to *The Golden Notebook* (1962) Lessing has insisted that her "major aim was to shape a book which would make its own comment, a wordless statement: to talk through the way it is shaped."[2] These often quoted words refuse to think of pattern without meaning. Within a short time of this essay/preface, a number of articles addressed themselves to the patterns of the novel.[3] Most critics have accepted Lessing's claim that the novel is about fragmentation and unity. Others prefer to shift the ground of discourse, for Lessing herself seems to be sending out a paradoxical message about these polar terms. She says her two themes are fragmentation and unity, then, after describing the inner Golden Notebook as the end of division, interpolates this startling statement: "there is formlessness with the end of fragmentation" (vii). This paradox should make the reader beware of overdoing any judgment that the inner Golden Notebook — or even the outer for that matter — represents unity or synthesis. The existence of alternate-discrepant endings (Blue 4 and Free Women 5) should be enough to suggest continuing process, contradiction, irony, uncertainty — anything but clear, unambiguous unity.

An example. The opening line of *The Golden Notebook* has no magic until one returns to it after having read the entire novel — or at least until it reappears as Saul's line in the inner Golden Notebook. It then acquires an extraordinary resonance. No one could expect the pointedly ordinary, almost wholly monosyllabic line, "The two women were alone in the London flat," to acquire such resonance. But it does — especially when placed against the closing line of the novel, "The two women kissed and separated." The seeming simplicity and actual intricacy of these provocative framing lines seem to me an emblem of Lessing's craft in *The Golden Notebook*.

Lessing also suggests that Anna and Saul " 'break down' into each other" and "into other people" (viii). "They hear each other's thoughts, recognize each other in themselves" and in the inner Golden Notebook they write collaboratively so that we "can no longer distinguish between what is Saul and what is Anna, and between them and the other people in the book" (viii).

I should like to suggest an additional way of defining the merging and separation of characters in *The Golden Notebook*, one that proposes these permeable selves as another structural pattern that works effectively and together with the narrative pattern. In other words, structure inheres in the disposition of protagonists as much as in the collision and interweaving of the five notebooks and the Free Women sections.

If Anna's other selves are called doubles, then another rich layer of meaning emerges. If these doubles are divided and examined by gender, the results are startling, for the central character conflicts are not between Anna and her female doubles but between Anna and her male doubles. Anna sees herself in her other female selves while she sees men as "others" for almost the entire novel. The male doubles are connected with destructive powers whose existence in herself Anna evades or denies.[4] Lessing's naming strategies are a witty and important indicator of the larger explorations of gender.

Although Lessing directs reader attention to the presence of split and merging selves, she doesn't direct it to the complex interaction between Anna's female and male selves. Her rather testy use of the cliché "the sex war" in her preface trivializes her own meticulous attention to the relations between men and women in the novel. It is an ironic echo of Paul Tanner's pronouncement that "the real revolution is women against men" (213).

In a novel filled with colliding forms and chronologies, the symmetry and clarity of the opening and closing lines of the Free Women sections is at once particularly pleasing and particularly deceptive. The novel is not primarily about the two women, Anna and Molly, for Anna and Molly are effectively separated at the beginning of the novel. The opening line is not Doris Lessing's line. It is Saul Green's who gives it to Anna who gives it to the reader. Anna writes Free Women with Saul's help. Saul says: "I'm going to give you the first sentence then. There are the two women you are, Anna. Write down: 'The two women were alone in the London flat' " (639). Doris Lessing's presence is nearly obliterated.

While the reciprocity between Anna and Saul is self-evident and even brutally forced upon the reader's attention, Saul's relationship to his earlier selves, to Tommy, Paul Blackenhurst, Paul Tanner / Michael is less obvious. Anna / Molly and Anna / Saul are, so to speak, the archetypal explicitly defined upfront doubles in the novel. Free Women tells us Anna is two women, making it easy to accept the female / female double as a structural layer in the novel. Lessing's seemingly simple and actually devious strategies should make us wonder at Saul's arrival onstage as a full-blown secret sharer. The explicitness of the Anna / Saul relationship is an invitation to notice earlier versions of Saul. Tommy, the two Pauls and Michael are major predecessors, Willi / Max, Nelson, De Silva lesser ones. Names are as usual a clue to connections. Lessing's Pauls become a Saul, in a witty reversal of the biblical Saul's conversion to Paul. The major male characters, Tommy, the two Pauls, Michael and Saul, are insistent, cynical inquisitors, and consciences as Anna's female selves are not. We might even say that the nineteenth-century madwoman in the attic has in *The Golden Notebook* become the madman in the attic.[5] The male doubles create motion in the novel. Only one woman, Anna, the mother of them all, is an active principle. She is present everywhere, from beginning to end and back again as her palindromic name suggests.[6]

There is, in short, a complex layer of doubling in *The Golden Notebook*. That layer includes mixed as well as same sex doubles. Like the more obvious Free Women / Notebooks overall patterning of the novel, this pattern has its disguises and ambiguities — its meaning is also slippery. But the pattern is there. When the novel opens, the two women who appear to be reuniting after a year apart are already psychically separated. The female / male doubling, disguised at first, ascends in clarity and significance as the novel proceeds. The final collision of Anna and Saul is climactic. Their separation ends the inner novel as the deceptive separation of Anna and Molly ends the outer Free Women novel.

An extended definition of the double in its various psychoanalytic and literary uses would take us too far afield.[7] We can agree that the second self normally exhibits displaced asocial characteristics that the public or the more compliant self cannot acknowledge. This basic distinction is a useful starting point. The self that divides in two, as it does in Jekyll and Hyde or in Dorian Gray and his portrait, has been less interesting to novelists of our time than the more complex figure whose other self has an objective existence. In the phrase, "secret sharer," Joseph Conrad fixed for us the fascination and the complexity of that free-standing other self. Virginia Woolf's Clarissa Dalloway and Septimus Smith, and Saul Bellow's Asa Leventhal and Kirby Allbee are more recent examples of secret sharers. Lessing's contributions to the genre are remarkable and heretofore unacknowledged. Her doubles are, for example, regularly female / female and female / male, unlike the classic male / male double. She develops her conception of the "free" self and its relation to the primary self with wit and originality, in part accepting, in part contradicting, and in the process extending our conceptions of the double figure.

Like other doubles, Molly Jacobs is in part what Anna would like to be, Jewish and more spontaneous, for example. Anna could never say, with Molly's "loud jolly laugh: I've got the curse" (340). Molly may seem and even be "freer," but neither she nor her other versions can be linked with the criminal or the mad self as several of the male doubles can be.

At the opening of Free Women, Anna and Molly, separated for a year while Molly was abroad, have not been living together for a while. Once so close as to be mistaken for sisters or lovers, both are over 35, divorced, "free" women currently living without men. Both are mothers; one has a son, the other a daughter. They have shared an apartment, the services of Mrs. Marks / Mother Sugar and sometimes men — De Silva sexually, Richard (Molly's former husband) almost sexually. Molly sends men — Nelson, Saul, Milt — to Anna. Both women became Communist Party members despite themselves. They call themselves "free" women in a very limited ironic sense; they are not attached to a particular man at present and are open to affairs. Both want to remarry. Even their differences seem more complementary than antagonistic. Like other literary doubles, they are almost twins.

To their friends, who simply cannot see their physical differences, they are interchangeable. Molly is tall, boyish, light-haired; Anna, "small, thin, dark, brittle, black-eyed" and "always the same" (4). The "always the same" identifies a crucial difference between the two women. Anna envies Molly's pleasure in role-changing, her "capacity to project her own changes of mood" (9). Molly admires Anna's single talent for writing. Molly's many talents and many selves seem suitably embodied in her profession as actress. Her acting, like Saul's, defines her ability to risk, to change, while Anna seems fixed in her role as writer-observer rather than writer-actor. Anna develops the capacity to role-change only privately, only in the long dark night of the soul she acts out with Saul.

Anna is, however, much stronger than she seems. Although her earlier move to her own flat seemed undertaken in order to accommodate her lover Michael, it accomplishes more. Anna and Molly will never again live together. Furthermore, Anna has begun to find her conversations with Molly too ritualized. She has tired of talking about how men fail women. When Anna and Molly talk, it is usually about Tommy. Only Tommy and Saul see Anna's notebooks. Molly is not even permitted to know they exist. Molly is Tommy's more passive mother; Anna his more active one.

Indeed, Anna functions within Free Women as an informal social worker, mediating between Tommy and Richard, between Molly and Richard, between Marion and Richard, trying to save Tommy. Hence the ironic Free Women 5 assignment of Anna to welfare work is neither inappropriate nor entirely unprepared for. It recognizes one of Anna's very female gifts. The increasing strength of her mediating function is an additional sign of Anna's growing independence from Molly, who had once "frankly domineered Anna" (9–10). (Isn't that independence an unremarked result of Anna's analysis?) It is a paradox that Anna's mediating role expands as she herself comes closer to breakdown. The most crucial sign of Anna's independence from Molly is what she withholds from Molly—her writing self and her relationship with Saul. Anna has in effect written Molly off. The concluding line of Free Women 5 belatedly confirms the Anna / Molly separation that has occurred before Free Women opens.

Of Anna's other female selves—Ella, Julia, Marion, Maryrose, Mrs. Marks—Ella is the strongest and most developed "other" besides Molly. Although Anna, like Lessing, warns readers and critics against finding autobiographical analogues in her writing, she is quite open in using her own life in her fiction. In naming Ella, she says; "I, Anna, see Ella. Who is, of course, Anna" (459). Anna also transforms her daughter Janet into

Ella's son and names him Michael after her departed lover. Ella and her former lover, Paul Tanner therefore function as shadow doubles of Anna and Michael just as Ella / Julia function as shadow doubles of Anna / Molly. Presumably Lessing sits above her creations paring her fingernails as she contemplates their movements.

Ella and Paul are primary characters in what may become Anna's second novel, "The Shadow of the Third." Within that novel, Ella is writing, and does finish a novel about a young man who commits suicide (Tommy? herself?) apparently on the spur of the moment. In fact, without his knowing it, the young man has been planning suicide for a long time. The apolitical Ella, an editor for a women's magazine, is a kind of Miss Lonelyhearts. Her double, Julia, "plump, stocky, vital, energetic, Jewish" (170) is a communist and a minor actress with minimal function in this novel within a novel within a novel. Ella seems an altogether more conventional Anna, although Anna has "to fight to write about sex" (482) and Ella can talk about orgasm. Unlike her creator Anna, Ella does not suffer from writer's block and, as a professional journalist, is, to use Molly's ironic phrasing, "integrated with British life at its roots" (666). Ella's sexual discussion is less "free" than it seems, for it mirrors conventional 1950s thinking about vaginal vs. clitoral orgasm. Her "Integrity is the orgasm" seems more parodic than genuine. Yet Anna can tell us more about Michael through Ella's Paul than she can in her own voice.

Turning Michael-her-lover into Michael-her-son gives Anna rather transparent power over and revenge against the lover who left her.[8] She had no such power over Michael-as-lover when they were together. Anna was in fact imprisoned, tied to illusions about their relationship, tied to waiting for Michael to show up, tied to serving him food and love without complaint and on his terms. The metamorphosis of Michael into a son is a metamorphosis into powerlessness; Anna can dominate Michael the son as she was unable to dominate Michael the lover. Perhaps Michael's transformation is predicted by his name, the M he shares with Molly.

Anna, on the other hand, begins her fictional life with a name that suggests greater independence, greater power than Michael or Molly can ever have. For in the name Anna, Lessing reverses the explosion of male A's and female M's that characterize the Martha Quest novels. Anna is stronger than Molly as Alfred, Adolph, Anderson, Anton, Athen, Andrew are, on the whole, stronger than the Marthas, Mays, Marnies, Maisies, Marjories who pervade the Martha novels. Anna takes on the male A and gives the female M to Molly, for, as we have seen, Anna creates Molly who may be as fictive as Ella. From this point of view Anna and Molly may even be considered a male / female double. From this point of view Anna is by her very conception more male than female.[9] Anna can be said to begin life as an androgynous figure, rather than become androgynous because of her interaction with Saul.

What happens to male names in *The Golden Notebook*? As suggested earlier, the profusion of male-A names and female-M names in the Martha Quest novels are reduced and often reversed in *The Golden Notebook*. Molly, Ella, Marjorie, Maryrose, Muriel, Mrs. Marks continue the female pattern of names. Male names tend to follow the female pattern — Michael, Max, Milt, or to fall outside the A / M pattern entirely — Paul, Saul, Tommy. However, Tommy as a name is close to Molly; both have internal double consonants, middle and final vowels. Like the Pauls, Michael and Saul, Tommy prods, questions, annoys. Like them, he is malicious and cynical — the Doppelganger figure so often is. Anna's submerged violence, cynicism, nihilism is mirrored in Tommy as it is in Michael, the Pauls and in Saul. Anna probably displaces her own contemplation of suicide into Tommy and into Ella's young unnamed male protagonist. Tommy can be aptly called the destructive principle of the Free Women sections as the Pauls and Saul are the destructive principles of their respective Notebooks.

Tommy accuses Anna of dishonesty, of masking her divided existential state by calling it a phase, by calling Tommy's own perilous condition a "bad phase." He insists:

> If things are a chaos, then that's what they are. I don't think there's a pattern anywhere — you are just making patterns, out of cowardice. I think people aren't good at all, they are cannibals, and when you get down to it no one cares about anyone else. All the best people can be good to one other person or their families. But that's egotism, it isn't being good. We aren't any better than animals, we just pretend to be. [275]

In this passage Tommy effectively "names" his own version of doubling. What he describes is the victim / cannibal concept developed more fully by Paul Blackenhurst, by Ella's father and by Anna and Saul. The victim / cannibal principle "names" the human / nonhuman material later dramatized in the Mashopi pigeon shoot episode. Tommy's naming provides the reader with a crucial link between the Free Women and the Black Notebook sections, sections that will not be pieced together until much later when Anna, becoming her own projectionist at last, reruns her divided experience in montage.

Paul Blackenhurst, the central actor of the Mashopi episode, is kin to Tommy. His brilliant cynicism dominates a section filled with unstated human / pigeon / insect analogues. Anna's recall of that African episode is precipitated by "a fat domestic London pigeon" who is kicked and killed in a comic-grotesque street drama. The brief episode, reported without comment, triggers Anna's memory. In her recall, five members of the African group, Anna, Willi, Maryrose, Paul, and Jimmy, undertake to collect pigeons so that Mr. Boothby may have a pigeon pie.

The remarkable afternoon that follows is a tale of coupling and death. The analogies with the general human condition and with the five who see and act are disturbing. Thousands of "apparently identical" grasshoppers couple while Paul, the "projectionist" of the afternoon, toys like a god with the insects, shifting sexual partners, killing some, announcing the death by evening of thousands more (418). In the meantime, Maryrose thinks of her brother's death, Jimmy fights with his fear of death, but Paul, the handsome, the fearless, will die first — in perfect absurdist fashion. The pigeon shoot is interrupted by another concurrently played drama of death between an ant and an anteater which proceeds while Willi reads *Stalin on the Colonial Question*,[10] while Paul tries to get Willi to acknowledge the existence of a "principle of destruction" he can never acknowledge, for Willi's communism cannot accept the cannibal within. Paul parodies present and future myths of progress and purpose as he continues his pigeon shooting. A beetle intervenes between anteater and ant. Paul shoots his ninth pigeon. The final image: "Now we saw the jaws of the ant-eater were embedded in the body of the beetle. The corpse of the ant-eater was headless" (432). That image, reminiscent of Virginia Woolf's similarly mutually destroyed snake and toad in *Between the Acts*, produces its special ironies among the group.[11]

This extraordinary section is Lessing's most successful dramatization of what Anna, Tommy, Paul, and Saul accept as "the principle of destruction." The actors are now victims, now cannibals; the action is copulation, combat, and death. Paul is the most memorable projectionist in *The Golden Notebook*. Anna's "self-punishing, cynical tone" is writ large in him (90). History fascinates him because it so perfectly satisfies "his intellectual pleasure in paradox" (77). Although Anna shares Paul's passionate perception of incongruity, she cannot so easily or so powerfully display her mockery. His "spirit of angry parody" foresees the ironic mediocre sameness of workers' housing and workers' lives under both socialism and capitalism (93). His predictions fail only for himself; he dies by walking into a plane propeller, perhaps in parallel with Maryrose's brother who is crushed by an Allied tank. By his life and death Paul exemplifies the principle of destruction and incongruity.

Paul and Maryrose make " 'a perfectly matched couple' " (433–44), really a magazine cover couple, but, like the grasshoppers which the human actors rearrange to couple by matching size who then return to their outsized partners, the matched human pair will not couple. Maryrose prefers the memory of her incestuous affair with her brother. Her attitudes toward incest, jargon, and ideology have the ring of truth. Immune to ideas and feeling imposed from outside, "She had a capacity for silencing us all. Yet the men patronised her" (90). This "unattainable beauty" of the group may be its only genuine radical — an incongruity Paul and Anna must relish. She can say to the intense ideologues who surround her; "I have no view of life" (423). Maryrose seems a transparent wish fulfillment projection of Anna as Paul is a projection of her "negative self."

The second Paul, Paul Tanner, appears in the Yellow Notebook. His wife is a Muriel, but his sexual life is with Ella, as the earlier Paul's actual sexual experience was with Anna not with Maryrose. This Paul is a psychiatrist like the Michael who is his original. He is negative-critical like Tommy, African Paul, Michael, and Saul. All five men are connected with death and great energy like the male-female dwarf in Anna's recurrent joy-in-spite dream, like so many other second selves (e.g., Conrad's Leggatt, Stevenson's Hyde, and the alter ego in "The Jolly Corner"). Paul destroys in Ella the knowing, doubting, sophisticated Ella, putting "her intelligence to sleep, and with her willing connivance" (208). He rejects Ella as writer: "his voice is always full of distrust when he mentions her writing" (208). The other Paul, Tommy, and Saul want to strengthen the knowing, doubting Anna. Paul Tanner encourages Ella's artistic impotence. In effect, he encourages her suicide.

Paul Tanner can be described as a purer or less clouded form of Michael, a fictional figure Anna uses to distance uncomfortable truths about Michael, his criticism of her as "authoress" and mother, for example. Anna manages to play down Michael's erosion of these two crucial Anna selves as she manages to submerge the fact that Michael will never divorce his wife and marry her. On the night this realization sinks in, she fails to achieve orgasm. Naturally, Michael most dislikes "the critical and thinking Anna" (331). Anna cannot unite "Janet's mother, Michael's mistress" and doesn't try to, for they "are happier separated" (336). Although Michael's ironic discourse lacks the Tommy-Pauls-Saul malice, it nevertheless seems to undercut every comment Anna makes. A displaced Prague Jew, a survivor who is, like Thomas Stern, "the history of Europe in the last twenty years," Michael simultaneously responds to and mocks Anna's remaining shreds of optimism about the human condition (132). Michael is experience to Anna's innocence in a replay of the Julia / Jan interchange in *Retreat From Innocence*.

Lessing's naming game continues when her Saul who was Paul comes onstage. He complements, combats, and completes Anna. Once Anna acts out her long dark night of the soul with her destructive double and all her multiple selves, she can contain and separate from Saul. In a novel with many characters who either act on stage or consciously and frequently role-change—Molly, Tommy, African Paul, Julia, De Silva—Saul is the consummate chameleon: "in any conversation he can be five or six different people" (573). During their lowest point of mutual madness, Anna has a long night of dreams in which she and Saul play roles against each other:

> We played against each other every man-woman role imaginable. As each cycle of the dream came to an end, I said: "Well, I've experienced that, have I, well it was time that I did." It was like living a hundred lives. I was astonished at how many of the female roles I have not played in life, have refused to play, or were not offered to me. Even in my sleep

I knew I was being condemned to play them now because I had refused them in life. (604)[12]

This night of dreams marks the end of an era. It is a genuine turning point. Anna and Saul have indeed doubled, divided, and interchanged selves. Their relationship climaxes and pinpoints the novel's complex use of doubling. The next morning Saul pushes Anna to begin her new novel; she is able to admit her writer's block and to leave the flat where she has been holed up for days in order to buy her golden notebook.

The insights Anna / Saul derive from one another are prepared for through Anna's slow deciphering of her repetitive joy-in-spite dream: Its disguising elements are slowly worked away. At last the dream becomes identified with an actual person in Anna's life, with De Silva, the latest and most nihilistic exemplar of the principle of destruction: "incarnate, the principle of joy-in-giving-pain." He appears in the dream "without disguise, just as he is in life, smiling, malicious, detached, interested" (503). The description is perfect. The disguise has yet to drop altogether. Only in her final bout of madness with Saul does it drop totally, revealing to Anna that both she and Saul are De Silva, the malicious male / female dwarf: "I slept and dreamed the dream. This time there was no disguise anywhere, I was the malicious male-female dwarf figure, the principle of joy in destruction; and Saul was my counterpart, male-female, my brother and my sister" (594). Anna and Saul are each other, like Anna and Molly, Anna and Michael, Maryrose and her brother, Anna and Paul, Ella and Paul. Their climactic interchange illuminates the function of the other couples in the novel. Anna's breakthrough is, of course, liberating. It means she may be able to free herself from repetitive behavior patterns. The dream with "no disguise anywhere" permits Anna to wake up "filled with joy and peace" (562–63). She has at last dreamed her destruction dream positively as Mother Sugar had admonished her to. She has at last internalized the destructive principle.

At one point in the Anna / Saul combat Anna accepts the victim-cannibal view of human interaction proposed by Tommy and by Ella's father and accepted by Paul Blackenhurst. To Ella's father, "People are just cannibals unless they leave each other alone." For him, the human animal is isolated, solitary: "People don't help each other, they are better apart" (464). Anna, committed to social action yet antagonized and repelled by its evils and its limits, purifies her negative self through this father figure.

Anna can only accept the cannibal figure in her own voice in the inner Golden Notebook. "You simply don't get to be wise, mature, etc., unless you've been a raving cannibal for thirty years or so," she tells Saul, identifying serenity and wisdom with "a history of emotional crime" (626). In the continuing didactic discussion that follows, Anna defines the interdependence of victim and cannibal and the conditions under which role reversal will occur. The victim / cannibal construction, developed through Tommy's attack on Anna, the events of the Mashopia afternoon and the Anna / Saul interaction is convincing. It is dramatic; it is objectified; it allows for violence. It represents in fact another form of the doubling mechanism.

Saul is, of course, a cannibal. For Anna to see herself, however provisionally, as a cannibal is a considerable achievement. She has always preferred to see herself as victim, particularly in her relations with men. Despite her anger at her emotional imprisonment to Michael / Paul, she is always the dependent partner, waiting and anxious. Anna is not "free" with men unless she lacks special feeling for them. (Her encounters with the American doctor, Nelson, and others are examples.) Through Saul, she achieves some measure of freedom from repetition. So she achieves some release from the stereotype of woman as victim.

Anna's surnames, like her first name, underscore the fact and the ironic limits of her "freer" condition. She is significantly not Anna Freewoman, but Anna Freeman Wulf. Lessing has given her a triply masculine name.[13] Does Lessing believe that male power is writer power?

Max / Willi, Michael, Milt are shadowy doubles of Tommy, Paul, and Saul. Perhaps the male-M names in *The Golden Notebook* represent acts of mastery and revenge; perhaps they represent more "feminine" males? Certainly, as we have seen, Anna makes the naming of Michael an explicit act of mastery and revenge. By comparison with the Paul / Saul figures, Max and Milt are recessive and hence perhaps more suitably males with an M. In Free Women 5, for example, Anna and Milt (Saul's "fictional" equivalent) do not undergo a journey into the self together. They do not help each other to write. Milt has no diary; he doesn't read Anna's notebooks. Anna does not buy a golden notebook. However, Milt does close the four notebooks and remove all the newspaper clippings from Anna's walls. After five days, he and Anna separate.

The Paul and Saul names, so totally outside the A/M pattern, may represent a maturing movement away from the self and from father analogues. As names they probably also twist and / or duplicate an autobiographical source as Anna duplicates Michael as Ella's son or herself as Ella, and as Lessing duplicates her father, Alfred / Michael and her mother, Emily Maude, into the fictional Alfred and May Quest.[14]

Lessing's doubling habit works in other ways. It extends, for example, to Janet and Tommy. Janet is Anna's child; Tommy is Molly's. In fact, Anna is the functional mother of both. Late in the novel, Anna's dream about Janet and Tommy confirms her double mothering role. It also reflects Anna's anxieties about the relationship between being a woman and a writer. She dreams Janet is "plump and glossy with health," Tommy "a small baby" she is starving (651). Janet has emptied her breasts; there is no milk for Tommy who vanishes "altogether." Anna wakes "in a fever of anxiety, self-division and guilt" (652). Her waking self doesn't understand the dream. Has she failed herself? The dream occurs after Anna wonders if

Tommy's reading of her four notebooks has triggered his suicide attempt. The Tommy of the dream may represent someone else, as Anna, familiar with the disguises of dream, herself suggests. True. Given the prior expression of guilt about Tommy, however, the dream figure is at least Tommy. He may, more significantly, also be the writer self Anna obliterates in Free Woman 5.[15]

Doubling may also as a term usefully describe the overt structural antithesis in the novel between and within the Notebook and Free Woman sections. For, as Lessing has herself said, the notebooks are to the Free Women sections what antinovel is to novel or what raw experience is to the finished work.[16] The notebooks are richer than Free Women as our interior self is richer than our external self, as experience is richer than art. The Notebook / Free Women juxtaposition is the most evident juxtaposition in the novel. It can be called a form of doubling, one that forces us to consider structure and character together. We might then think of the Notebooks as the rich shadow to the public Free Women, as the storehouse of esoteric knowledge that is reshaped for public consumption.

Lessing's use of pattern to reflect personality and vice-versa is reminiscent of Poe's "The Fall of the House of Usher." In that story house is reflected in tarn, refrain lines reflected by echoes and Roderick reflected by his twin, Madeline. So in *The Golden Notebook* the various Anna / Molly and Anna / Saul juxtapositions parallel and intensify the overall juxtaposition of notebook to notebook and notebook to Free Women. Like all the various "fictions" within the larger or outer Golden Notebook, such as "The Shadow of the Third," "Blood on the Banana Leaves," or Saul's Algerian novel, these doubles and multiples force us to see at least double, force us to question any single view of personality or reality.[17]

The varied narrative forms — diary, letter, book review, parody, short story, film script, headline, news clipping, synopsis — are mirrors for Anna as much as people are. We would know this without Anna saying so. Part of her "welfare work" for the Party is to read and mark stories and articles published abroad that are suitable for British consumption. Anna describes these "great piles of magazines" as a "mirror into which I have been looking for over a year" (351). Her use of the term mirror for writing (it occurs often for people) occurs in the Blue Notebook, supposedly the notebook of truth.[18] The long entry for September 15, 1954, judged a failure at presenting truth, is totally crossed out. The reader is privy to this crossed-out material. Anna / Lessing, by her cross-outs, her inclusion of other handwritings, black lines, pinned in newsprint, typescript, musical symbols, the £ sign, interlocking circles, asterisks, doodling, brackets, clipped and banded material, speaks to the excisions that falsify in published writing. Lessing describes the cross-outs, handwritings, black lines, asterisks, doodling, pinned and pasted in materials. She does not show them. The reader sees only the brackets that head each notebook section. Did Lessing ever contemplate direct visual presentation of raw, worked over, interpolated, or discarded materials in the way of French experimental novelists?[19]

The narrative forms and mixed-media materials project the multiplicity of personality and truth. They also suggest that the much proclaimed theme of fragmentation has been over-simplified. The doubling, multiplication, and interchanging of the self is more good than evil. Anna says the notebooks represent a way of splitting the self to save it from chaos. She's right. The splitting works. Seeing the self in or as others is a necessity. We are multiple. The inner Golden Notebook, generally touted as the great synthesis of the novel, does not contain a single Anna. All the selves of all the notebooks are in it, occasionally merged (Paul and Michael), still interchanging (Anna imagines Ella in an affair with Saul), still identifiable. The inner Golden Notebook does not homogenize personality. (Anna's madness also continues in it.) Its other selves will continue to function for Anna much as Rinehart functions for the nameless narrator of Ralph Ellison's *Invisible Man*. Like Rinehart and the Martha of *The Four-Gated City*, Anna can try out different selves in her quest for possibility over fatality. She may contemplate herself as various Mollys, various Sauls in various roles. She may, for example, see herself as mother in Anna, Molly, Ella, and Marion, and through these acted and unacted selves exorcise guilt or explore unacceptable acts and attitudes.

In projecting so many female and female / male doubles Lessing explodes the classic novel of doubling which is wholly male. Her rich exploration of female doubles has few precedents: Charlotte Brontë's Jane Eyre and Bertha Rochester, Woolf's Mrs. Ramsay and Lily Briscoe. Lessing's exploration of female / male selves is equally bold. The Anna / Saul predecessors are also few: Poe's Roderick and Madeline Usher, Emily Brontë's Cathy and Heathcliff, Woolf's Clarissa Dalloway and Septimus Smith. Other examples will be hard to find, for opposite sex doubles are even more rare in clinical literature than they are in literature.[20]

But no other writer has both retained and burst the boundaries of twoness. The nineteenth century doubles novel did not go beyond twoness to the complexity of multiple mirrors. Twoness and multiplicity co-exist in *The Golden Notebook* to signify that being more than one is a fact of life and not necessarily a threat to identity. Lessing manages to convince us of this abstraction although we also believe in the reality of characters openly described as "fictive": Ella, Molly, the Anna of Free Women, etc. Anna is a cosmos. There is "the Anna of that time" (153), "that other Anna's eye is on me" (351), "the Anna who goes to the office, argues interminably with Jack" (362), "two other Annas" (562), "and this Anna will cease to exist" (583), "younger, stronger Annas" (592), "I was not that Anna" (614), "sick Anna" (623 and passim), etc., etc. *The Golden Notebook* overturns and redefines the nineteenth century version of split and merging selves.

The doubling, multiplication and interchanging of the self also brings to the realistic surface of the novel a mysterious reverberating level.

People, events and settings connect, merge and separate in ways not always easy to define. Anna's "others" are at once real and not real. They are almost free-standing figures, almost in the sense that so many are fictions created by Anna. Despite their presentation as fictions, they are real enough to invite belief in their existence. Thus they are both free-standing figures and creations with visible puppet strings.

As a principle, therefore, doubling both speaks and shapes. It contains, sorts, accepts, links, and questions contraries—joy and spite, male and female, anarchy and order, victim and cannibal, art and life. Some of Anna's selves are, like the traditional other self, freer, more uninhibited, closer to the criminal than to the socialized self. Jekyll's "My devil had been long caged, he came out roaring," can describe Anna's "devils" (Tommy, the Pauls, Saul), her hidden, violently energetic cannibal selves. Other Anna selves are not so clearly evil or overwhelmingly frightening. Some may be frightening enough (Ella / Tommy's suicide impulse) or socially unacceptable enough (African Paul's harsh irreverences) to displace into a double. Some may represent unrealized parts of the self (Molly's role-changing). As a whole, the doubles show that the self is multiple and must shed its single skin. Lessing goes further. In *The Golden Notebook* acceptance of the destructive male self seems necessary to survival, to the reunification of the self and to the process of writing.

It takes Anna almost the entire novel to realize that the destructive principle is inside as well as outside her. In a way, the novel is "about" her search for its location and meaning. Mother Sugar's instruction to Anna that she dream her destruction dream "positively" means that Anna must recognize its presence within herself. She has preferred to see the destructive principle outside her and in men only, in Tommy, Michael, the Pauls, Saul. On one level, then, men make war and women do not. But, as Anna's repetitive dream shows, women contain the destructive principle and are kept from recognizing its existence. The "male" principle of destruction is therefore both male and not male. It is fundamentally without gender or contains both genders. But Anna perceives it as male and must unlearn that perception. Thus her triply masculine name suggests complicity in sexual stereotypes, while other aspects of the novel question these stereotypes.

The act of writing is crucial. It frees Anna and Saul to separate. Their interchange and separation simultaneously suggest the androgynous nature of the writer and the eternal antagonism of Anna / Saul principles. Anna cannot live with Saul: he would destroy her; they would destroy each other. But Anna must, through Saul, accept her own cannibalism.

On another level, Anna / Lessing accept and play out to a parodic end the societal perception of the male as power, violence, aggression. On one level male power is indeed writer power. At its most reductive, this playing out makes Anna a writer in the Blue 4 and inner Golden Notebook and a marriage counselor in Free Women 5. Why does Anna obliterate her writing self in *Free Women*? The answer isn't easy. It must lie in Lessing's desire to juxtapose to the very end. Blue Notebook 4 contradicts Free Women 5. Anna chooses to finish her conventional novel conventionally. Free Women is not a portrait of the artist as a young man. In it Anna is neither artist, nor young, nor a man. So at every turn Lessing seems to resist and to mock her own composition of a portrait-of-the-artist-as-a-woman-near-forty-with-writer's-block.

On yet another level, Anna triumphs, for she is the maker of Saul and his avatars, of Molly and of her companions. Anna made the decision to turn Saul into Milt in Free Women 5. Anna's palindromic name suggests her great hidden circular or unending power — her possession of a kind of eternal fecundity that is a writer's power and a woman's power. Anna will come back; she is indomitable, forever returning, like her name, to and from herself. She is the maker and the mocker of the male and female myth.

Notes

1. Martha R. Lifson, "Structural Patterns in *The Golden Notebook*," *Papers in Women's Studies* II, no. 14 (1978):97.

2. Lessing's essay on *The Golden Notebook* was originally published in 1971 as an introduction to an English paperback reprint. It did not appear in the United States until 1973 in *Partisan Review* 40 (1973):14–30. It is also republished in *A Small Personal Voice: Essays, Reviews, Interviews*, ed. Paul Schlueter (New York: Knopf, 1974). The pagination in parentheses is from the Bantam edition of *The Golden Notebook* (New York, 1973). All subsequent references to *The Golden Notebook* are from this edition and are noted parenthetically in the text.

3. The first two books on Lessing were Dorothy Brewster's *Doris Lessing* (New York: Twayne, 1965) and Paul Schlueter's *The Novels of Doris Lessing* (Carbondale: Southern Illinois University, 1973). Selma Burkom's early essay, "Only Connect: Form and Content in the Works of Doris Lessing," *Critique* 11 (1968):51–68 should also be noted. The following articles were published within a few years of Lessing's essay and represent close appreciation of structure in *The Golden Notebook*: John L. Carey, "Art and Reality in *The Golden Notebook*," *Contemporary Literature* 14 (1973):437–56; Joseph Hynes, "The Construction of *The Golden Notebook*," *Iowa Review* 4 (1973):100–113; Lifson, as noted in footnote 1; Anne M. Mulkeen, "Twentieth Century Realism: The 'Grid' Structure of *The Golden Notebook*," *Studies in the Novel* 4 (1972):262–74; Annis Pratt, "The Contrary Structure of Doris Lessing's *The Golden Notebook*," in *World Literature Written in English* 12 (1973):150–60. Hynes and Lifson have a particularly rich analysis of the interrelationship between structure and theme.

4. From the Jungian point of view, Anna could be described as needing to recognize her animus self. There are parts in the novel that are clearly Jungian. The notions of "negative selves," for example, which Anna says are Mrs. Marks / Mother Sugar's mode of description. The male selves could be described as negative or animus selves. The Jungian element is in the novel, but so are other ways of seeing conflict and contradiction in our psychology, art, politics and history.

5. Lessing may indeed overturn the nineteenth-century pattern so persuasively argued by Sandra M. Gilbert and Susan Gubar in *The Madwoman in the Attic* (New Haven: Yale University Press, 1979).

6. I owe to Roslyn Stein the perception that Anna is a palindromic name.

7. Carl F. Keppler believes that the terms "double" and "Doppelganger" are so loosely used "they have no real meaning." He prefers the term "second self." We may be stuck with both. I find double preferable for Lessing; it gives the other self greater independence from the primary self. See *The Literature of the Second Self* (Tucson: University of Arizona, 1972), 2.

8. According to the Freudian view, a woman can, through her son, acquire the phallus she lacks.

9. Lessing's father, Alfred Cook Tayler, was known as Michael at home. (See Dee Seligman, "The Four-Faced Novelist," *Modern Fiction Studies* 26 (1980):7. Michael can be described as the hidden or anima side of Alfred if we play the game of biographical analogues. For Anna to have a lover named Michael makes for witty oedipal fulfillment. It also makes Anna / Michael one male person. Compare this hidden incestuous motif with Maryrose's open one.

10. I assume Lessing deliberately altered the title from "Stalin on the National Question," although other titles have been misstated in her work. Mrs. Van, for example, is said to have read *The Story of a South African Farm* instead of *The Story of An African Farm* and Olaf Stapledon's novel is listed as *First and Last Men* instead of *Last and First Men*.

11. Virginia Woolf, *Between the Acts* (New York: Harcourt, Brace, 1941), 99. Giles sees a snake still alive, "choked with a toad in its mouth. The snake was unable to swallow; the toad was unable to die." He ends the impasse by stamping on the two animals.

12. Anna and Saul have enacted what Freud describes as "all the unfulfilled but possible futures to which we still like to cling in phantasy, all the strivings of the ego which adverse external circumstances have crushed, and all our suppressed acts of volition which nourish in us the illusion of free will." "The Uncanny" (1919), in *Standard Edition of the Complete Psychological Works*, ed., trans. James Strachey and Anna Freud (1953–64), 17:236.

13. Lifson is the only other critic I know to have explored Anna's name. Her view is different from mine: "It has been her immersion in chaos and cruelty, in the 'Wulf' part of her name, that enables her to move towards the joy of freedom ('Freeman'), to peace, order, endurance, and even creativity." Lifson, "Structural Patterns," 105. Wulf doesn't have to be male, but in normal parlance it is and in conjunction with Freeman it is more so.

14. Lessing derives her middle name, May, from her grandmother who was a Caroline May. By giving her middle name to her fictional mother (Caroline is given to a fictional daughter), Lessing may displace and dominate her. Anna's mother is also a May, May Fortescue (467).

15. It is also possible that Lessing displaces and disguises the three children she actually bore, two boys and a girl, into the three children in the novel — Tommy, Michael, and Janet.

16. As Lessing puts it, Free Women "is an absolutely whole conventional novel, and the rest of the book is the material that went into making it." "A Talk with Doris Lessing by Florence Howe," *A Small Personal Voice*, ed. Paul Schlueter (New York: Knopf, 1975), 81.

17. In *The Four-Gated City*, as I have argued in "Without Contraries is no Progression," Lessing extends her use of doubling to environments, *Modern Fiction Studies* 26 (Spring 1980):99–116.

18. The "truth" of the Blue Notebook is by no means absolute. Anna has two ages as does Tommy, for example. In her 19 January 1950 entry, Anna says she is 33 which would make her birth year 1923 or 1924 (234). On 17 October 1954 Anna says she was born 10 November 1922 (467).

19. Thomas Stern's manuscripts in *Landlocked* are very much like the mixed forms in *The Golden Notebook*. Thomas's go further; they are written over, dense with marginalia, torn, rained on, spotted, ant-eaten. Compare the practice of French novelists like Michel Butor, and the English novelist, Christine Brooke-Rose.

20. Only two of Sybil Dorsett's sixteen selves were male; Sybil "had developed more alternating selves than had any other multiple personality." Furthermore, she "was the only known woman personality whose entourage of alternating selves included males" (Flora Schreiber, *Sybil* [New York: Henry Regnery, 1973], 214). See also Robert Stoller, *Splitting* (New York: Delta, 1973) and Robert N. Mollinger, "Self Defense: Comments on Multiple Personality," a paper presented before an MLA Special Session, The Divided Self: Literary and Psychoanalytical Implications of Multiple Personality, 28 December 1971, San Francisco.

The Marriages between Zones Three, Four, and Five: Doris Lessing's Alchemical Allegory

Roberta Rubenstein*

One might say that Doris Lessing has always been interested in space: from the vastness of the African veld to the bounded female spaces of rooms, houses, and flats. The author's move to space fiction in her work-in-progress, *Canopus in Argos: Archives*, is therefore not an altogether unexpected shift in narrative direction. Rather, it is a change of metaphorical location from realistic to symbolic; the author has gradually shifted her focus from the boundaries of selfhood (frequently symbolized by the forms of living spaces) to metaphysical space with its own invented territories.

Unlike the chaotic and sprawling narrative lines of the first volume of the series (*Shikasta*, 1979), *The Marriages between Zones Three, Four, and Five* (1980) is a condensed and highly allegorical narrative. The narrator, Lusik, "represents" the events in both senses — as a storyteller and as an exemplar of the events themselves. Within that frame, the principal characters of the story, Al·Ith and Ben Ata, literally become the "representatives, embodiments of their respective countries."[1]

The topography of the imaginary space in which the narrative takes place is central to the development of events: three zones, numbered Three, Four, and Five, are separated by differences in geography, social organization, modes of consciousness, and the very air itself (Zone Two is only mentioned late in the novel. Lessing does not describe what is presumably the highest zone in her schema; if there is a Zone One, only the occupants of Zone Two could even apprehend it.) Each zone is bounded from the others by invisible borders that cannot be crossed unless the traveler wears a protective shield to insulate him or her against the poisonous air of the alien zone. Zone Three, located on a high plateau, bounded by snowcapped mountains on one side and ravines on the other, is a matriarchal realm guided by the wisdom of the "Mothers" (p. 42).

*From *Extrapolation* 24, 3 (Fall 1983): 201–215. Reprinted with permission of *Extrapolation*.

Al·Ith herself, the queen of the zone, is five times a mother as well as the spiritual mother to fifty orphans in her realm. Her zone is a land of spiritual serenity, peace, and telepathic communication among human beings and all other life forms.

By contrast, Zone Four is stolid, brutish, patriarchal, and militaristic; the entire male population is in the permanent army, defending the borders of the zone against nonexistent enemies. It is a realm of fear, discipline, and compulsion, repressed in nearly every aspect — including its prohibition against "cloud-gathering" in the higher realm of Zone Three — except for a coarse, aggressive sexuality. On the far side of the fourth zone is Zone Five, a land of apparent deserts that proves much later to be a temperate zone much like Zone Three but without its harmonious social organization. Instead, it is characterized by sensuality, lack of inhibition, and the pursuit of pleasure and indulgence. (Zone Six, inhabited by an "evil race," is only briefly mentioned, p. 97.)

In all three of the designated zones of the title, the reduction of fertility in the animal world and stagnation in the human one are the first signs that something is seriously awry. At the same time, an Order from the Providers — the unknowable higher authority to which all the realms are subject, although its imperatives are generally communicated to the inhabitants of Zone Three — decrees an extraordinary marriage between Al·Ith of Zone Three and Ben Ata of Zone Four, the purpose of which is the "fusing [of] imaginations of two realms" (p. 34).

Lessing subsequently elaborates on the theme of marriage and male-female relationships (a subject central to her earlier realistic fiction). In charting the variations of emotional exchange between a man and a woman, initially strangers to each other but eventually loving spouses, she develops an anatomy of marriage through which two partners grow toward and through each other. Early in the narrative, Lessing alerts us to the symbolic dimensions of this liaison: one not only between bodies and ultimately minds, but also one within the mind or consciousness of each participant. Each is "completed" and thus changed in a radical way by union with the other. Marriage or union is the symbol for the individual's exploration of "frontiers of the mind"[2] as well as of the Other.

Lessing's many-leveled narrative encodes both exoteric and esoteric dimensions of meaning. . . . Like the layered topography of the zones it describes, the novel's esoteric dimension can be read on several levels. In the first sense, the "mystical marriage" is an allegory of Being: in each marriage the fusion of opposites furthers the emotional and psychic growth of consciousness in both personal and social contexts. The very hierarchy of zones metaphorically suggests the esoteric ascent toward wisdom. . . . Consistent with this metaphor, but with its own further symbolism, is the alchemical marriage, in which the sacred union represents an aspect of the "work" toward the ultimate goal of inner enlightenment. It is this symbolism that I intend to explore in Lessing's narrative.

Alchemy was an ancient and medieval hermetic practice which was not only the forerunner of modern chemistry but a spiritual exercise to its adepts. Though to the uninitiated alchemy seemed to be a vain attempt to transmute base metals into silver and gold, its processes were encodings for an inner quest for the "philosopher's stone" of pure Being. The fusion of certain metals, notably sulphur and mercury, symbolically represented the fusion of body, soul, and vital spirit; this process in turn was prelude to the alchemist's achievement of inner knowledge or enlightenment. The descriptions of certain chemical interactions in alchemical texts were actually encodings for a process taking place not in a laboratory vessel but in the inner "laboratory" of the spirit.[3] *The Marriages Between Zones Three, Four, and Five* can be read as an ingenious contemporary parallel to an alchemical text, as Lessing makes the marriage between Al·Ith and Ben Ata the analogue of important spiritual transformations both within the partners and in the cosmos of the several numbered zones.

Alchemical references appear at the very outset of the narrative. As one of the songs of both Zones Three and Four cryptically informs the listener (and reader),

> Great to Small
> High to Low
> Four into Three
> Cannot go. (p. 3)

In addition to the apparent reference to the impermeability of the borders between Zones Three and Four, the verse contains several esoteric allusions. In hermetic symbolism "four" refers to the four elements — earth, water, air, and fire. During her travels to Ben Ata's zone for the first time, Al·Ith encounters each of these elements, which are also emphasized as the chief feature of the respective zones. The impossibility of "four into three" also alludes to the symbolic problem of "squaring the circle."[4] The "three principles" (or principal substances) of alchemy are sulpher, mercury, and salt. Though "four into three" cannot go, a central hermetic axiom states that the reverse order is the essential series for the alchemical process: "one becomes two, two becomes three, and out of the third comes the one as the fourth."[5] Further, the two parts of the alchemical work are referred to as the "lesser" and "greater" work. The "lesser" work in *Marriages* culminates with the birth of a child to Al·Ith and Ben Ata; the "greater" work is Al·Ith's eventual solitary achievement of illumination, as symbolized by her admission into Zone Two.

Another narrative clue to the hermetic allegory is the Chronicler's frequent digressions in his account of the "exemplary marriage" between the two royal figures (p. 3) to describe other forms of its artistic representation. The paintings and musical compositions or songs created by artists of the various zones to celebrate the legend of the union between the two royal rulers are contrasted with the "true" version of events. Thus the Chronicler suggests the classical discrepancy between appearances and reality. . . .

Additionally, the tableaux described by Lusik echo the illustrations of various alchemical works, wherein colors, directional clues, zodiacal signs, and special objects or figures are, to the adept, symbols for stages in the "work." The actual or "true" spiritual meanings are thus concealed in visual metaphor. . . .

One event early in the story illustrates a provocative, if perhaps coincidental, correspondence between alchemical representations and Lessing's tale. When Al·Ith first descends on horseback to visit Ben Ata in Zone Four, she carries a protective shield, as must all of the travelers who enter one of the alien zones. A frequently reproduced alchemical illustration shows a king and queen facing each other on horseback, each holding a shield aloft. The shields in the illustration connote the truth that "each opposing principle contains its opposite."[6] That truth is ultimately borne out in the events of Lessing's pairing of Al·Ith and Ben Ata, each of whom discovers the opposites of his / her own being through the complementary qualities of the other partner. . . .

In alchemy, male and female are expressions of equal and opposite powers. Lessing seems to invoke these polarities of gender not only to comment on the varieties of their interconnection in a more deliberately stylized manner than in her earlier realistic fiction, but also to emphasize the necessity for their "marriage" or integration as a precondition for subsequent spiritual growth. As long as such qualities are arbitrarily defined according to gender, the imagination is restricted to being one or the other. The allegory of *Marriages* shows the larger capacities of the unified soul.

Shortly after Al·Ith receives the Order to marry the king of Zone Four, she travels from the high mountains of her zone to the dull, oppressive plain of the bordering zone; clothed in the dark blue and black clothes of mourning, she literally descends from the "higher" to the "lower." The meaning of Al·Ith's somber dress during her first descent is amplified in the fear and mourning of her people, who would willingly perform a "Grief" if Al·Ith signaled it (p. 5). (She does not.)

In one of the many stylized tableaux of that first journey, Al·Ith is shown in a scene with the night sky crowded with stars and a slice of moon (p. 14); the latter is a major symbol associated with both mercury and the female principle.[7] Late in the tale Al·Ith is specifically identified with the crescent moon. As befits her lunar associations, the dark-haired queen is comfortable in the night and darkness; celebrations in Zone Three often take place at night. Al·Ith's name resembles Azoth, one of the numerous names for Mercury,[8] who is also associated with the receptive pole, the soul, and Mother Nature. Communion with nature is a central feature of Zone Three; another tableau shows Al·Ith surrounded by animals (p. 10).

Mercury is a "volatile" substance, also known as quicksilver, which is "fixed" or stabilized by sulphur.[9] During one tryst between the royal figures, Ben Ata sees Al·Ith as a "*quick, volatile, flamelike* thing, and understood how he subdued and dimmed her" (p. 108, my emphasis). Elsewhere Al·Ith's eyes are described as "burning" and "glow[ing]" (p. 7). In contrast to the symbolism of Al·Ith's mercurial, lunar temperament and zone, Ben Ata and his Zone Four embody the "fixed" male substance of sulphur. Not only is the king of the lower zone stubborn, earthbound, and fixed in his ideas, but Ben Ata prefers daylight to darkness — suggesting his affinity with the sun rather than the moon.

The marriage between Al·Ith and Ben Ata is thus, as the Chronicler of the narrative reminds us, a "union of incompatibles" (p. 144). The pairing also alludes to the alchemical union: "the marriage of Sulphur and Quicksilver, Sun and Moon, King and Queen, is the central symbol of alchemy."[10] Titus Burkhardt also explains, "Sulphur, the original masculine power, and Quicksilver, the original feminine power, both strive towards the wholeness of their one and eternal prototype. . . ."[11]

As the dark Al·Ith (Mercury) and the fair, blonde Ben Ata (Sulphur) slowly learn to comprehend each other's alienness and the radically different customs and beliefs of their respective zones, they experience a panoply of variations on the male-female relationship, from rape to tender lovemaking, from possession and jealousy to friendship and intellectual companionship, from parenthood to separation and loss. Alchemically, "in their successive coagulations and dissolutions [mercury and sulphur] enter into a variety of combinations with one another."[12] . .

Initially, for every such temporary synthesis of separate entities there is dissolution: soon, as the merged lovers return "to their absolute separateness, their otherness, these two denizens of their different realms could not believe what they had won together during their hours of submersion in each other" (p. 70). They experience an estrangement as complete as their earlier merging had been. . . .

Al·Ith's periodic returns to her own zone suggest further "dissolutions" in the relationship. Each time she is also more a foreigner to her own people, and the object of their quiet blame for the impoverishment of the land, which they believe her absence has precipitated. Al·Ith herself sees how dramatically her sojourns in Zone Four affect her: through her fractious encounters with Ben Ata, she absorbs the "lower" emotions of guilt, envy, possession, and jealousy. These new qualities form a barrier between her and the people of her realm. . . .

Al·Ith knows that each time she crosses the frontier back into Zone Four she ceases to be her "real self" (p. 99). She has earlier reassured herself that, while she might be "in bondage to Zone Four . . . she had not lost the knowledge, which was the base of all knowledges, that everything was entwined and mixed and mingled, all was one . . ." (p. 58). This is a variant of the "perennial knowledge" shared through the ages not only by alchemists but by practitioners of various other esoteric or mystical doctrines including, of course, those of Sufism. The latter offers the view that all esoteric forms have the same inner core of meaning. The Sufis also practiced alchemy and understood its true spiritual purpose. . . .

Other aspects of *Marriages* reinforce the alchemical allegory. The marriage pavilion is a domed chamber built to specification by the Providers, much as the special domed chamber or vessel of alchemical work—in which the marriage of opposites took place—followed a strictly prescribed form. The seven fountains surrounding the central pavilion in which Al·Ith and Ben Ata live (the number is emphasized by repetition) echo an esoteric number with multiple references, from the seven planets and metals of alchemy and hermetic art and the seven gates on the path to the Absolute in Tibetan mysticism to the seven valleys of the Sufi pilgrimage. Seven also connotes the "union of the ternary and the quaternary [three and four]."[13] The nine spice trees of the pavilion may symbolize the nine months of Al·Ith's pregnancy, which is both initiated and fulfilled there. . . . The connection between Al·Ith and fire or combustion continues throughout the narrative until, near the end, she merges with the flamelike entities of Zone Two. Earlier, some time after the child Arusi is born, Al·Ith returns to her former slender shape, and is "full of fire" once more (p. 179). Ben Ata remembers her when her tantalizing sensuality had produced in him a sense of "unbearable separation" after lovemaking; the flames of passion had "roared up in a fire that consumed them both, and in a way that never happened now" (p. 180). More currently, he feels that Al·Ith wants him to "extinguish" her sexually (p. 181). Eventually, as Al·Ith ascends towards the even more rarefied flames and "flushed red" mountains of Zone Two, she appears as "a worn, thin woman who seemed as if she was being burnt through and through by invisible flames" (p. 228). Finally she appears to be a "burnt-out" woman (p. 240), preparing herself for admission into another form of being which is, appropriately, flamelike.

One of Lessing's most vivid adaptations of the alchemical symbolism is expressed in the variety of colors of Al·Ith's dresses. Lessing takes care to mention each change of the queen's garments—an unusual detail in the author's fiction, particularly in the *Canopus* series where, for example, Ambien II of *The Sirian Experiments* is attired in the unelaborated "basic Sirian."[14] During the course of her fusion with Ben Ata and the birth of their son, Al·Ith changes from the dark blue and black mourning clothes of her first journey to Zone Four (p. 5), to white (p. 47), to dark red (p. 57). These colors are the major colors and sequence of the alchemical process, although there are occasionally intervening colors, variations, and elaborations on this order and series. . . .

Al·Ith wears green (p. 70)—fittingly, at the beginning of her pregnancy—followed by yellow (p. 83), bright orange (p. 96), bright yellow (p.

108), rose-colour (p. 128), white once again (p. 132), and gold (p. 145). At the time when Al·Ith wears gold, Ben Ata is reviewing his troops with her; he wears a silver tunic, the color associated with the moon and quicksilver.

The reversal of their characteristic symbolic colors occurs just before their child is born, at the "culmination" of their marriage (p. 154), suggesting the total exchange of qualities which their connection signifies. Al·Ith is "Ben Ata's other self" (p. 144); in turn, he feels that without Al·Ith, "he would be only half of himself" (p. 150). Just before their final separation, Al·Ith realizes that "they two, she and Ben Ata, were so married now that they made one person" (p. 187). In hermetic illustrations the marriage of mercury and sulphur is represented in the form of an androgynous being.[15] . . .

Not long afterwards, Al·Ith returns to the marriage pavilion and gives birth to the child Arusi. Thereafter, the two partners become increasingly more involved with the members of their own sex. Al·Ith turns her attention to an earlier interest in the women of both her own zone and Zone Four. Through the wife of Ben Ata's army commander, Dabeeb, and the females of Zone Four of all ages, Al·Ith begins to piece together a forgotten knowledge preserved in the women's songs, ballads, and secret rituals. Of these, the most important is one in which the women gather four times a year to worship, repeating the forbidden gesture of "looking upwards" at the mountains of Al·Ith's own zone. . . .

Soon after her child is born, Al·Ith leaves Zone Four for the last time, her journey precipitated by another Order of the Providers for Ben Ata to marry the queen of the mysterious Zone Five. Dabeeb cares for Arusi (and ultimately evolves into Al·Ith's role). The symbolism of Al·Ith's continuing ascent is signaled in the colors and signs of both her eventual illumination and the final stages of the alchemical process. In her own zone once again, Al·Ith wears first blue (p. 169), then shiny pink (p. 171), and later yellow (p. 182); all of these are reflections of the colors she sees when she gazes towards the flamelike higher zone of being, Zone Two.

When she approaches the boundaries of the higher zone, she approaches a noncorporeal realm of pure spirit and feels herself already "lighter, dryer" in preparation for entrance into it (p. 189). The environment of Zone Two is simultaneously both flames and a "crystalline yet liquid substance that held her on its surface" (p. 193). Al·Ith dreams that she has already entered this rarefied zone, as she longs to do. . . . In all esoteric systems, the novice puts herself (himself) in danger if she attempts to achieve the "gold" — transcendence or enlightenment — before being fully spiritually prepared and purified for it. . . .

While Al·Ith waits to enter "the very high," Ben Ata reenacts her own earlier reluctant descent into the "very low" by marrying the barbarian queen of the lower Zone Five in accordance with the Order. The marriage of opposites recurs; as Ben Ata anticipates, the process itself will "all happen again . . ." (p. 205). Through his distaste for the task of the second marriage, he understands what Al·Ith must have felt in lowering herself to him. Yet all is not as it seems. When the queen of Zone Five arrives as a captive of Ben Ata's army, she wears a multitude of gold ornaments and colored stones, indicating her access to the symbols of wealth, elevation, royalty — and alchemy.

Vahshi is a sensual, physically vital, uninhibited woman — the very qualities lacking in Ben Ata and his zone. This second coupling brings together the discipline of Zone Four and the physical spiritedness of Zone Five, just as the marriage between Zones Three and Four had fused duty with higher consciousness. Ben Ata proceeds to educate Vahshi, a process described far more briefly than the soul-marriage between himself and Al·Ith. Their marriage and Vahshi's prompt pregnancy are expected to produce a girl child "because the strength of her wild femaleness could only give birth to itself . . ." (p. 216). Perhaps that daughter is to be the eventual spouse of Arusi, the son of Ben Ata's marriage with Al·Ith; the interpenetration of realms presumably continues through the successive generations.

As as result of his new vision, Ben Ata allows his son and the people of Zone Four to "look upwards" to the forbidden peaks of Zone Three for the first time. Concurrently, a group of women led by Dabeeb take it upon themselves to visit Al·Ith in her own zone, with Arusi in their company. . . . Ultimately, as Al·Ith ascends to the higher zone, Dabeeb parallels her movement by her own ascent into Zone Three. . . . The paintings and tableaux depicting Al·Ith during this time offer the last "truthful" representations of the queen before her virtual transmutation and ascension into Zone Two. Versions of the scene with Al·Ith and the visiting women of Zone Four include either a "vast yellow moon" or "a delightful crescent set off by a star or two" (p. 226). In addition, a "large peacock, whose shimmering tail fills the orchard with reflected lights" (p. 226) appears in some variations. These symbols are particularly important in connection with the alchemical process described above. The opposite phases of the moon — new and full — correspond to Al·Ith's own evolution from the new bride of Ben Ata to the full attainment of elevated consciousness and being. The peacock's tail symbolizes "the blending together of all colors" that signifies the completion of the alchemical reaction and totality in general.[16] . . .

Lusik . . . underscores the sense that male and female are but arbitrary labels for describing aspects of the self as defined by certain needs. Like the storyteller, each of us is capable of entering imaginatively into the other gender, of being both subject and object. Moreover, Lusik's sense of people as manifestations of different qualities at different times is central to most esoteric systems, wherein the seeker becomes progressively identified with what he seeks, as it is contained within him. ("I am the Word."). . . .

Lessing's *The Marriages Between Zones Three, Four, and Five* is a rich allegory of the alchemy of spiritual consciousness in representative individuals of both sexes and in the cosmos as a whole. While the layers of this cosmos of Being are initially stratified and separated (like the theoretical regions of id, ego, and superego), the introduction of an unknown outer catalyst (the Order of the Providers) facilitates the eventual growth of the most advanced aspect of that consciousness (Al·Ith) to a higher level of Being. In turn, the effects of this inner alchemy are felt throughout the "system," whether understood as an individual consciousness, a group, or an entire world. The author's earlier concentration on bounded female spaces and the descent into hell gives way to an allegory of ascent into the outer spaces of Being itself.

Notes

1. *The Marriages Between Zones Three, Four, and Five* (New York: Alfred A. Knopf, 1980), p. 45. All further references will be indicated in the text by parenthetical page numbers; the title is abbreviated as *Marriages*.

2. Doris Lessing, Introduction, *Learning How to Learn: Psychology and Spirituality in the Sufi Way*, by Idries Shah (San Francisco: Harper and Row, 1981). Unnumbered pages 3 and 4 have been transposed. Lessing's comment appears on the fourth page if read in correct sequence.

3. Stanislaw Klossowski de Rola, *The Secret Art of Alchemy* (New York: Avon Books, 1973), p. 8.

4. J. E. Cirlot writes that " 'squaring the circle'. . . was one of the preoccupations of the alchemists. . . . The square was seen to correspond to the four Elements. The aim of 'squaring the circle', then (which strictly ought to be called 'circling the square'), was to obtain unity in the material world (as well as in the spiritual life) over and above the differences and obstacles (the static order) of the number four and the four-cornered square." *A Dictionary of Symbols*, trans. Jack Sage (London: Routledge and Kegan Paul, 1967), p. 293. See also C. G. Jung, *Psychology and Alchemy*, Vol. XII of *The Collected Works*, trans. R. F. C. Hull, 2nd ed., Bollingen Series XX (Princeton: Princeton Univ. Press, 1968), Plate 59, p. 125 (" 'squaring the circle' ").

5. Jung, *Psychology and Alchemy*, p. 23.

6. Klossowski de Rola, plate 13 (unnumbered page). The same illustration appears in Burckhardt, plate 8a (between pp. 144 and 145).

7. Titus Burckhardt, *Alchemy*, trans. William Stoddart (Baltimore: Penguin Books, 1972), p. 81.

8. Idries Shah, *The Sufis* (Garden City, N. Y.: Doubleday-Anchor, 1971), p. 219.

9. Burckhardt, p. 139.

10. Burckhardt, p. 149.

11. Burckhardt, p. 125.

12. Burckhardt, p. 127.

13. Burckhardt, p. 78; F. C. Happhold, *Mysticism* (Harmondsworth, Middlesex, England: Penguin Books, 1971), p. 57; Cirlot, p. 223.

14. Lessing, *The Sirian Experiments* (New York: Alfred A. Knopf, 1981), p. 109.

15. Klossowski de Rola, pp. 104–05 and Plates 21, 28, and others.

16. Cirlot, p. 239; Jung, *Mysterium Coniunctionis*, pp. 209, 288, 290, 311; Burckhardt, p. 182.

FEMALE (OTHER) SPACE

Lessing and Lawrence:
The Battle of the Sexes
Mark Spilka*

Several critics have already noted the way in which the opening of Doris Lessing's *The Golden Notebook* (1962) recalls the opening of D. H. Lawrence's *Women in Love* (1920). Though there are forty-two years between them, the two openings convey a strikingly similar ambience. In each scene two uprooted women, alone and unobserved by men, are talking about the nature of modern men and modern marriage and the predicament it poses for them. Lawrence's women—the two sisters, Ursula and Gudrun Brangwen—are tempted not to marry: it means not experience but the end of experience for them. Its abstract advantages, its expectedness, give way before those concrete realities, the men who might ask them to marry; as Gudrun puts it, "The man makes it impossible." Yet both sisters are frightened by that impossibility; they are in their mid-twenties, their lives ought to be taking the expected turn, they have returned to their father's home as if preparing for it, and they are now in fact on their way to someone else's wedding. Lessing's women, Anna Wulf and Molly Jacobs, are similarly engaged in a what's-wrong-with-men-and-marriage session; they are older women, in or near their forties, each with a bad marriage behind her, and each sharply critical of the effeminate or merely affectionate or sexually ineffectual men around them, yet they too would marry again if the men they knew weren't so impossible.

Lawrence sets the Brangwens off as "sisters of Artemis rather than of Hebe," virgin huntresses rather than cupbearers; Lessing calls her friends "free women," able to live now "free" of men and marriage, like the "odd" women in George Gissing's turn-of-the-century novel of that name, and the word "odd" figures freely now in their discourse, not only as an index to how others see them but also as to how they see themselves, in their own long reliance, for instance, on Mother Sugar, their psychiatrist. That necessary crutch is one of many signs by which Lessing emphasizes the precariousness of such freedom; her approach to it is as skeptical as Lawrence's, and she shares his trepidation over the modern crisis in

*From *Contemporary Literature* 16 (1975):218-40. Reprinted with permission of *Contemporary Literature*.

69

marriage, its evident failure as a social institution, and the evident failure too of men as possible mates, which is their common opening theme. Whatever their differences, they take their common point of departure from the novel's long concern with love and marriage as the accepted resolution for ordinary lives; and their extraordinary heroines — uprooted intellectuals, women who paint, teach, write, perform — question its acceptability as sharply as they question male sufficiency. One has only to remember how confidently Jane Austen's novels open with the problem of finding suitable mates for difficult or too numerous daughters to see how fully Lessing and Lawrence share a common cultural predicament.

But of course there are crucial differences. Not the least among them are the gorgeous clothes which Lawrence's heroines wear as members of the post-Edwardian avant-garde. Gudrun, for instance, when we meet her, wears "a dress of dark-blue silky stuff, with ruches of blue and green linen lace in the neck and sleeves; and . . . emerald-green stockings"; whereas Lessing's Molly Jacobs appears in "trousers and a sweater, both the worse for wear." The difference in degrees of liberation is instructive, Gudrun's flamboyance being part of a complex assertiveness by which she cows provincials, Molly's casualness indicating how far her generation has gone beyond that need. More importantly, those areas of unrecorded experience to which Virginia Woolf pointed, in *A Room of One's Own* (1929), are being filled in now as only a woman with Lessing's wide range of experience and intense sensitivity and concern might fill them. The "new facts" . . . to observe," the "unrecorded gestures," "unsaid or half-said words," which Woolf had cited as the province of women writers in scenes where women who like each other converse alone, are very much Lessing's advantage over Lawrence.

It is not that Lawrence lacks sympathy with or imaginative comprehension of conversing heroines; on the contrary, he creates them so vividly and sympathetically that many readers mistake them for real women and begin defending them against him, in unwitting confirmation of his powers; and of course without some such capacity for sympathetic identification men could not write credibly about women, nor women about men, under any circumstances, though they have all been doing so with reasonable effectiveness for centuries. One might even state categorically that without such sympathy no communication and no rapprochement between the sexes is possible, in which case we are hopelessly and permanently at odds and always have been, as some people hold. Nevertheless, Lawrence, like other male writers, cannot possibly imagine the extent and range of women's existence apart from their relations with men, not at least with the particularity and authority of a sensitive and widely experienced woman writer. Irving Howe speaks indirectly of this difference in his brilliant review of *The Golden Notebook* for the *New Republic* (December 15, 1962) while getting at that complex and copious "fund of experience" which makes Lessing superior — as you might expect — to other women writers. [See Howe's review, reprinted in this volume.]

* * *

By "Bloomsbury writers" Howe means here those women novelists in England and elsewhere who deal too narrowly with "personal relations" for his taste. Lessing goes beyond them not only in her finer ear for feminine dialogue but also in the greater political and sexual range of discourse her heroines enjoy. But surely she goes beyond Lawrence too, and beyond Bloomsbury males like Forster and James, who also make "personal relations" their concern, in the fullness and authenticity of such discourse. Between Lawrence and Lessing there is no contest, then, when it comes to "the way intellectual women really talk to one another when they feel free and unobserved." There is, however, a striking continuity, and beyond that an affinity founded in apparent antagonism, by which both writers imagine and convey these prologues to the battle of the sexes.

Their antagonism seems to get more emphasis than their affinity. Thus "Anna is the kind of woman," says Irving Howe of Lessing's heroine, "who would send D. H. Lawrence into a sputter of rage. So much the worse for him," he adds, then lists the kind of complaints Lawrence might register with some justice: "She whines, she is a bit of a drag, she often drives her men crazy. She does not inquire closely enough as to her own responsibility for the failures of her men or why she seems so gifted at picking losers. In her steady groaning about writer's block, she does not ask herself whether it is caused by a deep contempt for the whole idea of the intellectual life — " and so on: and he concludes by saying "she is open to almost every judgment except that of having died before her death."

Well, yes, Lawrence might have made these complaints; but wouldn't he also concur in the stress Howe gives to that last exception? and wouldn't he elsewhere agree with Howe that Anna is, rather like himself, "Modern in sensibility, but traditional in her desires"? or that "Sick as Anna is, trapped as she often finds herself in a pit of anxiety, she still commands a burning sense of the possibilities of life"? Lawrence would be attracted — would he not? — to that kind of self-division in a man or woman; it would apply as well to some of his own characters — say, Ursula Brangwen in the latter half of *The Rainbow*, or Rupert Birkin in *Women in Love* — as to Anna Wulf. His own entrapments were of this order, and one wonders, in this game of speaking for the dead, or speaking at least in the spirit of their lives and works, whether he would not now be ready to recognize in such a woman writer a kindred spirit. Certainly when Anna says to Molly, "our real loyalties are to men," or when her lover Michael lays his face on her breast in his sleep and she thinks, "The truth is I don't care a damn about politics or philosophy or anything else, all I care about is that Michael should turn in the dark and put his face against my breasts," she seems as traditional as Lawrence in her desires and as honest in evoking them.

Indeed, what attracts men as well as women to Doris Lessing's fiction these days, we might conclude, is what attracted them to Lawrence's: namely, an autobiographical intensity by which images of the author's self are put on the line and exploited with an honesty so self-searching and unsparing as to anticipate most of our critical objections to those images: a prophetic arrogance, too, a projected self-importance by which such characters are taken as where we are now or where we should be heading—as when Anna and Molly see themselves as "the position of women" in the 1950s, even as Birkin sees himself as "the man with a new idea" about love in the 1910s. And finally, there is an immersion through such characters in some regional manifestation of the fate of a whole civilization in decline, the death-driven ways of the South African colonies in World War II, or of the industrial midlands in World War I, in which Anna and Birkin steep themselves each with a fatal yearning, yet which each also struggles to transcend. Here indeed are kindred spirits, so much so that what critics say of one novelist might well be said of the other. Who is "one of the very few novelists who have refused to believe that the world is too complicated to understand"? Which novelist says to us, "Take me at my own level of sincerity, of seriousness, and not at yours, and you will see that this is exactly right"? The first is Lessing, the second Lawrence, as seen by Margaret Drabble (in her *Ramparts* review of *The Summer Before the Dark*[reprinted in this volume]) and Mark Schorer (in *The World We Imagine*) respectively. But surely both writers have made the same refusal to be cowed by the modern world's absurdities and incomprehensibilities; and surely both demand of readers the same active faith in their audacity and sincerity as pledges to authenticity—with the surprising result that Lawrence, about forty years after the fact, and Lessing about ten to twenty years after, have found audiences they have themselves helped to create who approach them with just such activated faith.

Their differences as "modern sensibilities" are nonetheless considerable. Both are "modern" in that they have written major experimental fictions and have dealt substantively with unconventional themes; but Lessing is plainly more Joycean than Laurentian in her formal predilections. If she shares her theme—the fragmentation of society and of consciousness—with a great many modern writers, including Lawrence, her expression of it follows the example of Joyce, Faulkner, and Woolf, in their use of multiple perspectives upon common strands of modern experience to convey its many-sidedness, and of stream-of-consciousness techniques to express both alienation and the quest to get beyond it to some kind of wholeness or connectedness.

Lessing's devices are variations on these precedents—the dream sequences which are becoming increasingly frequent in her fiction, by which she indicates the division of conscious from unconscious life and, more interestingly, the unconscious struggle of her protagonists toward some new unity with conscious life; and the notebook device by which she compartmentalizes past and present aspects of her heroine's divided self; the black notebook devoted to African memories during World War II; the red notebook to political life among leftwing intellectuals in London in the 1950s; the yellow notebook to Anna's fiction, particularly as it transforms her own experience into the love affair of Paul and Ella; and the blue notebook, in diary form, devoted to Anna's present daily life. Finally there are the unifying devices: the golden notebook near the end which is supposed to bring Anna's conscious and unconscious life together; and threading through all these sections, the chronological sequence called "Free Women" which proceeds from the omniscient perspective of traditional fiction. The effect of all these devices is to give us an almost physical delineation of the fragmented consciousness of a woman whose impulses as a writer, a socialist, and a person are to unify her personal, social, and fictive experiences; and of course it is a mark of Lessing's terrible honesty that at this stage of her career she could conceive of nothing less than this multiple approach to the difficulties of such unification; and the mark, too, of her characteristic "arrogance and egotism" that she should conceive of these difficulties as somehow representative of the "position of women" in the 1950s.

Lawrence could never give himself up to such fragmenting devices; his stance is always that of the omniscent narrator, and his attempt in his experimental fiction is to find symbolic actions which will dramatize the disintegrating or integrating tendencies of his characters against some natural standard for wholeness; he breaks with traditional plot by being episodic or by describing ongoing states of mind brought into focus by symbolic actions; and he breaks with traditional characterization by attending in these contexts to unconscious levels of feeling, especially as they reflect connections or disconnections with the natural world. Oddly, for a writer with this kind of ongoing stake in the unconscious, he seldom investigates dreams, probably because of the kind of intellection which exploiting them might entail. . . . There is a sense in which each uses the other's characteristic faith to implement recovery, as if between them there obtains a kind of obverse affinity—with surprising ramifications, I might add, for those feminist critics who embrace one author but eschew the other.

In some way, for instance, Lawrence was the kind of writer Lessing admired and would like to emulate if she could. She never to my knowledge speaks of him this way, though she lists him along with Proust, Joyce, and Mann as one of her predecessors in exploring the artist's sensibility; and there is a passing reference early in *The Golden Notebook* to "the intellectual and bohemian circles that had spun around the great central lights of Huxley, Lawrence, Joyce, etc." But there is a passage early in the first black notebook in which Anna speaks admiringly of Thomas Mann in such a way as to suggest, at least to me, that Lawrence might hold a similar place in Lessing's thinking. Thus, while discussing her disappointing experiences as a book reviewer, Anna calls Thomas Mann

"the last of the writers in the old sense, who used the novel for philosophical statements about life"; and a page later she speaks of "the only kind of
novel which interests me: a book powered with an intellectual or moral
passion strong enough to create order, to create a new way of looking at
life." She feels incapable of such writing herself because she is too diffused,
has only "the curiosity of the journalist" to go by, and she has already
disparaged the novel's journalistic turn. . . .

It is one of the ironies of *The Golden Notebook* that it too may be
taken as a report "sold across frontiers" — by male readers like Howe or
myself for instance, as we eavesdrop on intellectual women, or even by
feminist readers looking for extensions of their own dilemmas; but I for
one wouldn't want to dispense with this old-fashioned orienting function
of the novel, except as Lessing sees it as degenerating into mere journalism
and expressing only our current fragmentation. What interests me, however, is how she sees even this disparaged function as a desperate reaching
out for wholeness; for wholeness is what the philosophical novel, which
she admires, helps to create through its moral and intellectual passions, its
hard-won ordering and revisioning of life. In his finest work, certainly,
Lawrence is this kind of novelist. In the preface to his greatest novel,
Women in Love, he states the philosophical and moral aim of creating that
"passionate struggle into conscious being" which his prototype in the
novel, Rupert Birkin, undergoes. This "man with a new idea" strives for
wholeness, then — articulated, conscious wholeness — in something other
than a journalistic report; and at least some of us can accept the
integrative intelligence which F. R. Leavis sees at work throughout this
novel as exemplary for Lessing.

When she speaks . . . of reports from South Africa or from a coal-
mining village, she recalls for most of us her own and Lawrence's early
fiction. Their development was parallel in that the Martha Quest series,
like *Sons and Lovers*, proceeds in the traditional naturalistic vein, at least
until the fifth volume. Three of Anna's four notebooks proceed in this way
too; they are informed by the same faith in setting things down objectively,
as they actually happen, which motivates those novels of reportage she
disparages; and though the reports are now about her own fragmentation,
her own desperate search for wholeness, there is the same disparagement
as each of the three notebooks closes. In the yellow notebook Anna
continues to write stories, although she has supposedly foresworn them in
the first black notebook as shapings, hence distortions, of experience.
Presumably a story shaped by a moral or intellectual passion would create
its own order, its own truth, through "the quality of philosophy" she
admires; so we may take her continued story-writing as a sign of that
different faith still working within her. Interestingly, it is in the shaped
story of Paul and Ella, which dominates this notebook, that she seems
most Laurentian.

Midway through the first black notebook there is a similarly contradictory impulse at work as Anna rebels against the idea of the dissolving personality she has herself asserted: "And so all this talk, this anti-humanist bullying, about the evaporation of the personality becomes meaningless for me at that point when I manufacture enough emotional energy inside myself to create in memory some human being I've known." She is thinking about her South African friends and her ability to re-create them "as in a slow-motion film," by smiles and gestures, visual indications of the integrity, durability, and reality of personality. Yet the reference to films frightens her, and we remember how the whole African sequence becomes a dream-film as the black notebook closes in disillusionment. She wonders even now if the "certainty" she clings to "belongs to the visual arts, and not to the novel," a form claimed by disintegration and collapse. "What business has a novelist to cling to the memory of a smile or a look," she asks, "knowing so well the complexities behind them?" Yet if she did not have this certainty, she concludes, "I'd never be able to set a word down on paper; just as I used to keep myself from going crazy in this cold northern city by deliberately making myself remember the quality of hot sunlight on my skin."

We will return to that hot sunlight in a moment. What is interesting now is that her faith in reportage, in getting things down as they actually happened, which she has earlier disparaged as a false quest for wholeness, has led to a kind of wholeness in others if not in her own questing self. It is as if she were rediscovering some of the originating impulses by which the novel as we know it rose in the eighteenth century, the impulse to send reports across social frontiers, the impulse also to affirm the worth and interest of ordinary lives, the orienting and humanizing functions of an artform devoted in its early vigor to social variety and plenitude. Now, as society and the form it fostered decline together, Anna doubly affirms what she doubly disparages.

As most readers would agree, there are a series of such disparaged affirmations in *The Golden Notebook*. They may be taken as exhausted possibilities, cancellings out; but for me they have the effect rather of suspended moral accretions, wobbly stepping stones by which our battered and exhausted heroine eventually moves beyond her several afflictions: her writer's block, her political paralysis, her excessive dependence on men. Among these suspended accretions there are a number of values Lessing shares with Lawrence, and my point about them is not that they dominate or truly define her outlook, but simply that she refuses—quite rightly, I think—to give them up. Returning now to that memory of African sunlight which checks the urban clamminess of London—here is how it works at the beginning of the first black notebook:

> Every time I sit down to write, and let my mind go easy, the words, It is so dark, or something to do with darkness. Terror. The terror of this city. Fear of being alone. Only one thing stops me from jumping up and screaming or running to the telephone to ring somebody, it is to

deliberately think myself back into that hot light . . . white light light closed eyes, the red light hot on my eyeballs. The rough pulsing heat of a granite boulder. My palm flat on it, moving over the lichens. The grain of the lichens. Tiny, like minute animals' ears, a warm rough silk on my palm, dragging insistently at the pores of my skin. And hot. The smell of the sun on hot rock. Dry and hot, and the silk dust on my cheek, smelling of sun, the sun. Letters from the agent about the novel. Every time one of them arrives I want to laugh — the laughter of disgust. Bad laughter, the laughter of helplessness, a self-punishment. Unreal letters, when I think of a slope of hot pored granite, my cheeks against hot rock, the red light on my eyelids.

Here Lessing draws on her childhood experience on a South African farm as an antidote to urban terrors and unrealities; she appeals not to Eliot's ecclesiastical dry rock in an urban wasteland, with its sheltering and rather deadly shadow, but to its romantic opposite, the reassurance of natural warmth and substantiality, the sustaining light and heat by which animal life and vegetarian thrive. Her predecessor here is Lawrence, who used his childhood experience of Nottingham farms and fields for similar contrasting effects; as Paul Schlueter notes in *The Novels of Doris Lessing*, she was considerably influenced by Lawrence in her first novel about African life, *The Grass Is Singing*, and in the early sections of the Martha Quest series. The importance of the African landscape for this early fiction can hardly be overstated; Lessing evokes it often with an almost loving concern for detail and effect, and at times, as in Martha Quest's adolescence, with a romantic sense of oneness with the natural world which differs from its precedents only by her usual contrary insistence on the pain and difficulty of such moments.

The subordination of this romantic experience to Anna's intellectual self-absorption is plain enough; but its use as a touchstone for natural good is nonetheless recurrent and important. There is for instance that moment in the third "Free Women" section when Anna leaves Richard Portmain's office after a sexist putdown in a state of near-collapse and panic, tries to resist collapse so as to stand by her daughter Janet, and is terrified that she defines herself now as "something that is necessary to Janet." Then, trying to define herself further by her work, she thinks of her notebooks and sees not herself but Molly's son Tommy standing beside them, like an indictment of the deathliness in them which apparently led to his attempted suicide. When a sick ugly man follows her off the underground, grinning triumphantly at her retreat from his lewd urgings, she again feels panic; and as if to regain her balance she buys fruit now at a stand, smells the tart clean smell, touches the smooth or faintly hairy skins. This appeal to the normal creative impulse through its tokens is like an attempt to restore sexual and parental relations to some natural basis. The appeal is further underscored by the rumpus with her homosexual boarder Ivor which follows. Ivor has asked Anna to let his friend Ronnie, short of money and out of a job, share his room. Disliking Ronnie's type, seeing him as a calculating man who uses Ivor and Janet alike, Anna feels uneasy:

> Suppose I were living with a man [she thinks], a "real man"—or was married. There would certainly be tension for Janet. Janet would resent him, would have to accept him, have to come to terms. And the resentment would be precisely because of the quality of sex, of being a man. Or even if there was a man living here I didn't sleep with . . . even then the business of his being "a real man" would spark off tensions, set a balance.

She reasons further that she is saying or assuming "that children need the tension to grow up," that the quality of men who like women rather than men "would be better for Janet than what Ivor has." Let us accept this heterosexual definition of "real men" for the moment as simply descriptive; we will inquire later into its other meanings; and let us recall for a moment that the homosexual Jimmy in the black notebooks is called a "good man." Ivor and Ronnie are being criticized less for homosexuality, here, than for not providing heterosexual tensions, and beyond that, for defensively mocking the need for them; the hidden premise seems to be that if it's wrong for heterosexuals to make fun of homosexuals, the reverse is also true. There is mockery of the feminine world in Ivor's voice, for Anna, as he reads a story about a hockey girl to Janet. Anna excuses this as only a step further than the false gallantry of the "real man" who puts bounds on his relations with women. But when she hears Ronnie's song from an upstairs room, mocking heterosexual love, it disturbs her. She goes into her kitchen and runs a glass of water, slowly, "running the water to watch it splash and sparkle, to hear its cool noise. She was using the water as she had used the fruit earlier—to calm herself, to assure herself of the possibility of normality." A moment later she realizes that she is also trying to quench her feeling of being dry and empty. "I've got to touch some source somewhere," she thinks in her mounting panic, and she opens her parlor door to find "a large female shape" sitting there in the dark, like a mockery of that source—Portmain's much-abused wife Marion, who completes our crazy sexual circle.

Anna succeeds in having Ronnie put out, at least temporarily, as the section ends. Meanwhile she has reached a determined conclusion: "By God, there are a few real men left, and I'm going to see that she [Janet] gets one of them. I'm going to see she grows up to recognize a real man when she meets one." Of course it is her own heterosexuality which is being threatened, not Janet's; that healthy child now asks to be put in a boarding school, outside this conflictual household, where she can herself become a hockey girl, with goals and games and friends of her own age and sex.

It is Anna, then, who fears the loss of her own femininity in fairly traditional terms. The references to sunlight, fruit, water, real men, are part of an ongoing critique of the free state as she lives it. If at this point it is largely her sharp critical intelligence which keeps her sane, it does so by choosing things Laurentian to hang onto, reminders of natural creativity; and there is also the emotional working-through of an asserted feminine sexuality, an asserted heterosexuality, in a time of much confusion about the whole vexed question of sexual roles and sexual identity — on which Lessing seems to side with Lawrence.

In the pigeon-shooting scene in Africa she even adopts his method of symbolic action against some natural standard for wholeness. This scene, which begins with the sordid pigeon-kicking episode in London in the '50s, is her most telling evocation of the death-drive in her South African friends and the lying nostalgia in her novel about those days. The shooting of nine pigeons when six are enough becomes a resonant action, reflective of the prodigal slaughter in the animal and insect worlds around the shooting party, but even more reflective of human sterility, cruelty, and deathliness. Beginning with the stupidity of mismatching in nature noted in the thousands of coupling grasshoppers around the party, and the scientific attempt of bisexual Paul and homosexual Jimmy to match them properly, we get a parody on human love and its errors which Jimmy punctuates by positing, to no one's amusement, the homosexuality of the matching couples; at which point Paul trods on two mismated pairs and invokes Stalin as his justification, explaining that millions of insects must die to maintain nature's ecology. One of the party, Maryrose, has lost her beloved brother in the war, but Paul ignores her feelings by continuing to harp on natural doom for pigeons as well as insects, using Jimmy all the while as his human dog for fetching the dead birds. Meanwhile the group laughs at their intellectual leader, Willi, when he predictably explains the principle of destruction in nature by the class struggle. An anteater's trap for ants and some passing blacks are brought into the developing parable on that principle, the simple savagery of the African past is also invoked, and the death-struggle of beetle and anteater completes the debacle. Maryrose stops Paul from further shooting as the group returns, and Jimmy remarks on how Maryrose and Paul at its head would be a perfect couple if it weren't for his homosexual and her incestuous preferences. Here, surely, is Lessing's closest parallel to the cultural disintegration which Lawrence catches so powerfully in *Women in Love* through drownings, head-bashings, mare-spurrings, rabbit-slappings, pond-stonings, and other deadly sexual quarrels in and with nature.

The "real man" theme is of course the more significant connection with Lawrence. In *St. Mawr* and *Lady Chatterley's Lover* Lawrence had strongly emphasized the theme of male default and had posited the same shortage of real men in England to which Molly and Anna so frequently recur. There is a tendency nowadays to write such judgments off as instances of the male myth of *machismo*, but it is a little odd to find Lessing subscribing to that myth, and surely Lawrence too had opposed it, in *Women in Love* for instance, through his devastating indictment of the industrial *macho*, Gerald Crich. As with the problem of distinguishing between racism and racial pride, we are dealing here with virtues in the Greek sense—attractive traits or attributes—which may be overstressed or misapplied and so transmogrified into obvious social vices. Surely manliness and womanliness are virtues in this sense, real but subject to abuse, as Lessing and Lawrence present them; but the odd and significant thing is that they present them in short supply at a time when the cultural attack against them runs extremely strong. The attack is nominally against their abuses, but as our current emphasis on unisexual or androgynous standards suggests, the virtues themselves have been denied. In *The Golden Notebook* Lessing doesn't want this to happen. Her prototype speaks freely and positively of "real men" and "real women" and in certain sections gives us examples of what she means by them. Her most obvious example of a "real man" is George Hounslow in the African notebook. Hounslow is a forty-year-old philanderer who supervises road gangs by day and makes love to all and sundry by night; it is he who has the affair with the black cook's wife on which Anna bases her nostalgic first novel about a young British flier and a black girl, and certainly Anna is right that the actual situation is more interesting than her novel. Hounslow gets the woman pregnant, and though forced by his communist friends and the pressures of the time to do nothing about it, he is genuinely wracked by his and her dilemma.

He appears in Anna's recollections only after we learn about the cold sexuality of her intellectual lover, Willi, the fashionable homosexuality of her friend Paul, the bona fide homosexuality of his friend Jimmy, and the incestuous passion of Maryrose. In this context George's sexual appreciation of women seems rather attractive. Though it is qualified by his unfaithfulness to his wife, his compassion for her as a fellow victim of the economic trap which binds them, their common care for three children and four grandparents, impresses Anna. If she calls George the trapped man who put his wife in a cage, she nevertheless defines him as a "good man," says at one point that he and his wife love each other, and at another calls him "one of the most lovable people I have ever known" and "certainly one of the funniest," so that he figures as the key example for her of the problem of intact personality mentioned earlier. Interestingly, his goodness and his sexuality interfuse as she tries to resolve the problem. She can write about her friends with a kind of passion through visual clues to their remembered selfhood; but that selfhood also includes their goodness, meaning their humanity or lack of it, and their sexuality in its varied forms: both are crucial to the humanist credo for writing she is trying to think out. George's compassion and sexuality become Greek virtues in this context, attractive norms against which her other friends may be assessed—hence the pains she takes to define him first as a good man, and next, and for our purpose most relevantly, as a sensualist:

> I mean, a real sensualist, not a man who played the role of one, as so many do, for one reason or another. He was a man who really, very much needed women. I say this because there aren't many left who do. I mean civilized men, the affectionate non-sexual men of our civilization. George needed a woman to submit to him, he needed a woman to be under his spell physically. And men can no longer dominate women in this way without feeling guilty about it. Or very few of them. When George looked at a woman he was imagining her as she would be when he had fucked her into insensibility. And he was afraid it would show in his eyes. I did not understand this then. I did not understand why I got confused when he looked at me. But I've met a few men like him since, all with the same clumsy impatient humility, and with the same hidden arrogant power.

The passage is ambivalent, certainly, in its references to the sexual politics of submission and power; but as already indicated, it differs from current attitudes on *machismo* in suggesting the absense of sensual power in modern men rather than its threatening presence; and it differs in its appreciation of male desires, an act of sympathetic comprehension which again brings Lessing close to Lawrence. She comes closer still by making those desires something Anna feels personally as "a powerful sexuality, from which she fled inwardly, but then inevitably turned towards." If she went to bed with George, she would "learn a sexuality that [she] hadn't come anywhere near yet"; and she speaks of it as something "unbelievably sweet and lovely," as "this beautiful thing" from which she is now excluded. It is in this context that she repeats that she liked George, "indeed loved him, quite simply, as a human being" — which implies, among other things, that sexuality is human. Though it may involve domestic cages and problems of power, it cannot be eliminated from what we mean by our common humanity. This is strikingly close to Lawrence's sense of human wholeness and seems to be a novelistic as well as an ethical premise with both writers.

It is also something of a *modus operandi*. Among women writers Lessing comes closest to Lawrence in the fullness and frequency of her sexual presentations. A British reviewer, Kathleen Nott, has even suggested in *Time and Tide* (April 26, 1962) that she does this by deliberate parody that *The Golden Notebook* "is a kind of female counterrecrimination to Lawrence, which is sometimes almost parodic":

> [T]he sexual situations are almost as repetitive as Lawrence's and they are less boring only because they are more concrete and have a flavour of cynicism. But just as Lawrence estimates the "reality" of "real women" in terms of their capacity for orgasmic surrender, so Mrs. Lessing's Anna looks at the male in terms of his capacity to bring this surrender about. And she doesn't play fair, for she blames him because she doesn't quite want it herself.

There seems to be a certain resistance here to the "tyranny of the orgasm"; but along with it comes a rather appealing image of our two battling novelists: Lawrence, known far and wide for his recriminations against women, meets Lessing, with her long-savored store of feminist recriminations against men, in a 22-round knockout no-holds barred contest called *The Golden Notebook*. The trouble is that Lawrence concurs in the recriminations against men, as Lessing knows; and Lessing is scarcely sparing in the criticisms Anna makes against herself and other women. Nevertheless, there is a section of the novel, the Paul and Ella affair in the yellow notebook, which is largely a fictive response to issues raised in *Women in Love* and *Lady Chatterley's Lover*; but Kathleen Nott to the contrary, it is a sympathetic response, a sharing and modification of Lawrence's premises as they appear to a woman novelist who, like most of us, isn't quite sure what she wants.

When Anna' fictive heroine Ella, a writer like herself, walks to the party where she will meet her lover Paul, she feels responsible somehow for the grey ugliness and meanness of the London streets through which she moves. Next day, when she and Paul go for a drive through London, she tells him how much she hates the new and ugly England which has supplanted the old, how she hates the fact that people put up with it, and she concludes — like Birkin in *Women in Love* or like Connie in *Lady Chatterley* — "It ought to be swept away — all of it": then she makes a wide sweeping movement with her hand, "brushing away the great dark weight of London, and the thousand ugly towns, and the myriad small cramped lives of England." To check this Laurentian sweep Lessing adds now the experience of several more decades of lower-class advancement: Paul, who comes from that class, defends things that are as "better than they were," and so forces Ella to refine her borrowed vision. Like her creator, Anna, she argues that everything is now split up, even as Paul has been split by the struggle he has made to overcome class barriers; he has done this successfully, yet at such a cost, she senses, that he now questions its worth by defending it. She sees also that he is not appraising her sexual potentialities, as he has done before, so the argument, the opposition, puts them at ease, a little closer together, as in the early confrontations between Birkin and Ursula in *Women in Love*. . . .

But of course it is in the depiction of sexual relations, as mentioned earlier, that Lessing comes closest to Lawrence. She insists with him on the value of the heterosexual love-act, and she agrees unwittingly on the difficulties of depicting it. Thus in the first yellow notebook Anna writes:

> Sex. The difficulty of writing about sex, for women, is that sex is best when not thought about, not analyzed. Women deliberately choose not to think about technical sex. They get irritable when men talk techni- cally, it's out of self-preservation; they want to preserve the spontaneous emotion that is essential for their satisfaction.
>
> Sex is essentially emotional for women. How many times has that been written?

How many times indeed — and by men, too, for whom sex is also essentially emotional or not, as the case may be. To avoid analysis, for instance, to get irritable at technical talk, to preserve spontaneous emotions — that is how Lawrence approaches sex in *Lady Chatterley's Lover*, in those irritable parlor scenes at Wragby Hall where Clifford's intellectual cronies talk technically or analytically about it while Connie — and Lawrence along with her — fidgets. The difficulty of bringing sex into consciousness is not peculiar to women, but to anyone who takes it seriously enough to want to change our attitudes about it; and in this enterprise one wonders who is more analytical, more technical — Lessing or Lawrence? Here is Anna telling us how Ella's love for Paul was sealed in the first few months by her experience of vaginal orgasm:

> When Ella first made love with Paul, during the first few months, what set the seal on the fact she loved him, and made it possible for her to use the word, was that she immediately experienced orgasm. Vaginal orgasm that is. And she could not have experienced it if she had not loved him. It is the orgasm that is created by the man's need for a woman, and his confidence in that need.
>
> As time went on, he began to use mechanical means. (I look at the word mechanical — a man wouldn't use it.) Paul began to rely on manipulating her externally, on giving Ella clitoral orgasms. Very exciting. Yet there was always a part of her that resented it. Because she felt the fact he wanted to, was an expression of his instinctive desire not to commit himself to her. She felt that without knowing it (though perhaps he was conscious of it) he was afraid of the emotion. A vaginal orgasm is emotion and nothing else, felt as emotion and expressed in sensations that are indistinguishable from emotion. A vaginal orgasm is a dissolving in a vague, dark generalized sensation like being swirled in a warm whirlpool. There are several different kinds of clitoral orgasms, and they are more powerful (that is a male word) than the vaginal orgasm. There can be a thousand thrills, sensations, etc., but there is only one real female orgasm and that is when a man, from the whole of his need and desire takes a woman and wants all her response. Everything else is a substitute and a fake, and the most inexperienced woman feels this instinctively. . . .

This passage is intensely analytical, but it is saved from coldness by its honesty, its strong conviction, and perhaps also by its unconscious borrowings of ideas; phrases, even satiric speech rhythms (like "Very exciting" and "a thousand thrills, sensations, etc."), from Lawrence. When Anna speaks of the orgasm created by the man's need for a woman she aligns Paul with George Hounslow in the black notebooks, and herself and her creator with Lawrence. When she speaks of the vaginal orgasm as the real female orgasm she subscribes to one of the male myths of our day which Lawrence helped to create. Her distinction about the clitoral orgasm he had made before her, in *The Plumed Serpent* for instance, where he speaks of "the white ecstasy of frictional satisfaction, the throes of Aphrodite of the foam," and of the "strange externality" of this "foam-effervescence," which comes from without rather than from within; and he even uses the term "mechanical" in other contexts to describe such frictional ecstasy. Again, when Anna speaks of "dissolving in a vague, dark generalized sensation like being whirled in a warm whirlpool," she echoes Lawrence's watery metaphors for the vaginal orgasm, of fountains gushing from volcanic depths, waves rising and heaving with a great swell, "ocean rolling its dark, dumb mass." In Lessing's terms Lawrence is much more womanly, more passional, and in *Lady Chatterley* at least, more tender in his sexual descriptions than Lessing in her characteristically analytic manner; and I make this observation not to score debating points but to emphasize that men *have* to be imaginatively sympathetic to women's feelings, and women to men's, to make love at all with any kind of mutual satisfaction, that we are all blessed to some degree with "understanding bodies."

There is thus much unintended irony as Lessing, with her Laurentian borrowings, goes on to satirize masculine views through Paul's account of Professor Bloodrot's lecture on the female orgasm, from which all the lady doctors walk out because, as one later tells Paul, "women of any sense know better than to interrupt when men start telling them how they feel about sex." As the recent Masters and Johnson experiments have shown, Professor Bloodrot is technically correct in his contention that there is no physiological basis for the vaginal orgasm, that all orgasms in women are clitoral in origin; and one branch of the feminist movement has even seized on these findings as evidence of the expendability in the love-act of penises and of those who hold them dearest; they have used Masters and Johnson, that is, to attack the male myth that penetration of the vagina is vital to sexual fulfillment. It is nice that Doris Lessing, writing before these slightly whacky events, still finds the penis vital. Of course she is right about the tone and attitude she criticizes in Paul and Professor Bloodrot, a kind of priggish superiority which women properly resent, always to our male surprise.

But why, if these priggish men are nonetheless technically correct, do women like Lessing, along with men like Lawrence, *feel* there is such a thing as the vaginal orgasm? Well, one could talk about the relaxing of pelvic muscles not recorded by these experiments and about the accompanying sense of letting go which excites men as well as women; but surely the answer lies in the word *feel*, that is to say, in the feelings, and in this respect Lessing and Lawrence seem to me right. They are both describing an act of *love*, an emotional experience in which men and women are as they say *one flesh*, in which E. M. Forster's phrase, "only connect," applies in physical, emotional, creative, even procreative ways. Probably it is one indication of the craziness of our times that we may quarrel so about where the love and the fun are found, that we fight such odd biological battles; but there is an acuteness nonetheless to Lessing's observation that preference for orgasm through what is often called foreplay *may be* a sign of distrust or withdrawal of affection, and she is acute also in insisting on the indistinguishability of emotion and sensation when connective love is felt. There is much validity to the attempt, which she shares with Lawrence, to make distinctions about the quality and meaning of relations much exploited, these palmy days, but seldom sensitively explored. Still, there is a good bit of sexual puritanism, also shared with Lawrence, in Ella's pride about her emotional honesty, her incapacity to have vaginal orgasms without love, as in that now famous passage, "Integrity is the orgasm." If there is one thing that the polymorphous perversity of the love generation of the late sixties has taught us, it is that love-making works in mysterious ways its wonders to perform.

But then orgasm was not everything to either writer, Kathleen Nott to the contrary notwithstanding. Lessing follows and prefaces her sexual manifesto with evidence of Ella's dependency on Paul even in her orgasmic happiness. Of the naiveté which Paul created in her Anna writes: "He destroyed in her the knowing, doubting, sophisticated Ella and again and again he put her intelligence to sleep, and with her willing connivance, so that she floated darkly on her love for him, on her naivety, which is another word for a spontaneous creative faith." Ella is like a Lawrence heroine in reverse, trying to hold onto a condition toward which his women sometimes yearn, or into which they half-unwillingly acquiesce. Anna herself feels incapable now of such trust, such faith; and yet she measures its loss in terms of her own artistic creativity: "*What Ella lost during those years was the power to create through naivety*" is her italicized conclusion. In some measure her own ability to write, to create, has been blocked by her loss of sexual faith. Ella's story tells us then of the sexual contribution to her dilemma, tells us more about it, in fact, than she is able to convey by a direct account of what actually happens in her affair with Michael, on which *The Shadow of the Third* is based. It is a nice proof of another disparaged affirmation, another suspended moral accretion, that the shaped story is more revealing than the journalistic account. It is at this point, of course, that she parts with Lawrence and with that fusion of sexual and artistic creativity by which his novels supposedly proceed.

There is, however, another source of creative energy in both writers, most evident perhaps in the emphasis each gives to the drive for independent selfhood in their leading characters, in the determined intelligence by which Anna survives as a free woman, in Birkin's more passionate but scarcely less articulate struggle into conscious being. One of the premises of Lawrence's moral and intellectual passion, and I think it is a premise applicable to Lessing's world, is that the opposite of love is not hate but individuality. It is a paradoxical premise, since selfhood is initially nourished and later sustained by love; but as both writers knew, it is also often denied by love, as the amazing parades which each creates of women who destroy men and of men who wrong women, leave them, use them, put them down, attest. There is in these writers a terrible distrust of, hostility to, the opposite sex, which, if Lawrence is correct, is not a hopelessly destructive opposition; rather, it is an indication of unbalanced love—a happy thought, if so, for our conflictual times. The imbalance, moreover, is not with hate but with individuality; it is the self which is jeopardized by love; its insecurities, burdens, and dependencies, make it subject to absorption, usurpation, by stronger personalities. For Lawrence as for many male writers of his generation, women seemed to possess the emotional strength and certitude which men could only struggle to achieve; for Lessing and for the present generation of women writers, women, though not the weaker sex, are the more embattled in their claims of selfhood. In either case it is not love or hate which matters, but selfhood, as Lessing and Lawrence seem to know, each for his or her own sex chiefly, but also in some sympathetic measure for the other.

Looking at the long curve of their careers, moreover, an odd configuration occurs in Lawrence's forties and Lessing's fifties. The pregnancies at the end of *Lady Chatterley's Lover* and *The Man Who Died* are significant allowances for Lawrence, rare in his previous fiction, absent from his prototypical pairings; they indicate an acquisition of sufficient ego-strength to match that of the beautiful, imperious, passionate woman whom Norman Mailer posits in *The Prisoner of Sex* as possessing Lawrence's soul, as determining his lifelong struggle to be a man of sufficient strength to be her equal. The original possessor of course would be Lawrence's mother, later replaced by his wife Frieda as the outward manifestation of his problem. Without quarreling as to whether it was his soul or his ego, or better still, his super-ego, which these ladies threatened to usurp, we may take his later attempts to define himself through gamekeepers and the like as repossessions of his father's traits and strengths. The greatest of these seems to have been a capacity for tenderness, a fearsome quality which takes some courage, some inner strength, it seems, for a belatedly masculine man to give.

Similarly, Lessing seems to have arrived at a point where her heroines are no longer dependent on men, as the burning out of Anna's extreme dependence at the end of *The Golden Notebook* exhaustedly attests. In her latest novel, *The Summer Before the Dark* (1973), there is a similar burning out of dependence, sexual and parental, and a more positive arrival at determined selfhood. That the heroine of this novel is beyond childbearing and indeed childraising years makes for an interesting counterpoint to Lawrence: this woman is strong enough *not* to rely on sex or children for self-definition. She is at an age which somewhat undercuts the value of that achievement, and one wonders too at the reduction of George Hounslow's sensualism to the whistles that follow or fail to follow the changes of her hair: there is a diminishing here, surely, of the complexities of sexual love and hate. But the same sense of belatedly earned selfhood comes through that we get from watching the curve of Lawrence's life and work, and I for one am willing to settle for it. These writers are ready at long last to be themselves — which means perhaps that the battle of the sexes, while not exactly over, has for the time being at least ended in a draw.

"Woman of Many Summers": *The Summer before the Dark*
Virginia Tiger*

> . . . you can only begin to discover the difference between what you really are, your real self, and your appearance, when you get a bit older . . . A whole dimension of life suddenly slides away and you realize that what in fact you've been using to get attention has been what you look like . . . it's a biological thing. It's totally and absolutely impersonal. It has nothing to do with you. It really is a most salutary and fascinating experience to go through, shedding it all. Growing old is really extraordinarily interesting.
>
> — Doris Lessing[1]

Like *The Golden Notebook*, *The Summer before the Dark* seems to be a contemporary, intelligent — if troubled — woman's guide to intelligent women.[2] The ineluctable conclusions Doris Lessing draws here about contemporary womanhood and, by extension, the passionate identification which her female characters inspire among women readers derive from her exploration of private consciousness and grievance. Yet Lessing always links the turbulent inner lives of individual women to the grave chain of political, social, and biological pressures.

All Lessing's women live (like Anna Freeman Wulf) in social and economic worlds and the forces of history as much as individual conscience determine their sexual, intellectual, and moral development. Though Martha Quest carries the burden of the five-part novel cycle, she is meant to be just one of the children of twentieth-century violence. Similarly, the moral purpose of *The Summer before the Dark* — the novel here under discussion — is funneled through the growing self-awareness of a middle-aged woman as she discards feminine roles. Kate Brown's maniacal interior journey is tied to an explicit historical context: global starvation, the congealed irresponsibility of international managers of the world's diminishing resources, the calamitous consequences of widespread tourism, and the general dementia of ill times. For unlike many contemporary heroines, Lessing's women are never merely private soothsayers, though they often plunge into themselves. Nor do they limit their defiance

*This essay was presented at a Symposium on Women Writers sponsored by Rutgers University in 1974 and is published here for the first time with permission of the author.

to their own privations as sexual creatures, though they unashamedly criticize the masculine world.

Briefing for a Descent into Hell remains Lessing's only book to date which does not have an explicitly feminist character or (as in *The Four-Gated City*) feminist idea as part of the argument's lint, though familiar themes of alienation, madness, and prophetic fragmentation inform the fable and its protagonist's quest. Significantly, it lost her that female audience[3] which delighted in the concrete frankness, the sociological and emotional exactness achieved in her realistic depictions of lives lived and recorded. With the novel, *The Summer before the Dark*, Lessing appears to have recaptured — indeed, expanded — that audience; interestingly, it is her first novel to have, upon publication, immediately reached the best-seller list. Sharing with *Briefing*, and *The Temptation of Jack Orkney* (another work concerned with middle-aged doubt) the common question — what happens when experience is dulled by "the prison of adulthood?" — *Summer* returns to the woman question as it is refracted through the conventional domestic life of Mrs. Michael Brown, a woman whose shaky marriage makes her go (as Lessing remarked to an interviewer) "to pieces in a way I've witnessed women go to pieces."[4]

Obviously, the subject of women and their improper marriages has long attracted Lessing and the female voice so deeply felt in *The Golden Notebook* or short stories like "Winter in July" and "A Man and Two Women" once again emerges in *Summer*. Here, however, Lessing uses woman's awful descent into nullity (which for a similar heroine, Susan Rawlings of "To Room 19," ended in suicide) as a stage in a psychic voyage to integration as Kate Brown urgently attempts to locate herself. To judge from her comment to Joyce Carol Oates that the novel amounted to a "regression,"[5] Lessing may well have intended *Summer* as a deliberate reply to those feminists readers who nominated her (as she once wryly observed) Mrs. Pankhurst, the Fifth. What, the novel asks, *actually* happens to a forty-five year old female when her children have matured beyond her duty to them and her husband continues to dally in anonymous sexual liaisons?

By the 1970s this predicament of middle-class, middle-aged women had become a fictional commonplace. Works as different as Evan Connell's *Mrs. Bridge* and Penelope Mortimer's *The Pumpkin-Eater*, for example, used marital infidelity as the narrative occasion to force their heroines to scrutinize their past and confront their gender-identity. To many readers, Lessing's treatment of this theme seemed too detached.[6] Was *Summer's* emotional austerity, its insistence that women must develop an impersonal sense of self, evidence that Lessing was now alienated from the authentic female perspective?

To what degree in fact does *The Summer before the Dark* focus on a female dilemma? As in much female fiction, submergence in self is a defining characteristic of the narrative's thrust as Kate descends through layers of illusions and finds, at the novel's dramatic center, the respectable matron she has hitherto been grotesquely metamorphosized into a crazy old hag, obscenities tripping from her tongue, hair frizzed and poking out like some scatter-brained Medusa's. Her undiagnosed illness shares traits in common with much female illness which, as Adrienne Rich remarked of *Jane Eyre*, represents "an acting out of her powerlessness and need for affection."[7] But it also relates to general psychic processes which, ever since *The Golden Notebook*, Lessing has used to indicate what happens in the lives of both men and women when some crisis of function or belief catapults an individual into intense self-doubt, even lunacy.

As critical commentary has amply demonstrated, Lessing's preoccupation with mental disorder and the possibilities of psychic mutation reached their most doctrinal transcription in the novel which immediately preceded *Summer*, *Briefing for a Descent into Hell*, whose initial premise rested on the Laingian notion that insanity might be a kind of holy madness. In this view, an individual often escapes his bondage to oppressive personal circumstances (or coercive social institutions) by inventing special strategies which cut him off from an untenable situation. Far from being an illness — though judged so by the conventional world — neurotic, even psychotic and schizophrenic breakdown may be a healthy avenue into transcendent experience. In *Briefing's* evocation of this hypothesis a man (suffering from amnesia and hallucination in a London hospital) undergoes a psychic inner voyage to enter the gnomic world of myth; here, he celebrates and affirms those vital intuitions of the spirit which have been blunted during his normal life as a Classics professor because they were inappropriate to that imaginatively impoverished community. Imagining himself adrift and turning in the Atlantic, the protagonist / narrator, Charles Watkins, associates himself with legendary seafarers like Sinbad, Jason, and Odysseus; thrust upon the Brazilian coast, he discovers the ruins of an ancient city, then in horror and guilt, watches orgiastic couplings and savage fighting defiling its pristine order. Finally saved by a great white bird, he enters a celestial disc and is given a panoramic view of the Earth and its faulty evolution.

The overriding thematic meaning of this vivid archetypal journey is to give an allegorical report of Watkins's recovery of his personal capacity for oceanic wholeness as well as his initiation through symbol and myth into the truths of mankind's collective spirit: the peace of the mandala, the atavistic brutality of the rat-dogs, the cosmic harmony of the Crystal, the restorative rubrics of his planetary briefing before his rude descent into the hell of normalcy. For, after psychiatrists administer electric shock treatments to awaken him from his deep sleep, Watkins recaptures his social, professional, and domestic identity. But the recovery becomes, of course, a bitter and ironic loss of that essential identity he had constructed while voyaging in quest of a genuinely integrated self. The meanness of his daylight life brings to mind R. D. Laing's description of the numbed state of much contemporary life: "the condition of alienation, of being asleep, of being out of one's mind."[8]

The Summer before the Dark is concerned with a similar crisis of life-function, a crisis which Lessing argues in *The Temptation of Jack Orkney* might have been termed Religious Doubt in the past; in our time, it takes place in political and psychological contexts, but the pattern of upheaval is akin. Experienced first as a state where conflicting emotions swing back and forth between nostalgic self-pity and cranky cynicism, the crisis introduces a condition — often of extreme wakefulness — where a person feels convinced that *something* lost, hidden, or forgotten is trying to announce itself: erratic physical gestures, inexplicable stutterings, heavy dense dreams, each carries some obscure message which must be decoded before ordinary life can be undertaken with absorption. While *Briefing* dramatizes this theme by moving from the universal allegory of Everyman to the specific history of one individual, *Summer* assembles concrete details about one figure which, as the novel progresses, become representative of generic female history. The amnesia Kate Brown realizes she has been suffering from for the past twenty-five years is specifically female, "a spell of madness that had lasted all the years since that point . . . when her nature had demanded she must get herself a man."[9] Her struggle to recapture her past, during this summer before an ambiguous dark, represents the progress of Everywomen though five typical stages.

The novel opens with a fashionable matron standing, her family assembled before her in what might appear to be serene domestic security: late afternoon tea on the lawn. But the woman is irritated, restless; feeling as though "for some time now she had been 'trying on' ideas like so many dresses off a rack," she nags at herself with questions: "trying to catch hold of something, or to lay it bare so that she could look and define" (3). The novel closes with questions answered, romantic illusions stripped and laid bare, a dream about approaching death lived through and finished, and a woman, unlike Nora in *A Doll's House*, prepared to open the door of her suburban house and return to children and husband. Lessing, of course, has always been at pains to question and transform traditional stereotypes; her characteristically blunt, querulous style is just one of the vehicles she has assembled against the tradition of feminine sensibility.[10] In *Summer* there are other ironic uses of female conventions, for example the "cow session." Far from being the trivial gossiping of female cronies as medieval literature depicted the activity, Kate's old wives' talk with Mary Finchley offers her the opportunity to view with ironic detachment the essentially ridiculous — finally irrelevant — nature of domesticated life.

More than merely adroit, these subversions of previous accounts of femininity are of central importance to *The Summer before The Dark*'s ultimate insight into lives lived in these times. Though coerced by a determinate number of biological stages (aging or adolescence, for example) like modern man, modern woman is open to an indeterminate number of consciousness-transformations. Thus most of the subsidiary female characters in this novel serve as embodiments of the alternate possibilities for Mrs. Michael Brown — a point made clear in the rather heavy-handed naming of the two contrapuntal characters, Mary and Maureen. All of these figures have one common problem endemic to their specific historical situation: that of maintaining or establishing anew principles of order in the face of increasingly threatening world crises. As we know from the ominous "power cuts" that begin the novel, attempts to root order in the public reality (where the crucial events of most lives are "invasion, war, civil war, epidemic, famine, flood, quake, poisoning of soil, food, and air"(5) may well fail. Lessing here, as in *The Memoirs of a Survivor*, makes it pretty clear that she has no great hopes for political or economic projects for a new order. But what about Kate's attempts at the construction of order in her private reality? What function has her "private stock-taking, her accounts-making" (8) in the general circumstances she feels her future will hold: the "dwindling away from full household activity into getting old?" (8)

Lessing obviously wants to make palpable how delusive the notion of choice is in the *impersonal* processes of life, how the apparently unique emotional need of an individual is, in fact, the expression of some general *biological* stage in that person's life.[11] Kate warily explains this point to Maureen when, towards the novel's conclusion, the young girl seeks advice on marriage. Answering from that ribald detachment which is Mary Finchley's constant perspective, Kate replies: "Love and duty, and being in love and not being in love, and loving and behaving well and you should and you shouldn't ask and you ought and outn't. It's a disease" (252–53). And the narrative is deliberately structured by means of five chapters (each of whose headings ironically recalls the once agreed-upon public function of 19th century novelistic practice) that demonstrate how irrelevant are twentieth century solutions to woman's current lot.

Engaged in exploding individualistic conceptions of behavior — in particular, romantic love — Lessing has her heroine try on (only to discard as irrelevant) the various garments and social roles any woman in Kate's situation might adopt: the primordial Earth Mother in the first chapter, "At Home"; the Career Woman in chapter two, "Global Food"; the Sexual Adventurer in the third chapter, "The Holiday"; the anonymous Crazy Old Hag in the fourth, "The Hotel"; and in the final chapter, "Maureen's Flat," the Wise Old Woman with her soothing complacencies. Mother, Worker, Mistress, Madwoman, Witch: any one of these five roles might be offered by other novelists as a possible resolution to the predicament facing a middle-class, middle-aged matron banished from the garden of conjugal and familial certainty. Lessing, however, uses each as a means for what is to come, rather than as ends. The heroine's introduction to different social roles and their associated public worlds in each chapter is a departure point for Kate's real venture into another region of being, that state of heightened perception in which (unwittingly) an individual may become immersed upon some crisis of belief or function.

Even before the family's summer departure destroys forever the taken-for-granted routines of the past, Kate feels the seemingly durable elements of herself in suspension. She has the impression of being caught in some urgent condition which is nudging aside her customary view of things: "I'm telling myself the most dreadful lies. . . . There's something here that I simply will not let myself look at. Sometimes with Mary I get near to it, but never with anyone else. *Now*, look at it all, try and get hold of it" (15). And while *The Summer before The Dark* assembles a rich assortment of sociologically specific figures ranging from the higher officialdom of tourism to the differing social milieu of international businessmen, impoverished peasants, underground dropouts—there is even a fairly detailed sketch of a neo-Nazi nationalist—as well as depicting (with the precision of acute antipathy) the ways in which women, old and young, are treated as sexual objects, the real thrust of the novel is inward. Only when she has ceased *performing* in the midst of everyday reality can Kate voyage to her paramount reality: the necessity of recovering the past and grappling with her identity, a descent into the painful arenas of self.

As is so often illustrated in Lessing's work, the process of capturing the autonomous self may occur in the archetypal world of dream. Speaking of a serial dream about a seal which has haunted her sleep over the summer, Kate remarks:

> Looking back—over this time, you know, since that afternoon, the afternoon everything changed—it was like a thunderclap or an announcement or something, at any rate, *out* I went, *out* of my life, since then, what I think has been really going on is my dream. It hasn't been all the other things at all. Or if so . . . all the things that went on outside, the job I did and the travelling, and the affair . . . fed the dream. Yes. It was the dream that was . . . feeding off my daytime life. Like a foetus. (23)

The allusion here to the restorative mystery of the psychic life is familiar to any reader of *The Golden Notebook* who remembers how Anna's voyage through a final all-inclusive dream delivered her into autonomy—"all of myself in one book"—and that integration of self-hood. For Kate, however, the dream unfolds progressively. Like *Memoirs* and *Briefing*, external reality and dream allegory run their independent courses. Accompanying evasively and elusively every step in her review of the past is Kate's dream effort to carry a scarred seal through bleak wastes to water.

She is, of course, carrying herself; but until she chooses to tackle the total situation of her life "alone and outside a cocoon of comfort and protection, the support of other people's recognition of what she had chosen to present," (190) she cannot identify the landlocked creature, nor succeed in saving it from the alien waterless cold. At the same time, performances in the daylight world feed the dream; for example, on taking the translator job, Kate realizes that the essential Kate has been in "cold storage" for some time; she enjoys the fluid of her colleagues' approbation — "she was wanted, needed" (58) — until it becomes clear that she is simply repeating the role she has performed so effectively for two decades of motherhood, fussing. When she finds later that the impersonal thermostat of sexual availability has brought her an obligatory lover, she is amused to note that he has, in fact, sought out a "mother-woman," not a "love-woman": a female who would smile, and listen, and understand, and smile again. Indeed, her own response to Jeffrey is maternal, she must emancipate herself from the pervasive role of nurturing, protective, sympathizing compassion. This is the "dementia of motherhood" against which, she remembers in pain, her youngest child had rebelled one afternoon.

Alone in a small courtyard, Kate begins slowly to strip away her false "official memories," trying to rescue the past from nostalgia. This stripping away of artifice and the search for the autonomous self is now a persistent pattern for female heroism in literature. In *Summer* this common metaphor for rebellion against the confinement of woman's place is fused with the more general theme of self-therapy. For Kate must suffer a radical breakdown of her normal perceptions in order to begin to meditate on the place self-pity (and the hungry need for flattery) has played in her life's pretense at compliance. Overtaken by an illness which turns the competent bustling organizer into her shadow-self — a querulous sick old woman who must be taken care of — Kate attends a production of "A Month in the Country" and imagines the masks of social roles being torn from the faces of the men and women in the audience, revealing the animality beneath their civilized decorum. Perceiving Natalia Petrovna's weltering emotionalism as "the mirror of every woman in the audience who has been the centre of attention and now sees her power slip away from her," (171) Kate understands the meaning of performance and its humiliating centrality in the lives of women. "For the whole of her life, or since she was sixteen — yes, the girl making love to her own face had been that age — she had looked into mirrors and seen what other people would judge her by" (178). At the same time, she knows there is a core of genuine identity. It can only be confronted if she chooses — for the first time — to live outside the cocoon of social approbation.

In large measure, the final chapter of *The Summer before The Dark* recapitulates all the earlier themes and resolves them. Here Kate actively tries to locate her genuine self amid the shifting social roles of women. She must fight against her impulse to mother a young woman; struggle against the resentment she feels when shopmen do not pay her the homage required for Mrs. Michael Brown. Alone on London streets, she suffers the shame of old women who are no longer flattered by lascivious eyes and the anger of attractive women who are treated as sexual objects. By experimenting with different roles, she tests how much her inner self (beneath the costume's mask) fits into the expectations which her appearance alone has created. Her effort to solidify this self involves detaching her emotions from the conventional strains of bitterness, self-pity, and anger.

Through her solidarity with another woman Kate begins to search her memory for happiness. Dipping into episodes from the past, she recounts those golden days with Michael and the children as Maureen huddles at her knee. These nursery stories are brought to an abrupt, unsentimental end when the specter of Mary, with her insistent lessons about the need for detachment, appears. Taken together, however, the ideal world of the past and the real world of the present fuse the personal with the impersonal. And the compassion which the summer's rage has buried is released; genuine and unfettered. Miraculously, the dream completes itself: "She was no longer anxious about the seal, that it might be dead or dying; she knew that it was full of life, and, like her, of hope" (266). Except for this dream which Kate insists does not belong to her alone, the older woman cannot help Maureen since the overriding message of the novel is that quandaries or crises must be lived through alone and understood. Yet the final resolution of Kate Brown's predicament involves a new paradigm for women to sustain their autonomous selves. And Lessing's representation of Kate's final statement about herself, that marvellously female metaphor of streaky, greying hair saying "*no: no, no, no, NO*" (270) amounts to a rejection by inversion of the classic female condition of acquiescence — Molly Bloom crying, "Yes I said yes I will yes."

Notes

1. Lessing in interview with Josephine Hendin, "Doris Lessing: The Phoenix 'Midst Her Fires.' " *Harper's* July 1973. 85.

2. The title phrase "woman of many summers" is from Doris Lessing's "Older Woman to Younger Man"(1), in *"Fourteen Poems"* (Middlesex: Scorpion Press, 1959), 10.

3. See, for example: Susan Brownmiller, "Best Battles are Fought by Women and Men Together," *Village Voice*, 22 May 1969 (reprinted in this volume); Joan Didion, "Briefing for a Descent into Hell," *New York Times Book Review*, 14 March 1971, 7 (reprinted in this volume); and Annis Pratt's examination of the issue: "Introduction," *Contemporary Literature* (Autumn 1973). 4–5.

4. Lessing in conversation with Joyce Carol Oates, "A Visit with Doris Lessing," *Southern Review*, 7 (Autumn 1973), 877.

5. Ibid., 877.

6. See, for example, Anatole Broyard, "What Price Authenticity," *New York Times*, 7 May 1973; Elizabeth Hardwick, "The Summer Before the Dark," *New York Times Book Review*, 13 May 1973.

7. Adrienne Rich, "Jane Eyre: The Temptations of a Motherless Woman," *Ms.*, October 1973, 68.

8. R. D. Laing, *The Politics of Experience* (New York: Pantheon, 1967), 12. For a treatment of the parallels between Laing and Lessing, see Douglas Bolling, "Structure and Theme in *Briefing for a Descent into Hell*," *Contemporary Literature*, 14 (Autumn 1973). 550–64.

9. Doris Lessing, *The Summer before the Dark* (New York: Alfred A. Knopf, 1973), 140. Subsequent citations will be taken from this edition and will be indicated in textual parentheses.

10. Michael Joseph, see Doris Lessing, "Preface," *African Stories* (London: 1964), 9. For a brief consideration of the matter, see Lynn Sukenick, "Feeling and Reason in Doris Lessing's Fiction," *Contemporary Literature*, 14 (Autumn 1973). 516–7.

11. Lessing insists that "Growing up is after all only the understanding that one's own unique and incredible experience is what everyone shares." "On *The Golden Notebook*," *Partisan Review*, 40 (Winter/Spring 1973). 15. See as well Lessing's comments in Hendin, "Phoenix 'Midst Her Fires,' " 84.

Martha Quest and "The Anguish of Feminine Fragmentation"   Jean Pickering*

Elaine Showalter contends that, rather than originating in an innate female sensibility, "the female tradition comes from the still-evolving relationships between women writers and their society".[1] Because, from Paul and Freud and beyond, women have always been defined as "other," they have always written self-consciously as women, mediating, often explicitly, between their vocation and their female identity in their fiction. As Sandra Gilbert and Susan Gubar point out in *The Madwoman in the Attic*, "for the female artist, the essential process of self-definition is complicated by all the patriarchal definitions that intervene between herself and herself[2] thus, "in order to define herself as an author, she must redefine the terms of her socialization" (49). Since western literary genres are essentially masculine, "devised by male authors to tell male stories about the world," the woman writer who tries to mediate between her own gender and the patriarchal plots available to her may find herself blocked by irreconcilable contradictions (67). Thus women writers historically have been driven to subversion: during the nineteenth century, while they appeared to conform to patriarchal expectations, they covertly constructed a plot that is "in some sense a story of the woman writer's quest for her own story; it is the story, in other words, of the woman writer's quest for self-definition" (76).

Although *The Madwoman in the Attic* focuses on the nineteenth century, the same covert plot is clear in the work of twentieth century women writers. Defining oneself as a female and as an author still engages all the resources of the imagination. As Grace Stewart has shown, many novels written during the last hundred years have artist heroines,[3] and there are many more where the identification of the heroine as an artist is

*This essay was presented at a Modern Language Association meeting sponsored by the Doris Lessing Society in 1981 and is published here for the first time with the permisison of the author.

almost, though not quite, explicit. Martha Quest is an obvious example. That we "read" her as an artist even though she is not overtly identified as such is suggested by Nancy Topping Bazin's article comparing *Martha Quest* with two other autobiographical novels, *A Portrait of the Artist as a Young Man* and *Sons and Lovers*, where the protagonists are identified as artists.[4] Although Martha never develops into an artist in her own right, she does collaborate with Mark on *The City in the Desert* (which is built on her long-held vision of the four-gated city); furthermore, Mark is in some respects Martha's double: "the names suggest a narcissism, a twinning of the self, which is at the heart of the doubling phenomenon."[5] In short, the bildungsroman is essentially a *kunstlerroman*; furthermore, Lessing who "always knew [she] would be a writer," and who "has always been a writer by temperament,"[6] in her entire body of work has written and continues to write the story of her struggle to identify herself as a woman and as an author. Her covert plot thus resembles that of her nineteenth century sisters: it is her "quest for her own story."

Because "the twin images of angel and monster,"[7] presented by the patriarchal looking-glass have haunted women writers, their novels frequently align a "good" protagonist and an insane double, "the madwoman in the attic," on whom they project the anger and fear provoked by the literary and social confines in which they are imprisoned. Jane Eyre has her Bertha Mason, Clarissa Dalloway her Septimus Smith. By means of this doubling, women writers have been able to articulate their desire, if not to conform, at least to compromise with patriarchal norms, and simultaneously to express the negative emotions such unnatural submission inevitably arouses.

Lessing, as Gilbert and Gubar point out, "divides herself between sane Martha Quest and mad Lynda Coldridge" (78). This perception may console those who, sensing the autobiographical elements in Martha's character and thus assuming that she speaks for the author, are disturbed by the retreat from her feminist position in the first volumes of The Children of Violence. The Martha who abandoned Caroline in order to free her from the crippling mother-child dependency relationship becomes the middle-aged mistress of the Coldridge household, "living a life almost entirely formed by the needs of others."[8] But it must be remembered that Caroline's mother also felt a "painful and insistent craving" to "start the cycle of birth again";[9] the battle against the maternal, nurturing self may be fought more than once, with different outcomes. Furthermore, the Martha of *The Four-Gated City* does not host all ambivalencies of her younger self: in the last volume of the series, the expression of her antinurturant resentments has been taken over by Lynda Coldridge, who, though perfectly competent to talk to antique dealers about quality and price, is "unfit for ordinary life," particularly for the wife and mother functions.

Lynda permanently refuses her position in the patriarchal scheme, avoiding as far as possible "their" roles and "their drugs." She maintains her tenuous identity by refusing all the tender roles the patriarchy tries to assign her: she will be neither a loving wife to Mark nor a nurturant mother to Francis, though she manages, albeit with great difficulty, to establish some kind of relationship with him when he is almost grown. Thus the younger Martha's characteristics are divided between the older Martha and Lynda, and the urge both to nurture and to abandon finds expression without the apparent contradiction of A Proper Marriage.

As an adolescent, Martha developed a "detached observer," mostly by reading books on economics, sociology, and psychology provided by the Cohen brothers. This judging observer, critical of herself as well as others, is the one constant factor in her personality: "as she sat there being that adolescent girl, she remembered that, even then, there had been that other person, that silent watcher. Nothing else had been permanent."[10] In the earlier novels this acute observer was the hallmark of Lessing's narrative style as well as of Martha's personality: many critics have commented on Lessing's sensitivity to contemporary trends, which in her earlier fiction she both reported and evaluated. In Martha's later years, under the tutelage of Lynda Coldridge, she transformed her talent for observation into a kind of egoless receptivity, tuning in like a radio to different attitudes and emotions, "flounder [ing] about in a total loss of personality" (FGC, 539). In her interview with Jonah Raskin, Lessing said, "Since writing The Golden Notebook . . . I don't believe any more I have a thought. There is a thought around."[11] In the preface to Shikasta, she elaborates further: "Yes, I do believe it is possible, and not only for novelists, to 'plug-in' to an over-mind, or Ur-mind, or unconscious, or what you will" (ix). Here she seems to be approaching the tenets of the female aesthetic according to Dorothy Richardson and Virginia Woolf, who, as Showalter has shown, associate "egolessness . . . with the highest form of female perception" (290).

Lynda Coldridge, the "nothing-but Cassandra" (FGC, 225), was born with the talents Martha had to grow, but to the end her capabilities remain the greater. "Her antenna for atmospheres and tensions and what was behind words was her first developed organ" (FGC, 521). From the time she was very young, "she had always known what people were thinking" (FGC, p. 522), and had assumed that everyone else knew too. She resists the psychiatric establishment, which, diagnosing hallucinations, prescribes electric shock, insulin, drugs. The treatment damns her: the voices, "once friendly and helpful, are now dreadful" (FGC, 522). Thus Lynda has been made a psychological cripple, her visionary talent turned against herself: "accepting the evidence of her senses against the climate of orthodoxy [has] cost her health, and, for long periods at a stretch, her sanity" (FGC, p. 624). It is this same "climate of orthodoxy" of the patriarchal culture which is responsible for the unidentifiable final catastrophe, prophesied by Lynda in spite of her damaged state: "England has been poisoned." In the Appendix to *The Four-Gated City*, somewhat restored by enlightened treatment, she becomes "a first-class 'listener,' . . . a first-class 'seer' " (635). Though Martha manages to develop some of Lynda's talents, she never supplants her as prime visionary; thus, while Lessing goes far towards integrating the "good woman" with the "mad-woman," making them allies rather than enemies, they remain separate personalities, testimony to the continuing fragmentation imposed on the woman writer by the patriarchal culture.

The relationship between Martha and Lynda represents a significant modification of the traditional relationship between the good woman and the mad double. Bertha Mason dies so that Jane Eyre may marry Rochester; Septimus Smith kills himself so that Clarissa Dalloway may be integrated into society; both must be victims of authorial homicide so that the good woman may be regenerated and reintegrated into the patriarchal culture. At the end of *The Four-Gated City*, however, Lynda is thriving, her visionary powers more fully developed than ever before. It is true that Mark believes her dead, but Francis is sure she is still alive, though her whereabouts unknown. She reappears in *Shikasta*, which amongst its many documents includes a report she has written. Martha, on the other hand, spends her last years as she did her middle years, nurturing the next generation; the last we hear of her, she feels her death approaching. Lynda, apparently, is the survivor, battered but not destroyed by the patriarchal culture and the catastrophe its policies have brought about.

It is significant that neither Lynda nor space fiction appear in the Lessing canon until after *The Golden Notebook*, which describes "the dichotomies and divisions" (x) comprising the disease of the woman writer in a patriarchal culture. The inevitable fragmentation of her life and personality appears both in the structure and the content of the novel. Ironically, the multiple diaries, "those disconnected bits and pieces of feminine existence,"[12] Anna keeps in an attempt to ward off chaos actually leads to the creation of Ella, her fictional double. The novel outlines the problem of the fragmented personality and posits the solution of a breakdown, a crack-up which will lead to regeneration. But the solution to the problem of a fragmentary structure — "how to integrate the world of the diaries into that other world of the novel," as Rapping puts it — is not so easily found because *The Golden Notebook* "was too much a statement of it."[13]

Lessing herself has said that the writing of this novel, "and not only the experiences that had gone into the writing," changed her (x). One expression of that change appeared as a new authorial attitude towards her material, which many critics have noted but none more succinctly than Katherine Fishburn, who pointed out that Lessing's mimetic mode is characterized by "a single center of consciousness whose voice blends with hers so thoroughly that the two are indistinguishable"; on the other hand, "the narrators of her science fiction exemplify the role that Lessing herself is playing as a novelist, which is that of a creative and perceptive intellect forming itself and the world it inhabits."[14] These two centers of consciousness are reflected in Martha and Lynda respectively. Clearly Martha has provided the narrative mode for all the novels up to *The Golden Notebook* while Lynda just as clearly provides the mode for *Briefing for a Descent into Hell*, *Memoirs of a Survivor*, and the Canopus in Argos series. It is conceivable that the *Memoirs* are in fact Lynda's memoirs: who else could they be the autobiography of? And the dissolving of the walls which forms the remarkable end of this novel is the precise object of Lynda's compulsive journey round the boundaries of the Coldridge basement: "if you go on always, testing the walls for weakness, for a thin place, one day you will simply step outside, free" (FGC, 494).

Thus, unlike Brontë and Woolf, Lessing has refused to kill off the madwoman so that the good woman may "choose not to think when [she is] reaching out for happiness" (GN, 542). Instead, she has chosen "the more interesting route . . . of madness" by redefining it as an answer to the problems brought upon us by the patriarchal culture. As Lynn Sukenick has demonstrated, for Lessing it is "the mad who are sane."[15] Lynda is alive, well, and rebellious; the patriarchal world, blown apart by a catastrophe of its own making, has given way to another in which visionary talents are raised to a higher power. These talents, it should be noted, are traditionally feminine ones: Nancy Topping Bazin has quite rightly pointed out that these qualities, the primary values of *Briefing for a Descent into Hell*, *The Summer before the Dark*, and *Memoirs of a Survivor*, are necessary for realizing "what many feminists refer to as the 'androgynous vision.' "[16]

In her most recent interview, Lessing maintained that the Catastrophe is already upon us: "This is the apocalypse, here and now."[17] Even if the present state of affairs doesn't constitute quite the conflagration we've been expecting, the current administration's flirtation with the neutron bomb certainly encourages the expectation that Armageddon might descend at any moment. Thus the question of prophecy arises. Is the Catastrophe so central to Lessing's later work the inevitable result of patriarchal institutions, on which the "nothing-but Cassandra" can have no effect? In short, are the Lynda novels prophecy or revenge?

It is, of course, possible that these alternatives are not contradictory: the answer to both may be *yes*. The fact that Lessing's apocalyptic vision may yet come to pass does not mean that the madwoman is not angry enough to destroy. As early as 1972 when the only unequivocal indication of the Armageddon approaching in Lessing's work was the Appendix to *The Four-Gated City*, Frederick Karl pointed towards the latter interpretation: "One wonders . . . [whether] still another novelist is succumbing to apocalyptic visions as a way of settling personal problems."[18]

Although feminists may be gratified by Lessing's determination to do away with planetary patriarchy (to use Mary Daly's euphonious phrase), her visionary new world doesn't seem much of an improvement. It's true that it is inhabited by, amongst others "the new man about to be born" she predicted as early as 1957,[19] but even after the Catastrophe at the end of *The Four-Gated City*, National Areas are still indulging in Cold War espionage. Further, the new world Lessing has "made—or found—for herself"[20] in Canopus in Argos does not seem any better than the one she blew up at the end of The Children of Violence. Conspicuously it lacks a Herland, its nearest approximation, Adalantaland, being inundated after a very short history.

Spacks has pointed out that "only recently has it become possible for women to express directly in print the rage that responds to the world's insistence that they be 'good' (285); it is still difficult to abandon completely the cover story of good protagonist and her insane double. Such a reading of Lessing's work explains many of the contradictions so embarrassing to her admirers: her refusal to confront or even acknowledge the feminism of *The Golden Notebook*; the contradiction, in the preface to the second edition, between her assertion on the one hand that readers must look only for what is relevant to their own lives and her complaint on the other that desperate feminists had misread her authorial intentions; her hostility, while she claims to be an intellectual herself, to the academics who constitute her main readership—all these are manifestations of the deep division forced on the woman writer by the patriarchal establishment. In her case, the excesses of the patriarchy have made her nervous not merely about her identity but the very survival of the species.

The onward sweep of patriarchal technology hurtling us all to destruction has caused a counter balancing push for women's liberation. Lessing's analysis to the contrary, women's liberation in its widest sense is not an issue peripheral to the survival of the species; as Dorothy Dinnerstein has convincingly argued in *The Mermaid and the Minotaur*, the liberation of women—and of men—from the psychological maladies caused by the traditional patterns of child care is absolutely necessary if the human race is to master the destructive effects of modern technology. The sense of crisis which so clearly grips Dinnerstein also informs all of Lessing's later work. In spite of her pronouncements, she is still vitally concerned with "the ongoing struggle for personal and artistic autonomy,"[21] which characterizes the novels written by women during the last twenty years. Showalter maintains that "the change in Lessing's fiction . . . [has been] a systematic, willed process of escape from a very painful encounter with the self, with the anguish of feminine fragmentation."[22] In her work the female tradition has thus undergone a significant modification: the madwoman is out of attic and basement and powerfully loosed upon the world. Up to this point, women writers have always implicitly recommended some kind of authorial compromise with the patriarchal establishment: after Lessing, such a compromise may no longer be possible.

Notes

1. The title phrase of this essay is from Elaine Showalter, *A Literature of Their Own* (Princeton: Princeton University Press, 1977), 309; 12.

2. Sandra M. Gilbert and Susan Gubar, *The Madwoman in the Attic* (New Haven: Yale University Press, 1979), 17.

3. Grace Stewart, *A New Mythos: The Novel of the Artist as Heroine, 1877–1977* (Montreal: Eden Press, 1981).

4. Nancy Topping Bazin, "The Moment of Revelation in *Martha Quest* and Comparable Moments by Two Modernists," *Modern Fiction Studies* 26 (1980):87–98.

5. Claire Sprague, " 'Without Contraries is no Progression': Lessing's *The Four-Gated City*," *Modern Fiction Studies* 26 (1980):106.

6. "Interview with Doris Lessing by Roy Newquist," *A Small Personal Voice*, ed. Paul Schlueter (New York: Vintage, 1975), 68.

7. Gilbert and Gubar, 44.

8. Patricia Meyer Spacks, *The Female Imagination* (New York: Avon, 1972, rpt. 1975), 401.

9. Doris Lessing, *A Proper Marriage* (New York: Plume, 1952, rpt. 1964), 322.

10. Doris Lessing, *The Four-Gated City* (New York: Bantam, 1969), 229.

11. *Small Personal Voice*, 68.

12. Elayne Antler Rapping, "Unfree Women: Feminism in Doris Lessing's Novels," *Women's Studies* 3 (1975):32.

13. Rapping, 33.

14. Katherine Fishburn, "The Eye of the Storm: Narrative Technique in the Science Fiction of Doris Lessing." Unpublished manuscript presented at an MLA meeting of the Doris Lessing Society, 1980.

15. Lynn Sukenick, "Feeling and Reason in Doris Lessing's Fiction," *Contemporary Literature* 14 (1973): 530.

16. Nancy Topping Bazin, "Androgyny or Catastrophe: The Vision of Doris Lessing's Later Novels," *Frontiers* 5 (1981):11.

17. Nissa Torrents, "Doris Lessing: Testimony to Mysticism," *Doris Lessing Newsletter* 4 (1980):13.

18. Frederick Karl, "Doris Lessing in the Sixties: The New Anatomy of Melancholy," *Contemporary Literature* 13 (1972):33.

19. Jonah Raskin, "Doris Lessing at Stony Brook," in *Small Personal Voice*, 8.

20. Doris Lessing, *Shikasta* (New York: Knopf, 1979), ix.

21. Showalter, 302.

22. Showalter, 309.

The Golden Notebook: "Female Writing" and "The Great Tradition"

Elizabeth Abel*

"I am incapable of writing the only kind of novel which interests me: a book powered with an intellectual or moral passion strong enough to create order, to create a new way of looking at life," Anna Wulf announces at the beginning of her black notebook.[1] Anna's confession signals a break with a literary tradition resembling that which F. R. Leavis defines as "great," a tradition in which fictional shape emerges from "an unusually developed interest in life . . . a vital capacity for experience, a kind of reverent openness before life, and a marked moral intensity."[2] Leavis scrupulously includes both male and female novelists in this tradition, whose animating moral and emotional energy presumably transcends the experience of gender. Yet the very notion of a single "great" tradition based on uniform criteria and composed of unifying works of art may reflect a characteristically masculine perspective. Anna's alienation from such a tradition is shaped by gender as well as history. "It is because I am too diffused," she says. "I have decided never to write another novel" (61). Anna's awareness of her own heterogeneity reflects the modernist's disbelief in the unified self, yet it also anticipates feminist distinctions between the attitudes characteristic of the sexes — between singleness and multiplicity, coherence and diffusion, unity and heterogeneity. Interestingly, Anna's one exemplar of the old tradition is Thomas Mann. The gender designated by his name is appropriate, if perhaps coincidental, and in a novel which extensively considers the problems of Marxism and grants the name "Mrs. Marks" to the maternal Jungian analyst, the gender implications of names should not be overlooked. In this paper I will argue that *The Golden Notebook*, Lessing's most self-conscious novel, allows us to consider gender a factor as decisive as chronology in distinguishing Lessing from the "great tradition." The inclusion of a male text, Saul's novel, in *The Golden Notebook* bolsters the argument that Lessing's work implies a theory of gendered writing.

Such an argument is in part anachronistic, for the notions of female writing with which I wish to ally Doris Lessing were formulated after the composition of *The Golden Notebook*. Yet contemporary French definitions of *écriture féminine*, of female writing as heterogenous and disruptive, as a radical tool for exploding symbolic structures, describe a potential always available to the woman writer. The French emphasis on the function and character of writing provides an alternative to modernism as a conceptual framework for Lessing's experimental work. While

*This essay was presented at a Modern Language Association meeting sponsored by the Doris Lessing Society in 1981 and is published here for the first time with the permission of the author.

Lessing shares concerns and values with her British female predecessors, her play with form in *The Golden Notebook* distances her from a female tradition defined primarily through recurrent themes, images, plots, and characters.

The intricacies of French feminist theory must be drastically oversimplified in such a brief presentation. Here, I will simply note a few recurrent tendencies. Self-consciously female writing, according to these theories, gathers its force from woman's cultural status as Other, as embodiment of that which culture represses to achieve a coherent identity. To render in language the density and complexity of female experience is to challenge fundamental cultural structures. By articulating the unacknowledged rhythms and sensations of the female body, reduced in psychoanalytic theory to the negative image of the male, to absence and silence rather than activity, female writing can subvert the hierarchies codified in language and theory. According to Hélène Cixous, "Women must write through their bodies, they must invent the impregnable language that will wreck partitions, classes, and rhetorics, regulations and codes. . . ."[3] Female writing, rooted in the diffuse sensuality of the female body, generates a syntax that fractures distinctions between subject and object and makes impossible "all discrimination of identity, all establishment of ownership, thus all forms of appropriation."[4] Female writing thus is marked by a dual gesture of disruption and connection. The most fundamental pattern it struggles to subvert is the system of binary oppositions that surround the sexual division, for "the complete set of symbolic systems—everything said, everything organized as discourse— art, religion, family, language—everything that seizes us, everything that forms us—everything is organized on the basis of hierarchical oppositions which come back to the opposition man / woman."[5] Writing herself, her polymorphous sexuality, her unsevered bond with the body of her mother and thus with other female bodies, woman replaces structures of opposition with versions of continuity. In "When Our Lips Speak Together," the utopian conclusion of *This Sex Which Isn't One*, Luce Irigaray evokes the emotional and physical bonds between women as a model for new language and new concepts of identity: "we are always one and another, at the same time. Thus we can not distinguish ourselves without all of us ceasing to be born. Without limits or edges, except those of our moving bodies."[6] Writing from a different theoretical perspective, Julia Kristeva contrasts the symbolic register, which expresses propositional meaning, with the semiotic mode through which one communicates by rhythm, sound, and gesture. Woman's enduring pre-Oedipal relation to her mother accords women's writing a privileged relation to the semiotic mode which precedes verbal communication. Female writing will simultaneously subvert symbolic structures and enact new modes of connectedness.

The Golden Notebook is aesthetically and politically radical. The novel's form subverts literary structures; its characters challenge political structures. Lessing, however, gradually differentiates male from female struggles for change. Political action becomes a futile masculine endeavor, while the radical impulse shifts to the literary realm, gaining force in Anna's hands. Anna's nightmare vision of opposing soldiers placed interchangeably before a firing squad, a vision she relates the day she decides to leave the Communist Party, encapsulates her sense of political futility, her fear that "there is no right, no wrong, simply a process, a wheel turning" (345). Significantly, her vision is given literary expression in a male text, Saul's novel. By interpolating a male text within *The Golden Notebook*, Lessing delicately traces an axis between political frustration and masculine writing, while suggesting an alternative female defiance manifested in Anna's web of texts.

Lessing also implies that biology differentiates female from male styles of radicalism. Anna's detailed record of 15 September 1954, the day she decides to leave the Party, succinctly and subtly indicates the pull of gender. The record plays dramatic, definitive events against seemingly trivial, but equally definitive ones. On the one hand, Anna leaves the Party after realizing that her two male comrades play roles analogous to those of her nightmare vision, and she understands that Michael, a Party member who sees himself as "a man who is the history of Europe over the last twenty years" (332), is leaving her; her most important ties to men and politics thus are severed simultaneously. On the other hand, Anna participates in routine, physical, female activities: she wakens, tends to, and puts to sleep her daughter Janet, revelling in their physical intimacy; lovingly cooks for Michael, who doesn't return to eat; and begins her period, an acute reminder of her female body. A subtle dialectic between male and female realms of experience punctuates her day. Anna's identification with the female realm contrasts with the stance of the Party's loyal secretary Rose, an unpleasant, unkempt woman who blindly identifies with male politics and neglects her body to such an extent that its very presence is offensive to Anna. Rose provides a counterexample to Anna's awareness of her physical being, an awareness that suggests a biological alternative to Marxist definitions of materialism. The means of reproduction, not production, ground female perspectives on change.

Although the attitude toward female sexuality in *The Golden Notebook* is basically conservative, and very different from the polymorphous *jouissance* celebrated by Cixous and Irigaray, the novel shares with the French perspective the belief that female biology shapes female experience in ways that are resistant to male codes of liberation and that serve as a touchstone of female authenticity. For women like Ella, Anna's fictional surrogate in the yellow notebook, "integrity isn't . . . any of the old words. Integrity is the orgasm," a physical response that, within this novel, functions very differently for women and for men. When Tommy complains that Anna perceives him as an evolving (rather than completed) individual, she offers a biological explanation for her perspective on human experience: "But I think that's how women see — people. Certainly their own children. . . . When a woman looks at a child she sees all the things he's been at the same time. When I look at Janet sometimes I see her as a small baby and I *feel* her inside my belly and I see her as various sizes of small girl, all at the same time. . . . That's how women see things. Everything in a sort of continuous creative stream — well, isn't it natural we should?" (269). Similarly, Anna acknowledges the impact of biology when she reflects on her unsatisfying record of September 15: "it is the same as the 'experience' with Mother Sugar. I remember saying to her that for the larger part of our time together her task was to make me conscious of, become preoccupied by, physical facts which we spend our childhood learning to ignore so as to live at all" (468). In her writing, as in her analysis, Anna struggles to reclaim her physical experience, but the task if problematic, for a literal transcription violates our habitual, unconscious response to our biology. Finding a literary equivalent for the female body is an important undercurrent in *The Golden Notebook.*

What might some of these equivalents be? Lessing hints at one typically female mode of communication in her descriptions of female relationships, in which nonverbal interactions play an important role. Anna's relationship with her daughter is presented primarily as a physical bond enacted through songs, laughter, crooning, and occasional stories, largely rhythmic, nonsignifying exchanges, remnants of the pre-Oedipal babble Kristeva describes; Anna's relation with her closest friend Molly is highly verbal, yet Anna also depends on "reading" the expressive gestures of Molly's hands; Mother Sugar "conducts" her psychoanalytic sessions with Anna through smiles, nods, shakes of the head, and impatient clicks of the tongue, as well as through verbal analysis; and Anna and Maryrose, in the black notebook, communicate almost exclusively through glances and smiles that contrast with and puncture the abstract political language employed by their male peers. The physical "language" of female bonding suggest a way of displacing the symbolic structures that shape, and therefore domesticate, even radical politics.

The larger form of *The Golden Notebook* also suggests the desire to fracture confining structures. Disruptions occur not at the level of syntax, as Cixous exhorts, but at the level of narrative structure. Writing is Anna's political tool; if she can no longer write the kind of novel she admires and no longer participate in radical politics, she turns her literary fragments to a radical purpose. *The Golden Notebook* disrupts and blurs traditional categories, suggesting new forms of continuity. The form of the novel dramatically challenges the structure of binary oppositions. Anna's ironic recitation of the oppositions that shape our experience — "Men. Women. Bound, Free. Good. Bad. Yes. No. Capitalism. Socialism. Sex. Love. . . ."(44) — sketches the deconstructive impulse underlying her composite work of fiction.

The structure of *The Golden Notebook* dissolves the division between fiction and reality into a continuum of possibilities. Lessing deliberately gives us both "story" and "plot" — both the disorderly flux of experience, represented in the notebooks, and its orderly recreation in such works of fiction as "Free Women," "The Shadow of the Third," and the synopsis of *Frontiers of War*. The novel is a heterogenous web of fictions, haunted by allusions to absent fictions, traversed by one fiction presented as "reality" and another explicitly presented as fiction yet essential to our knowledge of the characters, and completed by the narrative of diaries which self-consciously question their own accuracy. As it winds its circuitous path between truth and fictionality, the novel subverts the notion of authority. Our ostensible anchor to reality, "Free Women," is finally revealed as a fictional creation, while the placement of the yellow notebook stories before the blue notebook events they describe creates the illusion that the fiction shapes, rather than reflecting, reality. The double ending of the novel — in which the "real" Anna writes "Free Women," whose fictional "Anna" abandons writing and decides to become a social worker — prevents a definitive sense of closure, disrupting a formal convention that separates the shape of fiction from that of life. The deliberate subversion of formal conventions conforms with Anna's claim that the most provocative aspect of art is formlessness: "People don't mind immoral messages. . . . What they can't stand is to be told it all doesn't matter, they can't stand formlessness" (474). The formal challenge to fixed categories is the most effective, most radical, tool for opening possibilities. By suggesting formlessness through form, Anna / Lessing uses writing to dissolve another opposition.

In contrast to the rest of *The Golden Notebook*, the male text interpolated in the novel emphasizes binary oppositions. Saul's novel (in synopsis) is heir not only to Anna's nightmare vision, but also to a recurrent pattern of male opposition. Men in *The Golden Notebook* tend to pose alternatives in terms of unresolvable conflicts: Tommy, for example, is paralyzed by the choice between chaos and constraint; George Hounslow vacillates between desire and remorse; Michael struggles futilely to resolve his faith in the Communist Party with his faith in the innocence of the comrades denounced as traitors by the Party. Static opposition is also represented in the pattern of male relationships, frequently polarized by political conflict. Willi and Paul argue endlessly and to no avail; Michael and Jack, the men to whom Anna claims she feels closest, do not trust each other politically enough to speak together; Charlie Themba quarrels with and splits from his closest friend, Tom Mathlong. Anna's nightmare vision encapsulates this dynamic of frozen opposition. By transferring this relation to the center of Saul's text, Lessing implies a view of gendered writing in which the male text inherits the structure of oppositions the female text struggles to undermine.

Saul's novel emerges from the sentence Anna gives him: "On a dry hillside in Algeria, a soldier watched the moonlight glinting on his rifle"

(642). In Saul's hands, this soldier appears automatically to generate his intellectual and political opposite: a French soldier who feels burdened and defined by the structures of western thought. The Algerian complains that none of his feelings conform to expected patterns; the Frenchman craves a spontaneous thought or feeling "not willed on him by Grandfathers Freud and Marx" (643). This confrontation between the bondage imposed by systems and a blank and meaningless freedom dramatizes the opposition between form and formlessness that *The Golden Notebook* explodes. In the male text, however, the opposition generates mutual destruction instead of creativity. The conversation between the men is interrupted by a Commanding Officer, the representative of "an invisible *they*, who might be God, or the State, or Law, or Order" (642), who distrusts their intimacy and orders both men shot together, side by side. Cultural law forbids any dissolution of opposition. Saul's text, though ironic, ultimately sanctions the power of this law. The tone implied by the synopsis reproduces the "bitter, accepting smile" exchanged by the two men in Anna's nightmare vision, a smile she claims "cancels all creative emotion" (345). Saul's novel laments, but does not challenge, the dynamics of his culture. The conventional form of the novel reflects the resigned point of view. As Saul can not envisage any resolution of form with formlessness, his writing cannot experiment with these categories. Saul, like Anna, keeps a journal, but the chaotic flow of experience represented in a journal finds no entree to the orderly plot of his novel. Saul's work of fiction is closed against disruption, and the double death that seals its closure inverts the double possibility that broadens the conclusion of *The Golden Notebook*. The male text sanctions the stasis that the female text dissolves.

While Anna regrets the passage of the great tradition, the composite novel she creates suggests the prospect of a different tradition, explicitly radical, implicitly female, a tradition moulded less by moral concern than by the disruption of moral and aesthetic categories. It is the woman writer, Lessing implies, who can initiate this new tradition. Shaped by a different biology, less entrenched in certain cultural dynamics, woman can enact Cixous's faith that "writing is precisely *the very possibility of change*, the space that can serve as a springboard for subversive thought, the precursory movement of a transformation of social and cultural structures."[7]

Notes

1. Doris Lessing, *The Golden Notebook* (New York: Simon and Schuster, 1962; rpt. Bantam Books, 1973), 61. Future citations will appear in the text.

2. F. R. Leavis, *The Great Tradition* (New York: New York University Press, 1964), 8–9.

3. Hélène Cixous, "The Laugh of the Medusa," trans. Keith Cohen and Paula Cohen *Signs* 1 (Summer 1976); 886.

4. Luce Irigaray, *Ce sexe qui n'en est pas un* (Paris: Editions de minuit, 1977), 132. My translation.

5. Hélène Cixous, "Le sexe ou la tête?" *Les Cahiers du GRIF* 13 (October 1976); 7, cited and translated by Domna C. Stanton; "Language and Revolution: The Franco-American Dis-Connection," in *The Future of Difference*, ed. Hester Eisenstein and Alice Jardine (Boston: G. K. Hall and Co., 1980), 73.

6. Irigaray, 216.

7. Cixous, "The Laugh of the Medusa," 879.

The Woman Writer as Exile: Gender and Possession in the African Stories of Doris Lessing

Clare Hanson*

Doris Lessing's African stories are valued highly by critics, perhaps because in them Lessing writes about a landscape and a culture which she knows as she could not know her later countries of exile. These fissured, disjointed, problematic texts should not be viewed as a discrete unit somehow separable from Lessing's other work but as consistent with the main body of her fiction. They must be approached as representing a decentered subject and object: an exiled woman writer's response to Africa.

The *form* taken by these stories is that of the *free* story, a type of short fiction defined in my book *Short Stories and Short Fictions, 1880–1980*; the free story is essentially a "plotless" story and its freedom consists largely in its potential for narrative inconclusiveness. It has been suggested that the free story is a very apt form for the exiled writer because it seems suited to the expression of an ambivalent or an uncommitted world view. However, I'd argue that there is a conflict in Lessing's African stories between the form (or the expectations created in us by the use of the free story genre) and the content, and that it is in exploring such a conflict that we may locate some of the major sources of energy and interest in the texts.

I would like to open up the question of gender before going on to talk about "Africa," for I think that for Lessing herself *as a writer* the question of gender choice precedes and shapes some of the experience of Africa which she presents. It is as though Lessing feels that in these short stories she has the option of writing either in a "masculine" or a "feminine" way: this implies a kind of detachment from form and content, or a gap between feeling and form, which it would be hasty to judge as necessarily

*This essay was presented at a Modern Language Association meeting sponsored by the Doris Lessing Society in 1984 and is published here for the first time with the permission of the author.

disabling. (I use these terms because Lessing does — I do not take them to designate essential, but cultural differences. What is interesting is the fact that Lessing herself makes these assumptions about the possibility of choosing a masculine or feminine style. We as critics must reproduce, before questioning, such assumptions.)

Gender is signalled as problematic in the African stories on many levels, including language. First, one is struck by the uncertainty about the sex of the narrator in the opening stages of many of the stories — "Old John's Place," "The Story of a Non-marrying Man," "Flavours of Exile," for example. For several paragraphs the sex of the narrator is left in doubt, while the text presents a detailed account of sex- or gender-less activities which baffles and frustrates the reader. We remain in a state of impatience and unease because we are unable to settle down to identify with our protagonist until the key pronoun is dropped. The effect is to foreground the issue of gender, making clear to the reader the extent to which he or she relies on gender differentiation as a means of coding, sorting, making sense of the world and experience, in ways which may be entirely arbitrary.

The second signal in the texts comes from the frequent use of a young boy or girl as the main protagonist or observer. These observer figures may — just — be pubescent, but they have not yet entered into their sexually differentiated adult roles, and so if gender is initially made problematic in these texts through our uncertainty over the sex of the narrator, the problematic continues through the texts' apparent reluctance to engage fully with adult, gendered experience. The adolescent perspective skews the texts, giving strength through the scope it offers for the observations of an innocent abroad, but also acting as a kind of negative filter, blotting out large areas of experience. The reader identifies with the adolescent perspective because the texts themselves offer so little other leverage: there are so few occasions on which the language generalises itself to the extent that we emerge from this narrow point of view.

Through most of Lessing's African stories there is a shrinking away from sexuality, from what Pound would call "direct treatment of the thing": the texts seem to refuse sexuality but leave the trace of their refusal as a second troubling question for the reader.

Thirdly, there are disquieting shifts of tone in the "African Stories," to put it crudely, but in terms taken from Lessing herself, there are shifts between a direct, free "masculine" prose style and an indirect, intense "feminine" prose style: to extrapolate from Lessing's own terms, there are shifts between a style which is abstract, analytic, predominantly metonymic, and one which is concrete, sensuous, and predominantly metaphorical. Often the shifts in style or tone may occur within a single story, as these brief quotations from "The Black Madonna," a story to which Lessing has said that she is "addicted," might show. First of all the wordy "masculine" prose:

> Zambesia is a tough, sunburnt, virile, positive country contemptuous of subtleties and sensibility: yet there have been States with these qualities which have produced art, though perhaps with the left hand. Zambesia is, to put it mildly, unsympathetic to those ideas so long taken for granted in other parts of the world, to do with liberty, fraternity and the rest.

Now the "feminine," informed with a tone of longing or regret:

> Yet he spoke of her now to Michele, and of his favourite bush-wife, Nadya. He told Michele the story of his life, until he realised that the shadows from the trees they sat under had stretched right across the parade-ground to the grandstand. He got unsteadily to his feet, and said: "There is work to be done. You are being paid to work."
> "I will show you my church when the light goes."[1]

Lessing has discussed her use of masculine and feminine prose styles with specific reference to two of her "African" stories, "The Trinket Box," and "The Pig." She has written:

> ["The Trinket Box"] . . . intense, careful, self-conscious, mannered— could have led to a style of writing usually described as "feminine." The style of "The Pig" is straight, broad, direct; is much less beguiling, but is the highway to the kind of writing that has the freedom to develop as it likes.[2]

"The Trinket Box" and "The Pig" are both stories about possession. "The Pig" is open, direct, and above all composed. The prose seems plain and unadorned, but if *we* analyse *it* we find that it is analytic and abstract to a degree. The sentence structure is simple, but the sentences accumulate in a relentlessly logical way—we have the feeling that all the different elements in the text have been well weighed and judged before the story ever came to be written, and that nothing can now divert or deflect the narrative from its willed and chosen course. Take this paragraph, for example:

> Jonas did not reply. He did not like being appointed official guardian against theft by his own people, but even that did not matter so much, for it never once occurred to him to take the order literally. This was only the last straw. He was getting on in years now, and he wanted to spend his nights in peace in his own hut, instead of roaming the bush. He had disliked it very much last year, but now it was even worse. A younger man visited his pretty young wife when he was away.[3]

Lessing feels that such writing "is the highway to the kind of writing that has the freedom to develop as it likes," and her statement must be respected. Yet it is my impression that this writing does not have freedom on the level of text or language: its freedom exists, if it exists at all, in the public, historical domain. In stories like these Lessing by her own admission writes "like a man" and in so doing attempts to enter the field of male discourse, male history, and male power. "The Pig" is thus not only about male power on the most obvious level — the story is concerned with one man's possession of another man's wife — but also exhibits a kind of textual possessiveness, through its relentlessly analytic prose style, which it would seem fair to call "masculine."

In calling Lessing's style "analytic" I do not mean that it is necessarily either very cerebral or very complex — clearly the style of the African stories is not in the remotest sense Jamesian. But the style is very selective: it is as though perceptions and language have been sifted through so that only the *typical* rather than the particular event or perception comes through to us. The texts are thus in a curious way bodiless, even when they are directly concerned with physical or sensuous experience.

Lessing's "masculine" prose is a language of selection, excision, expropriation: the law of (masculine) language becomes the law of being: (masculine) syntax does not so much mimic as construct the experience of Africa which we take away from such texts as "The Pig" and "The Sun Between Their Feet."

In the context of contemporary feminist theory, and in particular the writings of Julia Kristeva, I think it legitimate to claim that in "masculine" stories — or in parts of stories — like "The Pig" Lessing attempts a takeover, a possession of Africa which is doomed to fail. Recent feminist theory has stressed the repression of female desire which takes place in conventional representation: in the Lacanian "symbolic order" (the phallocentric order of language), utterance is made possible precisely through the repression of the feminine, the heterogeneous, the other. Kristeva goes on to argue that in literature femininity can characteristically be located in the breaks and *"pulsions"* of a text, where desire as it were "bounds back," and she particularly associates the feminine with the kind of disruption and fissuring of the text which occurs in modernist and postmodernist writing (e.g. Joyce, Sollers). This of course raises a problem — how can it be that the feminine in this sense is expressed by men? Kristeva has in fact been taken to task by some writers for failing to acknowlege that the feminine as she presents it is not truly other: it is defined by difference from the masculine, not otherness. This brings us up against the perennial different / other question in feminist theory. I would like to offer a way out of this by suggesting that "masculine" and "feminine" as Kristeva's crities, for example Juliet Mitchell, use them are not stable terms and are not ultimately tied to sexual identity — they are to do with *qualities* which can shift. In a sense therefore the debate about otherness takes us far beyond the notion of a "real" feminine: the notion of the other in this sense can be seen as rather like the Derridean postulate of the "third term" which would ideally break the antithetical relations of the word / the world. I'd like to stress the link between this "ideal" pursuit of the feminine and Derridean theory, before going back to discuss Lessing's stories in the very contingent terms which she has given to us — masculine and feminine.

It is in those stories of Lessing which seem most fissured and disjointed that we come closest to the subject, Africa, that "inexplicable majestic silence" as she calls it, and I would argue that the question of exile and possession in the African stories (the question of their "Africanness") is intimately bound up with a choice of "masculine" and "feminine" modes of writing. The "feminine" writer Lessing makes closer contact with, effects some kind of rapprochement with Africa, just as the feminine characters do in the texts we've been considering. It's actually very striking that in these texts (white) male and female attitudes to Africa are absolutely polarized. The men characteristically feel that they own Africa in both the literal and the metaphorical sense: they organize it, partition it, drive roads and railroads through it, imposing European notions of order on it.[4] Men are associated with the hunt, the chase, guns and dogs — the young girl in the famous story "The Old Chief Mshlanga" feels safe when walking about her father's farm only when she mimics her father, takes over his accoutrements ("I had my rifle in the curve of my arm, and the dogs were at my heels"). The women settlers are by contrast alienated from Africa in both cultural and physical terms. Some may make brief *sorties*, make initial attempts to impose their kind of order or civilization on Africa — Mrs. Lacey, for example, in "Old John's Place" creates a bedroom which is an organza fantasy in the midst of the "red dust" of Africa. But these baroque efforts soon dwindle and fail, as the women come to recognize the impassable gulf which exists between their assumptions and expectations and the physical reality of life in "Zambesia." So Julia muses in "Winter in July":

> "That is my home," said Julia to herself, testing the word. She rejected it. In that house she had lived ten years — more. She turned away from it, walking lightly through the sifting pink dust of the roads like a stranger. There had always been times when Africa rejected her, when she felt like a critical ghost.[5]

In "Winter in July" the contrast between male and female responses to Africa is described in terms which begin to suggest a certain wise passiveness on the part of the female:

> Her liking for the evening hour, before moving indoors to the brightly lit room, was the expression of her feeling for them [the two men]. The mingling lights, half from the night sky, half from the lamp, softened their faces and subdued their voices, and she was free to feel what they were, rather than rouse herself by listening. This state was a continuation of her day, spent by herself (for the men were most of the time on the lands) in an almost trancelike condition where the soft flowing of the hours was marked by no necessities of action strong enough to wake her. As for them, she knew that returning to her was an

entrance into that condition. Their day was hard and vigorous, full of practical details and planning. At sundown they entered *her country*, (my italics) and the evening meal, where the outlines of fact were blurred by her passivity no less than by the illusion of indistinctness created by sitting under a roof which projected shadowlike into the African night, was the gateway to it.[6]

In this text, the men embody the so-called "masculine" mode of possession: they are hard, practical, vigorous, driven by an instinct for self-preservation which forces them to annihilate, or to refuse the separate quality of "their" land, Africa. The woman is soft (indistinct), passive, more than willing to annihilate, or perhaps suspend herself in order to "feel" what her two companions and the landscape "are." The woman recognizes that presence ("what they were") cannot be freed from absence ("the evening hour" "an almost trance-like" state): she recognises not only her points of contact with but far more crucially her alienation from Africa. "In order to possess what you do not possess / you must go by the way of dispossession."

What of Africa, then, in "The Pig," the story written, in Lessing's own words, in the style leading to freedom? I would argue that "Africa" in "The Pig" is not free in that it is not fully nor openly recognized as an entity distinct from the consciousness of character or narrator—it isn't available to the reader as both subject and object. I can only support this charge by direct quotation from passages which purport to evoke the feeling of Africa:

> Hours passed, and he watched the leaping dancing people, and listened to the drums as the stars swung over his head and the night birds talked in the bush around him. He thought steadily now, as he had not previously allowed himself to think, of what was happening inside the small dark hut that gradually became invisible as the fires died and the dancers went to their blankets. When the moon was small and high and cold behind his back, and the trees threw sharp black windows on the path, and he could smell morning on the wind, he saw the young man coming towards him again.[7]

It's striking that here Lessing uses images which point us back to mechanization and civilization (particularly notable is the phrase "the trees threw sharp black windows"): it is as though there is some kind of confusion between an intention of conveying Africa and an inability to do so save through images which are literally mechanical or metaphorically so in the sense that they verge on cliché ("he could smell morning on the wind").

By contrast in the more disjointed, elliptical story "The Trinket Box" a dialectical relationship is set up between the characters and / or the narrator, and Africa. It is clear that, in the main, we are being presented with Africa as it has been perceived and imaged by "Aunt Maud"—there is not that ambiguity which still exists in "The Pig," where we are not at all sure through whose eyes we are viewing Africa — those of the farmer, Jonas, or an omniscient narrator. We see Africa in "The Trinket Box" through a series of "characteristic," quirky photographic images. A relation between subject and object exists and is made clear even in the largely picture-postcard view which we have of Africa in this story: though the perspective may be limited, it is only because we have a sense of tension between the object — Africa — and its neat presentation in white-settler language that we can perceive or acknowledge that such limitation exists. Africa is presented in similarly complex, mediated ways in other stories written in Lessing's avowedly "feminine" style — "Winter in July," "Getting off the Altitude," "Old John's Place," for example.

To conclude: I have been studying the implications of Lessing's apparent refusal, in some of the African stories, to take what Simone de Beauvoir has called the "negative way" of female knowledge. I would like to make one final suggestion about the relationship between the forms some of these stories take and their content. I don't want to tie too easily together concepts which should remain significantly juxtaposed, rather than merging and becoming confused. But it does seem to me that we should at least entertain the idea of a relationship between Lessing's "masculine" style and the theme of colonization. It could be argued that in writing about a colonial system she wholeheartedly deplores, Lessing nevertheless reproduces or perpetuates in the processes of some of these texts patriarchal, and by extension colonial, systems and values. One has perhaps to turn again to the all-pervasive thought of Derrida to explain the logic of the supplement whereby a liberal attitude proposed by the texts on the level of ostensible content is undone, shown to be incomplete through the workings of the text. It is perhaps not so much that Lessing is a recidivist colonial figure, as some critics of the Canopus in Argos series have suggested: rather we should recognize that the texts *as texts*, if Derrida is right, will almost certainly work to show that a good, a desideratum, is incomplete, because / if it is proposed too confidently as absolute.

Can I finally quote very briefly from the "Preface" to *The Diaries of Jane Somers*? This seems to illustrate again the point that Lessing herself is acutely aware of the possibilities (and dangers) of gender choice in writing. Here she talks about the dry (or wry) and the romantic female alternative voices:

> And it did turn out that as Jane Somers I wrote in ways that Doris Lessing cannot. It was more than a question of using the odd turn of phrase or an adjective to suggest a woman journalist who is also a successful romantic novelist: Jane Somers knew nothing about a kind of dryness, like a conscience, that monitors Doris Lessing whatever she writes and in whatever style.

Notes

1. Doris Lessing, *Collected African Stories* (*African Stories*) (Triad/Panther: London, 1979) 2:45, 56.

2. Doris Lessing, "The Small Personal Voice," quoted in Elaine Showalter, *A Literature of Their Own* (Virago: London, 1978), 309.

3. Lessing, *African Stories* 2:69.

4. For the "geography" of colonization, see the opening chapter of *A Passage to India* (1924).

5. Lessing, *African Stories* 1:219.

6. Ibid., 193–94.

7. Lessing, *African Stories* 2:72.

INNER AND OUTER SPACE

"Disorderly Company": From *The Golden Notebook* to *The Four-Gated City*

Dagmar Barnouw*

> So it must be said that if a man starts thinking a bit he gets into what one might call pretty disorderly company.
> —Robert Musil, *The Man Without Qualities*[1]

The Golden Notebook, thought by most critics to be Doris Lessing's best novel so far,[2] has been praised for its formal control. Lessing herself, in a 1969 interview at Stony Brook,[3] said she was "very proud" of the novel's form, describing, in contrast, the form of *The Four-Gated City* as "shot to hell." There is indeed a marked change in attitude toward the organization of the narrative as well as toward the protagonist; yet, the narrative anarchy and the insistence on the potential dimension in the development of the protagonist's consciousness, new in Lessing's work, deserve serious consideration. The new, much more open narrative structures may be seen as thoroughly functional: "shot to hell," after all, points to the central concern of the novel, the descent into the self which is partly hell. Assuming, as a working hypothesis, that the indeed surprising differences between *The Golden Notebook* and *The Four-Gated City* are indicative of changes in Lessing's concept of the function and responsibility of the novelist, I should like to explore these differences in some detail, starting with a reexamination of the function of the organizational devices and their influence on intellectual decisions in *The Golden Notebook*. . . .

Anna's fear of letting in chaos, "becoming that chaos" (*GN*, p. 313) is interrelated to her need to make fictitiously whole beings out of her child and the men she comes into contact with. These other selves can then be used by her to patch up, if only temporarily, the imperfections of her self. The central ambiguity of the novel is founded in the reader's inability to decide whether Anna is judged guilty of a fragmented vision by her author, or whether such judgment is rejected as meaningless, because fragmentation is inevitable. Significantly, the sexual basis of the woman's dilemma is dealt with in detail—realistically and very intelligently—in

*From *Contemporary Literature* 14 (Autumn 1973):491–514. Reprinted with permission of *Contemporary Literature*.

the most distancing form Anna is capable of: her fragmentary novel about Ella and Julia. . . .

Caught between her four notebooks, Anna cannot do without the protection of abstractions and generalizations about the "other." She is both waiting for the "real man" to come down like a *deus ex machina*, impossibly perfect, closing her wounds without getting himself infected by them, and ready to form such a man herself, forgetting for the time her own limitations as well as those of her materials. Irving Howe implicitly accuses Anna, though he explicitly accepts her on her own terms: "She wants in her men both intimacy and power, closeness and self-sufficiency, hereness and thereness. Modernist in sensibility, she is traditionalist in her desires."[4] With this, the central problem of the novel is summed up so neatly that it does not seem a problem anymore. . . .

The "small personal voice" which Lessing defended in her 1957 statement in *Declaration*[5] — the author's as well as the protagonist's — has contributed greatly to the success of her novels and stories. It has been a precise, nuanced, intelligent voice; but in its best performance, in *The Golden Notebook*, it disclosed most clearly its limitations. In the interview given in 1969 at Stony Brook Lessing said:

> Since writing *The Golden Notebook* I've become less personal. I've floated away from the personal. I've stopped saying, "This is *mine*, this is *my* experience." . . . Now, when I start writing, the first thing I ask is, "Who is thinking the same thought? Where are the other people who are like me?" I don't believe anymore that I have a thought. There is a thought around.[6]

This means, as Lessing herself points out, different narrative structures — the form of *The Four-Gated City* "shot to hell" — and a different attitude to her protagonist. It also means a different concept of what ought to be important in the relationship between a man and a woman. Quoted out of context, Lessing's Stony Brook statement, "I'm impatient with people who emphasize sexual revolution. I say we should all go to bed, shut up about sexual liberation, and go on with the important matters,"[7] is indeed startling after the four volumes of the *Children of Violence* and *The Golden Notebook*. In its context, the apocalyptic threat of "the bomb," it expresses a logical development. "The bomb," obviously, is much more than the physical power to destroy — though the physical effects produced approach the metaphysical; it is the mental operations and manipulations sustaining it, a mental state of frenzied exclusion that has to be opposed by restructuring human relationships. In *The Four-Gated City* Lessing has accepted this responsibility. . . .

Neither Lessing's statement in the Stony Brook interview nor the development of relationships in *The Four-Gated City* suggests in any way that the conflict is considered "resolved"; on the contrary, it has become much more painful. It is only suggested that the locus of the conflict has shifted. Relationships between a man and a woman remain "incredibly difficult"; it is, however, no longer enough to state that fact, no matter how intelligently and lucidly. Variations of "It's all very odd, isn't it?" are not acceptable anymore because they place too much importance on premature safety (*GN*, 51, 135 ff.). Sexual liberation is possible only if it includes the "other," the man who was so obviously not included in *The Golden Notebook*; it will have to begin again—from the beginning—as the process of contemplation of the "familiar problem of identity and will." Liberation as a conscious choice proved to be impossible in *The Golden Notebook* because the conflicts the women were caught in were kept too static. Now, though still only a potential, its very potentiality is recognized as an indispensable reality in the fight against a domineering destructive technology and the mental and physical acts that made this particular form of domination possible.

The Four-Gated City, as Doris Lessing points out with calm defiance, is a *Bildungsroman*, and as such its structure is informed by Utopia. All the protagonists of *Bildungsromane*, especially in the German tradition from Wolfram's quester hero Parsifal to Musil's Ulrich, the man without qualities, are moving toward the possibility of a conscious choice. In the nineteenth century the process of consciousness usually ended with the protagonist making a meaningful choice—though Utopia ended right there, if the choice (the author controlling it) was honest. In the twentieth century the protagonist has usually been shown unable to make any such decision. Honesty in this context meant renunciation in the nineteenth century; in the twentieth it has meant a fusion of hope and despair, accepting Utopia as a structural principle informing the barely begun process of the self rather than as a defined goal.

The first four volumes of the *Children of Violence* are not *Bildungsromane* in the strict sense of the concept. Matty is neither moving toward a choice, a determining decision she will make at one time or the other, nor is the fact that she is incapable of such a choice integrated into the substance and structure of her development. The first three volumes offer an absorbing examination of the tragicomedy of socio-political manners a young, intelligent woman finds herself caught in, especially illuminating because of the clearly outlined mechanism of the colonial setting. They are, however, already "dated" to a degree, belonging to that majority of novels that Anna describes in her black notebook as "a function of the fragmented society, the fragmented consciousness. Human beings are so divided, are becoming more and more divided, *and more subdivided in themselves*, reflecting the world, that they reach out desperately, not knowing that they do it, for information about other groups inside their own country, let alone groups in other countries" (*GN*, p. 59). Such "novel-reports" are continuously superseded by new information about, for instance, the political-social consciousness in the colonies, the consciousness of women. Lessing-Anna realizes that very well. The sheer expanse of the *Children of Violence*, the inexorably detailed account of Martha's political education, is mainly justified as sustaining and making credible—in different ways—the concentration in *The Golden Notebook* and *The Four-Gated City*. The 1965 *Landlocked*, however, anticipates, if only by implication, certain aspects of the new Martha who, on the whole, seems to have been born during that sea voyage, separating Africa from England, and *The Four-Gated City* from the rest of the *Children of Violence*.

Walking through London at night in the beginning of *The Four-Gated City*, Martha acknowledges precisely those dimensions of experience that Anna found overwhelming and turned away from. Though it did not expose Matty to a new stage of the self, *Landlocked* prepared her to an extent to become Martha. In this fourth volume, individuals and the relations between them are suddenly, if infrequently, penetrated by an understanding that has to be founded on an attitude toward psychological and narrative control different from that in the other three volumes as well as in *The Golden Notebook*. Matty-Martha's relationships with her mother and with Thomas Stern—both of great importance in her process of consciousness in *The Four-Gated City*—assume an illuminating immediacy, detached from any distinct perspective, even Matty-Martha's. In Mrs. Quest's dream about her own mother, which is interwoven in her daydreaming and preparations connected with the Victory Parade, her relationship to Martha can suddenly be understood. This dream also provides insight into Martha's need to explore the passionate pity and fear tying her to her mother, leading her toward madness in *The Four-Gated City*.

Matty-Martha's relationship with Thomas, "sucking her into an intensity of feeling" unknown to her before (*L*, p. 81), would have been unimaginable for Anna and Michael; they never achieve such degree of mutuality. If it is almost too much for Martha to bear this intensity of openness to the "other," it is explicitly so for Thomas. He is as vulnerable as she is, and as he tries to understand her needs, she tries to understand his. Thomas' peculiar desire for women can then be accepted by Martha as arising out of his individual need; it is not "the man" who inflicts pain on the woman merely by virtue of being a man. Neither can Thomas fail her in the role of the "real man," because Martha understands the unreality of such roles. If one chooses to speak of failure at all in this context, one would have to say that they both fail their own potentiality.

Martha may be stronger and more intelligent than Thomas—Lessing's women usually are, being part of their creator—but he is ahead of her on the way toward the self, having admitted chaos. Sensing this dimly from the documents of madness he leaves behind, she alone understands them as "messages" (*L*, p. 272), copying them, trying to make "sense" the way she will much later try to keep some control over her own descents into the self, mapping the route of his search. She takes Thomas' crumbling papers with her into her new life. Only much later will she come to understand the full meaning of his search outlined in one of the "stories" Thomas made up for himself: " 'Once there was a man who travelled to a distant country. When he got there, the enemy he had fled from was waiting for him. Although he had proved the usefulness of travelling, he went to yet another country. No, his enemy was *not* there.' (Surprised, are you! said the red pencil.) 'So he killed himself' " (*L*, p. 270). She will have to recover her past.

Martha, setting out on the search herself, having cast off Matty entirely for that purpose, is a strikingly different person, certain preparatory similarities in *Landlocked* notwithstanding. The change is clearly indicated by the author-narrator's attitude toward her. As narrator Lessing withdraws from the tone of omniscience, from explanations, comparisons, encouragements, and patient irony that had pervaded the first three volumes of the *Children of Violence*, the author-narrator now tries to preserve a high degree of immediacy, which is extended also to the relationships that Martha forms. Martha is given time and space for confusion, eventually even chaos. Lessing is much less protective of her than she is of any other female protagonist. Anna and the Matty of the *Children of Violence* are eminently more vulnerable, judging from their author's possessive attitude toward them alone. The degree of vulnerability seems to be connected with the insistence on "*my* experience" Lessing referred to in her Stony Brook interview. This very personal relationship between the author and the protagonist before *The Four-Gated City* is clearly reflected in Anna's creation of Ella for her yellow notebook, resembling her in mental and physical make-up, fascinating her by her state of being besieged: "She wore her hair tied back with a black bow. I was struck by her eyes, extraordinarily watchful and defensive. They were windows in a fortress" (*GN*, p. 393). Ella is a metaphor for Anna, including even Anna's absorbed interest in exact chemical measurements (*GN*, pp. 393 ff.), the elements in the experiment being members of a social group. Parts of the metaphor are then used independently, for instance Ella in the act of tying back her hair, fighting back chaos (*GN*, p. 394). In its mimetic simplicity this personal intimate gesture seems to defy abstraction; and the success of *The Golden Notebook* is partly based on this illusion. In reality, the abstraction and oversimplification inherent in the structural use of such metaphors—the four notebooks, the Anna-Ella projection as a whole and in details—have not been avoided. Attempting "to create order, to create a new way of looking at life" (*GN*, p. 59), Doris Lessing-Anna superimposes structures of order on chaos in a way that precludes mediation.

The structure of *The Golden Notebook*, then, hinders the process of self-knowledge. Neither the four notebooks, meant to guarantee flexibility, nor the stories, meant to guarantee multiperspectivity (*GN*, pp. 455 ff.), fulfill their purpose; they yield only prematurely arrested analyses of relationships, closing off precariously for a time what will destroy them anyway in the end. The enemy is intensely feared but not known. In this the novel's ambivalence, really a structural problem, is essentially different from the ambivalent endings of *The Four-Gated City* or *Briefing for a Descent into Hell*, where the concept of knowledge of the self as process is consistently supported by narrative means.

Walking toward Jack's house by night, Martha is suspended between two protective enclosures that she does not want or need: Baxter's cozily shabby self-evident upper-middle-class security and Jack's starkly outlined, threatened "pure" space, determined to shut out a chaotic outside. Martha already has a very different relationship to rooms, enclosures, than Matty or Anna. Anna's room (*GN*, p. 52) resembles Jack's (*GN*, p. 43) and Bill's in colors and the feeling of lines creating space; these are all rooms of defiance, in the center of which is a desperate need for protection from unexplored chaos and unexplored fear of chaos. Martha is ready for the room in Mark's house, which is open, unthreatened, admitting the presence of thoughts distilled from past inhabitants; the sycamore tree defines the room from the outside, suggesting shifts of space in the temporal flux rather than protective static space against time (*FGC*, pp. 100 ff.).

Walking, Martha is "nothing but a soft dark receptive intelligence," open to the "invasions" of people and places she has experienced (*GN*, p. 36). She is given by her creator the freedom of "narrated monologue"[8] to a degree which has no precedent in the *Children of Violence* or *The Golden Notebook*. Seeing Jack and calling Phoebe on the telephone are like two blocks in the swiftly moving sequence of pictures and sounds. The recognizable elements of her experience seem to be changing their meaning, oscillating between fear and "a state of quiet" which, however, she is losing fast. At the telephone box where she will arrange for an appointment that will end her "aimless" open wandering through London, she feels she has lost already what she had just found: "Yes, but remember the space you discovered today. It was gone, gone quite, not even a memory, and she sunk down out of reach of the place where words, bits of music, juggled and jangled and informed. And even the calm place below (beside?) was going, it was a memory, a memory that was going" (*FGC*, p. 39). Martha's "education" in *The Four-Gated City* is toward the conscious recovery of that space with its pictures and voices that she received here by chance, made sensitive, receptive by her "aimless" walking, talking, listening. Much later, when Martha is on her first willed, and now controlled, reconnaissance descent into the self, she will remember, when she reaches that space, that she had been there and forgotten. . . .

It takes Martha almost fifteen years and 450 pages closely packed with people, acts, and ideas to get back to where she had once been, prepared now to chart this landscape of the self in order to be able to use it. Repeatedly pointing out the extraordinary power of conformity to certain dimensions of experience, reinforced through centuries of standard education, to the explosive impulse contained in social ridicule, Lessing moves Martha very slowly and cautiously to the point where she thinks it possible to claim credibility for the "disorderly company" she will have to ask the reader to join.[9] Martha has proved herself a very shrewd, capable, skeptical woman, living in Mark's house, coping with very different but always difficult human situations, showing a great deal of common sense. Yet, social developments, on a personal and general level, make it imperative for her to pursue her search for identity through a descent into the unexplored self.

The richly detailed story of a group of men and women living through the fifties and sixties, participating, resisting, changing, and watching themselves change, discourages the reader from more than occasional identification with the protagonist. Martha does not emerge clearly enough from the symbiotic relationships she is drawn into, formed by and forming herself during those fifteen years in Mark's house. Shedding Matty, she has overcome the need to define herself against the "other," man: now she traces the process of self-defination within the group Martha-Mark-Lynda, the permanent center around which changing constellations of young and old people, lovers, friends, and enemies revolve. This center group, however, is itself constantly changing—an important element in Martha's preparation for the descent. Martha fully understands the meaning of this fluidity in their relationship during one of the peace marches where she sees variations of Lynda-Mark-Martha, Mark-Martha-Lynda pass by in the long line of marchers: she realizes that the only promise of permanence is in change (*FGC*, pp. 397, 518).

In this context Martha's position as secretary to Mark is of significance. She is not an independent intellectual like the writer Anna whose independence is, very importantly, extended to the economical aspect of her existence. She "serves" Mark in the archetypical role of the exploited female, the secretary. Yet, because of the individual situation in Mark's house and because of her essential participation in his work, the conception, birth, and precarious development of the four-gated city in the desert, she gains moments of true independence which were inaccessible to Anna because they are essentially informed by mutuality.

The plea for mutuality, potentially dangerous because it can be perverted so easily into liberal rhetoric, gains strength and substance from the detailed accounts in *The Four-Gated City* of men and women trying to achieve it through politics, through personal relationships, failing mostly, achieving it in rare vulnerable moments. In spite of its sprawling character, the novel moves fairly fast through those fifteen years of political change and changing attitudes toward politics. Martha, having gone through her communist phase when she meets Mark, seemingly has an advantage over him, as she knows what is going to come next from remembering herself moving through the different stages of passionate involvement and disillusion. And Mark does indeed follow those stages, but he is also granted his own rhythm of change. Lynda, beyond politics from the very beginning (*FGC*, p. 165), is not judged right or wrong. Lessing refrains from making her even sympathetic; the victim is by no means idealized. Lynda may know more than Martha, who has lived through all those stages as a healthy intelligent young woman; she also may not. For all of them, knowledge is a process they are engaged in; the movement of the process differs from person to person; it is open-ended for all of them.

The greatest strength of Lessing's argument for the possibility of truly mutual relationships lies in the manner in which these three people, Martha, Lynda, and Mark, are shown to move along together for some time so that they can part without bitterness. There is none of the brilliant bitterness of *The Golden Notebook* in *The Four-Gated City*: Mark, emotionally more immature than the two women, is a very cautious intellectual whose main virtue is to resist prematurely brilliant sentences on life; Martha is above all shrewd and commonsensical, patiently intelligent about herself and other people; Lynda, badly hurt and re-pressed in her specific talents, is largely inarticulate. The only certainty they have reached in middle age is their trust in the help they can give each other by understanding more and more clearly their own unresolved problems. Martha, for instance, fighting furiously with the various shapes of the self-hater (*FGC*, pp. 507 ff.) imposed on her by insufficient recovery of her past, understands now the particular form of defeat in Lynda; she also understands why Mark, too possessively "in love" with Lynda, is still unable to explore her defeat and needs to close himself off to that particular part of the search, though he accepts the responsibility for the partial results of Lynda's search and Martha's: tracing, charting on the "outside," on the walls of his study (*FGC*, pp. 282, 414) what their "working" (*FGC*, pp. 354 ff.) their way down into the self will make them see.

One could say, then, that is it not Martha who is the protagonist of the *Bildungsroman*, *The Four-Gated City*, but Martha, Mark, and Lynda together. This is underscored by the failure of Martha's relationship with Jack. Walking toward his house in the beginning of the novel, she knows that Jack is the only one in London who would allow her "to go on living as she was now, rootless, untied, free," which is, as far as she knows, the condition of reaching the inner space with pictures and voices:

> And she understood just why he lived as he did. She had "understood" it before; but she understood it differently now that she was in that area of the human mind that Jack also inhabited. Yes. But in that case, why did she shy so strongly away from Jack, from what he stood for — or at least, she did with a good part of herself. That part whose name was Self-preservation. She knew that. *He was paying too high a price* for what he got. (*FGC*, p. 38)

Jack at this point knows more than Martha; making love, he has discovered that "hatred is a sort of wavelength you can tune into. After all, it's always there, hatred is simply part of the world, like one of the colours of the rainbow. You can go into it, as if it were a *place*" (*FGC*, p. 57). But Jack cannot sustain that knowledge; when Martha sees him again years later, he has "become stupid"; once "all a subtle physical intelligence," his body has been taken over by hatred, by a degraded mind that needs to possess the other completely by degrading her morally (*FGC*, p. 386). This development is implicit in his relationship with women when Martha first makes love to him: his end is the body; the silences between her and him are not filled, contented (*FGC*, p. 62). The comfort he offers her (the acceptance, in her body, of the passing of time and death) isolates her further, as he makes even that acceptance part of his taking possession of her and, at the same time, frees himself from the changes that time works on his own body (*FGC*, pp. 54, 63, 381). The relationship with Jack is a step between Anna's love that did not reach such depth of intimacy through the body and Martha's attachment to Mark which goes beyond it (*FGC*, pp. 227 ff.).

The second part of *The Four-Gated City*, in which Martha really begins her life with Mark and Lynda, is introduced by a long quote from Robert Musil's *Man without Qualities*. It is taken from a chapter entitled "A chapter that can be skipped by anyone who has no very high opinion of thinking as an occupation"[10] in which Ulrich, the man without qualities, Musil's mathematician-protagonist, is straying in his thoughts from the research paper he is working on. He has just written down an equation of the state of water, and so he starts thinking about water. Musil, like any writer working with the *Bildungsroman*, concentrates on the development of his protagonist's consciousness. Ulrich, his creation and his friend, is speculative by temperament and shares with his author a discipline of mind and imagination that makes it difficult for him to accept the solid established reality of dailiness as real. His many abilities and qualities, highly favored by the twentieth century, have only been used to a very small degree in his scientific work that rewarded him with a promising academic career. When he realizes this, he breaks off his career, taking "a year's leave from his life" to test his abilities by applying them to the (assumed) reality of his time. He understands immediately that this reality is at least one hundred years behind what is being thought, behind its potential, in other words, and that anyone who consistently confronts reality with modern thought processes will get involved in recreating reality, that is, will have to admit chaos. Musil developed specific verbal forms to present these thought processes; he uses the term "essaysistic" to define them. . . . The basis of Ulrich's intellectual (verbal) discipline is his "sense of possibility," his *Möglichkeitssinn*.

To return to the passage that evidently interested Lessing: Ulrich, thinking about water, follows religious, scientific, and just daily, "normal" associations connected with that concept and, as usual, is stopped by the problem of communication:

> Ultimately the whole thing dissolved into systems of formulae that were all somehow connected with each other, and in the whole wide world there were only a few dozen people who thought alike about even as simple a thing as water; all the rest talked about it in languages that were at home somewhere between today and several thousands of years ago. So it must be said that if a man just starts thinking a bit he gets into what one might call pretty disorderly company. (I, 130)

Admitting this "disorderly company" into the decisions defining the main structures of the world, Musil and Lessing share essential assumptions about the novelist's function and responsibility. They are both basically unconcerned about the fate of the novel as form, declaring their quite extraordinary confidence that the novelist is indeed responsible for the whole potential stratum of an aware intelligent person's experience. It is true that Ulrich's is an exceptional mind; Mark and Martha have neither the trained mental discipline nor the dedication to epistemological problems that Ulrich has. His thought processes, immersing and dissolving the mimetic surfaces of the story he is part of, his need to shape and reshape each sentence until it is a sentence on reality, a judgment of the split between knowledge and experience, put the novel on an intellectual level which is very different from that of *The Four-Gated City*. Musil, a mathematician and behavioral psychologist — he wrote his dissertation on Ernst Mach and did considerable research in the field — deeply influenced by the Viennese School, spent three decades writing and rewriting the huge torso of his *Man without Qualities*; his idea of verbal precision and verbal discipline is, obviously, quite different from Lessing's. Yet, his primary concern as a novelist, to pursue the interrelationships between the potential and the real, is also Lessing's in her last two novels.

Musil sets the (intellectual) action of the novel in the years immediately before the First World War, 1912 to 1914; the novel, never "completed," was meant to end with Ulrich's mobilization, the apocalyptic disaster of the Great War. The First World War, as the first total war, had an effect on the imagination probably stronger than the explosion of "the bomb"; at least, the effect was intellectually more confusing and destructive. Musil always claimed that he was not writing a historical novel at all, as he was interested in the typical. The intellectual confusion he describes so brilliantly in his novel and in many socio-philosophical essays is indeed rather postwar; his analysis is meant to show that the intellectual problems that led to the disaster of the First World War could not be resolved by it, but were intensified, and led straight into the Second World War and — had he lived to know of "the bomb" — into the Third (Atomic) World War. . . .

It is easier to follow Ulrich than to follow Martha or Watkins because we will always be given the means to question, to doubt and to reject the "disorderly company" we have been invited to join. This, however, ought not to be misunderstood as a negative judgment of Lessing's attempts to push further into the inner space: as her fear is more urgent, more immediate than Musil's was, her means to document it have to be more drastic, and her prescriptions for hope both more striking and more vulnerable.[11] *The Four-Gated City* is a courageous and a necessary piece of work; Enright's negative review of it in *The New York Review of Books* in fact illuminates the justification of Lessing's development from *The Golden Notebook* to *The Four-Gated City*: "That Mrs. Lessing is so shrewd about things as they are makes me resent the more sharply her uneasy excursions into things to come."[12] Uneasy these excursions may be; they are now the indispensable basis for her precise observation of things as they are.

Notes

1. Robert Musil, *The Man without Qualities*, trans. Eithne Wilkins and Ernst Kaiser (London: Seeker & Warburg, 1960–61), 3 vols., I, 130.

2. "Form" does not refer to careful organization of small structural units, for instance, the sentence; many of her admirers admit Lessing's verbosity, her tendency to overwrite. "Form" refers here to the larger structures, for instance, the arrangement of the material by means of the four notebooks and the "frame" "Free Women," 1–5.

3. Jonah Raskin, "Doris Lessing at Stony Brook: An Interview," *New American Review*, 8 (1970), 170.

4. Neither Compromise nor Happiness," *The New Republic*, 148 (Dec. 15, 1962), p. 19.

5. *Declaration*, ed. Tom Maschler (London: MacGibbon and Kee, 1959), p. 27.

6. Raskin, p. 173.

7. *Ibid.*, p. 175.

8. I borrow this translation for the German expression "erlebte Rede," that is, "the rendering of a character's thoughts in his own idiom, while maintaining the third-person form of narration," from Dorrit Cohn's essay, "Narrated Monologue: Definition of a Fictional Style," *Comparative Literature*, 18 (1966), 98.

9. After her first descent, Martha starts gathering information on the greatest possible variety of aspects of the occult. She begins with Jimmy Wood's "potted library representing everything rejected by official culture and scholarship" (*FGC*, p. 486) — these books, of course, feed Jimmy's mind, triggering ideas for his machines which are perfectly acceptable to and exploitable by "official culture." Martha asserts her distaste for the "dottiness," "eccentricity," "shadiness" of most of the occult, but she is also aware of her conditioned response (*FGC*, pp. 488f.); see also Francis writing to Amanda about the powerful concept "superstition" (*FGC*, p. 584).

10. Chapter 28. Wilkins / Kaiser's translation is not very accurate and misses the irony; a more accurate reading is as follows: "A chapter that can be skipped by anyone who does not think very highly of getting involved with thoughts."

11. See Martha's letter to Francis (*The Four-Gated City*, pp. 596ff.). Her description of "the new children" (p. 608), tentative as it is, is still too much of a good thing.

12. D. J. Enright in *The New York Review of Books*, July 31, 1969, p. 23. See, however, Roger Sale in his review of *Briefing for a Descent into Hell*, *The New York Review of Books*, May 6, 1971, p. 15.

Doris Lessing and R. D. Laing:
Psychopolitics and Prophecy

Marion Vlastos*

I

There would seem to be only two basic ways to attack a social problem — from the outside or the inside, by reforming the structure of society or by revolutionizing the consciousness of man.[1] While the two processes cannot be completely dissociated, the crucial question is which concern must be placed first. To George Orwell, in his famous essay on Dickens in 1939, the Marxist solution seemed the most basic approach to the problem of injustice. Orwell showed that Dickens' commitment to social change was superficial, based on his feeling that those entrenched in positions of power should have kind hearts. Radicals in the first half of this century shared Orwell's belief in the preeminence of structural change, but radicals in the latter half are showing signs of a swing in the opposite direction. If we look at the novels of Doris Lessing with this fundamental question in mind, we can see a gradual movement away from Orwell's position toward a new kind of belief in the possibility of affecting the inner man.

As a Communist writer, Lessing in her first phase — the novels written before 1960 — sympathizes with the Orwellian view. *The Grass Is Singing, Retreat to Innocence*, and, to a great extent, the first four volumes of the *Children of Violence* series are marked with the stamp of historical determinism, and the Martha Quest of these early volumes — a heroine portrayed with striking realism — is personally committed to political action. However, even in these early novels, Lessing is consciously concerned not with promulgating an idea like Orwell's of the proper solution to social evil but with understanding the gap between the public and private conscience. As she says, *Children of Violence* "is a study of the individual conscience in its relations with the collective," and she believes that the hope of man lies in the resting point between his private and social selves.[2]

In the early sixties, with *The Golden Notebook*, Lessing continues her search for this crucial resting point, but from a changing political perspective. The heroine of *The Notebook*, Anna Wulf, is a writer in her early thirties who lives alone with her daughter Janet, has written one successful novel, and does volunteer work for the Communist Party. Through Anna's personal experience with the Party and Anna's view of the Western world in the middle to late fifties, Lessing conscientiously and

*From *PMLA* 91 (March 1976); 245–58. Reprinted by permission of the Modern Language Association of America.

carefully reexamines the Marxist solution and rejects it as unviable. For, during the fifties, radicals like Anna and her friends become disillusioned with established Communism, suffer the effective repression of independent leftist activism, and witness the development of Cold War phobias into terrifying facts. With the collapse of hope in the political answer to human misery, the struggle for a viable existence becomes again the onus of the individual self and its capacities for creativity and moral development.

But the self in *The Notebook* struggles with conscious weakness under its burden. Anna suffers not only from political disillusionment, but from failures in human relationships and the inability to overcome her recent "writer's block," to adjust her esthetic capacities to a new and realistic vision of a doomed world. Unable to bear up under the pressure of failure and despair, the self finally collapses into madness. However, here — in the self's descent into madness — can be found whatever small hope is offered by *The Notebook*. With her male counterpart, Saul Green, an American expatriate, fellow Communist, and fellow writer, Anna discovers new truths about her own nature and her relation to the world, and she emerges from insanity to a tentative but fresh state of balance, self-respect, and independence. Lessing's idea of madness as revelation and cure, initiated in *The Notebook*, is later explored in *The Four-Gated City*, the last volume of *The Children of Violence* series, [3] and finally carried into a supernatural realm — which literally transcends the troubles of the earth — in *Briefing for a Descent into Hell.*

While Lessing's recent preoccupation is for her a new alternative to political reform, the idea of madness as potential salvation for the contemporary world is not hers alone. Not only in her emphasis on madness but also in her very articulation of its value she shows a striking similarity to the views of R. D. Laing, unorthodox psychiatrist and cultural theoretician. Because of the conjunction of their insights, it is extremely helpful, perhaps even necessary, to study Laing along with Lessing. [4] Separately but simultaneously, Lessing and Laing are evolving a solution on the other side of the fence from Orwell but an enormous distance from Dickens and the nineteenth century. Unlike Dickens, Lessing and Laing believe not in hearts but in psyches; not in Christian ethics but in the rhythms of nature and the order of the universe; and, above all, not in a saving discrepancy between the evils of society and the possibility for perfection in the individual but, precisely, in the connection between what human beings are in their innermost selves and how they behave collectively. Because of this commitment to look as deeply as possible into everything and because of this capacity to see *connections* Lessing and Laing may be seen not only as social analysts but also as social analysts but also as social visionaries, prophets of contemporary culture.

In Laing's view madness functions in two ways to reveal society to itself. First, the mad person embodies in grotesquely exaggerated forms society's self-division; and second, in the heights and depths of his nature the mentally ill individual participates in those realms of existence that conventional man has either denied or never known. A schizophrenic person is a split person, often split in more than two ways but usually maintaining two basic categories of self: a "true" or "inner" self and a "false self" or "false-self system" which he has created in order to deal with a world that, psychically, he repudiates.[5] While the distance between the different aspects of being in the mad person is so great as to be outwardly absurd and inwardly unbearable, the phenomenon of the split personality is typical of "normal" man and of contemporary society. As Laing says at the beginning of *The Divided Self*, his purpose is "to show that there is a comprehensible transition from the sane schizoid way of being-in-the-world" (p. 17). Because of this "comprehensible transition" Laing believes it is essential to understand the mad person as symptom and as victim of a sick society[6] and finally as prophet of a possible new world, a world governed by forces of unity rather than of separation. . . .

II

As Lessing portrays them, there is no doubt that the sixties — colorful, stylish, superficially eclectic — *look* a good deal better than the fifties. But the sense of political hopelessness that reverberates through *The Four-Gated City* simply echoes the despair suffered by Anna ten years before. Despite the new fashion of protest, the world of the sixties is even more fiercely and efficiently headed toward self-destruction than the more repressive earlier decade. Only the youth on the antiwar Aldermaston March have any illusions as to whether their voices will be heard by those in power, and even the younger generation sense at bottom the futility of their protest: "the spirit of the march, the wry gaiety, its gentle self-mockery, was perhaps a salute to the knowledge that no one wished to own; and despair being its own antidote, it was breeding from its nucleus something like a laugh.[7] Furthermore, in case the readers of *The City* should entertain any hopes about what can be accomplished by leftist liberals within the conventional processes of government, Lessing takes great pains to document the futile case of Phoebe Coldridge, hard-working, self-sacrificing Laborite. Phoebe doggedly maintains her faith in "the people" and in the government always against the evidence reality has to offer, against the evidence of the billions of pounds being spent on war and on preparations for war and, at last, against the evidence of the total breakdown of society shortly before "the Catastrophe."

Just as Lessing's disillusionment with political activism carries over from *The Notebook* to *The City*, so does her preoccupation with fragmentation. However, although the London life of Martha Quest (now Hesse) is, like Anna Wulf's painfully divided, the emphasis on compartmentaliza-tion in the later book is both more abstract and more political than personal. Lessing writes: "It is at least possible that the most fruitful way of describing the human brain is this: 'It is a machine which works in division; it is composed of parts which function in compartments locked off from each other.' Or: 'Your right hand does not know what your left hand is doing' " (*FGC*, p. 496). The maps in the study of Mark Coldridge, Martha's employer, like the newspaper clippings on the walls of Anna's apartment in the final "Free Women" section, indicate a conscious attempt to combat this destructive mode of perception. By documenting areas of destruction and failure all over the earth, Mark is better able to see the world as a whole, to determine the true drift of man's intentions by fitting one fact with another.

In both Laing's and Lessing's views the principle of compartmentalization, applied to groups of people, usually takes the form of separating Them from Us in obviously spurious moral terms. Not only do we divide up humanity into "The Reds, the Whites, the Blacks, the Jews," etc.[8] but we make a false and fatal "absolute separation" between the sane and the insane (*FGC*, p. 217). Thus, when Martha begins work as secretary, editor, and household manager for Mark, she views the Coldridge house as a series of layers of different kinds of people and attitudes toward life. Predictably, in view of the idea revealed in *The Notebook* that the power of evil to possess the spirit is intensified when it is falsely dissociated from the good, the world of Mark's mad wife Lynda and her spiritualist friends becomes menacing to Martha: "The basement flat, its occupants, were isolating themselves in her mind, as if it was a territory full of alien people from whom she had to protect herself" (*FGC*, p. 211).

However, as Martha begins to talk to Lynda, she gradually comes to realize that Lynda's vision of life is not qualitatively different from her own. And when she wants to investigate further her own intimations both of the world's destruction and of a higher kind of existence to come, it is Lynda to whom she must go. Furthermore, it is from Lynda, victim of society's mistrust of the strange and the acutely sensitive, that Martha receives the warning that teaches her to be discreet about what she knows and later, in Paul's house, about what she is trying to discover. When she tells Lynda about the two persons within, the one who watches and the one who is watched, Lynda cautions her: "you'd better be careful, you mustn't tell them . . . About the two people" (*FGC*, p. 216).

The tremendous irony described by Lessing and Laing and other contemporary writers on madness is that, while social behavior is based on the principle of compartmentalizing, splitting, certain people are forcibly seized and locked up in isolation from society for admitting this condition in themselves. The institutionalized patient who is aware of the manifold ironies involved experiences the wild frustration and despair of a double bind, a dilemma that offers no logical escape. As Lara Jefferson, a schizophrenic, wrote in her terrifying and moving account of her incarceration, "Here I sit—mad as the hatter—with nothing to do but either become madder and madder—or else recover enough of my sanity to be allowed to go back to the life which drove me mad. If that is not a vicious circle, I hope I never encounter one."[9] Whether or not the patient is hospitalized, he remains subject to the control of a psychiatrist, who, more often than not, represents and enforces the destructive aspects of the society against which in some way the patient is rebelling. The essential fact about the doctor, as Martha realizes through her own confrontation with Dr. Lamb, is that he possesses all the power: the essential fact about the patient is that he is helpless, though, like an unruly child, he can and does cause plenty of trouble within the confines of his dependent role.

The relationship between patient and analyst as explored in *The City* is much more serious and threatening than in *The Notebook*. Like Anna, Martha comes to a doctor with a problem of psychic paralysis and, like Anna, she discovers that the onus of both defining and solving the problem falls back on herself. Both women, exceptionally intelligent and sensitive products of their time, are neurotics with a capacity for psychosis and an equally strong capacity for pulling free of madness when they must. But Martha visits Lynda's psychiatrist, Dr. Lamb, as much for Lynda's sake as her own—to test the truth of her ill friend's accusations that he is, at best, useless and, at worst, a positive danger to her mind. The cozy argumentativeness of Anna's discussions with Mother Sugar is missing in Martha's rather chilling investigation of the conventional process of therapy. For it is evident to Martha that power and truth are synonymous in the consulting room. Whatever Dr. Lamb says goes, whether or not his diagnosis makes sense to his patient. Reflecting society's tendency to protect itself by separating the unknown from the familiar, by compartmentalizing, the doctor labels the malady. In doing so he both defines the boundaries for exploring the illness and establishes his own control over the process. But, as in Lynda's case, open and frank communication by the patient of *his* view of existence may lead to hospitalization, and then, if the institutionalized patient has sufficient intelligence and force of will to comprehend the process which is victimizing him and to assert himself in rebellion against authority, drugs and shock treatments are used, in effect, to punish him. Shock "therapy" is superficially justified by changes in the patient's behavior, but, as an individual who has herself undergone such treatment suggests, its actual effect may be to drive the most powerful irrational impulses deeply underground. Thus, the next eruption comes from an unconscious level over which the patient has no control (Coate, pp. 156–57). Drugs and shock relieve both patient and doctor of responsibility for the truth and ultimately, as the conclusions of *The City*, and *Briefing* strongly suggest, of the responsibility for survival—both personal and generic.

R. D. Laing is a psychiatrist in rebellion against the authority of his own professional power. To Laing, as well as to Lessing, the social "values" on which the doctor's authority rests are hostile not only to the individuality, insight, and potential creativity of the schizophrenic but to the survival of the society itself. Not only do "we all," as Laing says, "live under constant threat of our total annihilation," but "by the most outrageous violation of ourselves" we have become adjusted to our own destruction (*PE*, p. 76). Clearly, it seems absurd for a doctor (a healer of humanity) to adjust an individual to a society adjusted to self-destruction. Thus Laing, in discussion the psychiatric relationship, emphasizes the necessity of distinguishing between what is false in the patient's attitude toward the world and what is simply nonconformist: "it is of fundamental importance not to confuse the person who may be 'out of formation' by telling him he is 'off course' if he is not" (*PE*, p. 119).

Furthermore, Laing believes, as Martha also comes to understand through her confrontation with Dr. Lamb, that the hierarchical nature of the typical psychoanalytic relationship is *in itself* inimical to a meaningful human experience and possible cure. In fact, Martha realizes, the conventional relation between doctor and patient is no relationship at all, for whatever happens when she talks with Dr. Lamb happens only to herself. Since "the ground being of all things is the relationship between them" (*PE*, p. 41), therapy in Laing's view can be successful only if the search for understanding is a personal interaction between equals. Laing's idea of the therapist's role is developed within the framework of existential phenomenology, which is an attempt "to characterize the nature of a person's experience of his world and himself. It is not so much an attempt to describe particular objects of his experience as to set all particular experiences within the context of his whole being-in-his-world" (*DS*, p. 17). Laing feels that "the therapist must have the plasticity to transpose himself into another strange and even alien view of the world. In this act, he draws on his own psychotic possibilities, without forgoing his sanity. Only thus can he arrive at an understanding of the patient's *existential* position" (*DS*, p. 34). Only by adopting what is in society's view the "disreputable 'subjective' " (as opposed to "the reputable 'objective' ") approach to the problem (*DS*, p. 25) can the therapist learn what he needs to know: that is, the nature of the experience of the patient's "true" or "inner" self, rather than as is too often the case simply the history of the "false-self system" (*DS*, p. 148).

What happens when Martha goes to live in the basement with Lynda during one of her "bad times" approximates much more closely the basic therapeutic principles or methods established by Laing. Although she is not a doctor and has no intention of "curing" Lynda, she attempts to help her friend not by keeping her "in touch with reality," as Mark suggests (*FGC*, p. 163), but by doing precisely the opposite transposing *herself* into Lynda's view of the world. Thus Martha allows herself to be initiated into madness, a process she describes as letting go of ordinariness to sink herself into Lynda. The crucial moment in their relationship occurs when

Martha follows her friend's example and drinks milk from a piece of the glass pitcher that Lynda has smashed. This symbolic act establishes Martha's willingness not to judge Lynda on conventional terms and eliminates in Lynda the hostility that is stimulated by any threat to her already circumscribed autonomy. Concurrently, Martha achieves insight both into Lynda's motives and into the source of her own existential restlessness. In Martha's memory of her own determination as a child to safeguard her freedom and independence from the metamorphosis into adulthood, Martha locates the reason for Lynda's desire to test the apartment walls. She realizes that Lynda is really trying to escape the confines of her "poisoned and hypnotised" mind (*FGC*, p. 469). Now Lynda's quest becomes Martha's quest: to relearn the awareness and the significance of the awareness of the child. Each child is a "potential prophet" Laing says (*PE*, p. 30), but, as Lessing suggests, the achievement of the child's potential depends on the conscious psychic rebirth of the adult.

Of course, Martha's ability to journey so successfully into inner space and time is not simply the effect of her humaneness and intuitive grasp of those psychoanalytical principles that Laing has articulated, but also the result of a long apprenticeship in psychic phenomena. In *The City* this psychic training, often called "work" by Martha, includes analyzing her dreams, painfully resuscitating her memory, studying esoteric literature, and experiencing hallucinations. The hallucinations, occurring during sex with Jack, her first lover in London, poignantly portray the Golden Age which Anna longed for but never envisioned and then shift into accurate prophecy of Martha's life in the Coldridge house. From the beginning of the novel, we are warned that extraordinary psychic phenomena are to be taken seriously, and there is a suggestion — in the conjunction of the image of unearthly hope and the image of reality to come — that the Golden Age may finally be more than a dream. Because of its psychic orientation, *The City* stands apart from the preceding four volumes of the series *Children of Violence*, but, suggestively, Martha's preparation for madness begins as far back as her experience of illumination on the African veld in *Martha Quest*. Intensely complex, this kind of experience is always remembered as an "ecstasy" but felt, during the actual moment, as an apprehension of the totality of existence and her own part in it: what Martha calls a "difficult knowledge."[10] Understanding is achieved as the result of a fine balance between a passive receptivity of spirit and conscious concentration, an attitude of the inner self that characterizes Martha's response to the mad Lynda as well as the other successful psychic occurrences of the novel. (Nor, in Lessing's view, should the ability to make judgments be impaired by opening one's spirit to psychic phenomena. Martha discovers that even in the depths of madness one can use one's ordinary mental faculties, "one's common sense," *FGC*, p. 508). Essentially, all of Martha's psychic experimentation and study in *The City* emanate from her vision on the veld as a teenager and are directed toward rediscovering that moment in such a way that she can incorporate its full meaning into her adult life.

Apart from her interaction with Lynda, Martha's trips, as private experiences, are complex, difficult to understand, and, sometimes, as in the case of her sojourn at Paul's house, disappointingly inconclusive. However, the essential patterns and effects of her trips are sufficiently comprehensible — Martha seems both to descend and to ascend psychically. Facing the "self-hater" and the "Devil," she confronts the depths of her own nature and of the collective consciousness of humanity. In some sense Martha is able to recognize her own participation in human evil, as Anna does in her mad dreams at the end of *The Notebook*, without being morally threatened, and the effect of her courageous descent is that, like Anna, she gains psychic strength and, in Laing's terms, greater "ontological security." Consequently, she is able to accept her personal life for what it literally *is*, for its reality ("Here, where else, you fool, you poor fool, where else has it been, ever," *FGC*, p. 559), and to see more clearly how she can work to save what is most valuable in the world from destruction. Moreover, as a result of her own experience of heightened psychic sensitivity and vulnerability, Martha understands precisely what happened to Lynda and why. Because Lynda as a young girl revealed her special sensitivity to other people's natures, her ability to hear their thoughts, she was punished with doctors, hospitals, and shock treatments by a society terrified of the truth about itself. When her friendly voices were repressed they turned hostile, and Lynda — now existentially weakened — became victimized by the self-hater. Eventually, through Martha's understanding, the special capacities that made a tragedy of Lynda's life become the crux of the psychic effort to save humanity from the coming Catastrophe.

The evil in humanity that Martha confronts in her mad descent provides only a negative basis for psychic strength and leads, of course, to the increasing disintegration of the society and its final destruction. But Martha's trips, especially the first, are deeply ambivalent. Having known, in Lynda's apartment, not only the horror of bedlam but also the golden light of quintessential beauty and happiness, she has achieved the fresh perception of one newly born to the world. As Jesse Watkins says, returning from a ten-day voyage recorded in *The Politics*, everything was so much more "real" than before and he himself was much more "aware" — not simply of appearances but also of the moral aspects of things (p. 166). When Martha leaves the apartment to walk in the street her fellow human beings seem mutilated in appearance and unbearably wary in attitude, but the sunlit sky reveals a balancing element in existence. "She stood gazing up, up, until her eyes seemed absorbed in the crystalline substance of the sky with its blocks of clouds like snowbanks, she seemed to be streaming out through her eyes into the skies" (*FGC*, p. 479). The elements of nature — sky, clouds, trees — seem both to embody and to represent "another world" (*FGC*, p. 483), and Martha's desire for union with natural beauty is so intense that psychic desire evolves for a moment into psychic reality. It is this movement of ascent in Martha's psychic experience that reveals a source for hope in the new breed of humanity rising from the ashes of the old.

The unearthly beauty and sweetness revealed to Martha in a London sky finally become embodied in the race of children born on the island she inhabits with a handful of people who escape the destruction of the old world following the Catastrophe. The children are physically lovely, peaceful in nature, wise with a wisdom that both comprehends and transcends human history. Most significantly, they possess extraordinary and strikingly diversified capacities for extrasensory perception and communication. As Martha says, it is the children who not only contain but also are sensitive to the "crystalline gleam" in the air. Moreover, there is an indication of divinity on the island, foreshadowing the gods and goddesses of *Briefing* and reminding us of Laing's conviction that opening the doors to the inner world can generate the emergence of "divine power" (*PE*, pp. 143–45). Lessing implies that representatives from another world may be accompanying and perhaps stimulating a new stage in the evolution of humanity. . . .

Predicting her approaching death, Martha, in much the same terms, recognizes that she and Mark's son Francis are evolutionary forerunners who must become obsolete: "People like you and me are a sort of experimental model and Nature has had enough of us" (*FGC*, p. 608). Ultimately, this new evolutionary theory leads to the suggestion that if schizophrenics were not locked up and mutilated by a self-protective society they might also have the capacity to create a new environment compatible with their advanced instincts and abilities. For, as Laing says, schizophrenia is, when analyzed, not a mysterious, absurd condition but *"a special strategy that a person invents in order to live in an unlivable situation"* (*PE*, p. 115).

The possibility of the eventual evolution of humanity into a different species altogether may seem tremendously exciting, but it can hardly be very comforting to us in the predicament of the present time. Moreover, even after the destruction of so much of the world at the end of *The City*, whatever hope Lessing offers through the conscious development of various capacities exhibited by mad people is very gently and tentatively suggested. For working against Martha's own rather hesitant faith are the indications, in Francis' letter to his stepdaughter Amanda, that espionage with destructive intent is still going on between "National Areas." "Is it any less true," Francis asks, "even after the experience of the last decades, that the human race cannot learn from experience?" (*FGC*, p. 563). And Mark, walking among the monstrous victims of radioactivity and of plague in his Middle East desert camp, is full of cynicism about the younger generation's faith in the future. Despite the implications of evolution and of divinity in the novel, the question of the survival of the world rests on the very dubious nature of the present human race. If man is *ever* to build "that perfect city, a small exquisite city with gardens and fountains" (*FGC*, p. 610) which Mark in his bitter sadness still dreams of, he must, Lessing is saying in *The City*, begin now.

III

In some ways, *Briefing for a Descent into Hell* seems to be an expansion of the two preceding novels; in other ways — most obviously in its form — it appears radically different. Moreover, the psychotic trip which classics professor Charles Watkins undergoes offers the most striking instance so far of Lessing's similarity to Laing (it is hard to believe that Charles and the sculptor Jesse, whose experience Laing records, have the same last name out of pure coincidence). However, there are differences between the two voyagers' approaches and reactions to their experiences that may suggest a basic divergence between the psychiatrist's and the novelist's views of the psychic journey. . . .

But, for the first time in Lessing, psychic reality provides the context for ordinary reality, rather than the other way around, and the judgment on humanity and the prescription for its survival comes from nonhuman beings. While undergoing a psychic voyage, Charles Watkins is found wandering around London in an apparently confused state and is taken to a mental hospital. In his hospital bed, he continues on his mental journey, traveling by sea, land, and air through a strange world inhabited by both grotesque and beautiful creatures. Finally he is "absorbed" by a divine Crystal that floats in the heavens and admits only those who are morally and psychically ready, and then deposited at a convocation of the gods where divine emissaries are being "briefed" for their descent into hell (earth) for the purpose of saving humanity from destruction. At the briefing, a god, Merk Ury, articulates the essential sin of humanity: "[Humans] have not yet evolved into an understanding of their individual selves as merely parts of a whole, first of all humanity, their own species, let alone achieving a conscious knowledge of humanity as part of Nature, plants, animals, birds, insects, reptiles, all these together making a small chord in the Cosmic Harmony."[11] Men are a necessary, but miniscule, part of the vast system of the Cosmos; they are a necessary but peripheral part of the small solar system of which the sun, not the earth, is the reigning center. According to "the briefing" which Charles presumably reexperiences during his psychic trip, some of the inhabitants of earth are former gods who have descended into "hell." With more or less success, these divinities disguised even from themselves, are struggling to overcome the dullness and destructiveness of their new human identities in order to alert the rest of humanity to the necessary conditions for survival.

It could be argued that the briefing is not to be taken literally, that the urgent convening of the reigning powers of the solar system is merely a metaphor, in Charles's mind, for the agitation of the system as the destruction of one of its parts becomes imminent. In fact, the height of Jesse Watkins' experience, transcribed in *The Politics*, offers a remarkably similar vision: a sense that becoming aware of everything is somehow synonymous with running everything. Jesse senses gods, "beings which are far above us capable of — er — dealing with the situation that I was incapable of dealing with, that were in charge and were running things." Most devastating to Jesse is the idea that everyone who achieves total awareness must "even for only a momentary period" "take on the enormous job at the top" (*PE*, p. 157). With knowledge must come responsibility.

But while Jesse's sense of — temporary — identification with the gods is consciously vicarious, in Charles's vision it appears to be literal. Moreover, although Jesse's statement conveys the sense of a metaphysically structured universe, it does not suggest the conviction of fate that is so emphatically and specifically delineated in *Briefing*. In Lessing's novel not only are the earth and all the planets locked in an "iron" web of influences emanating from the sun, but all the nations, within the earth, "were held in laws that they could not change or upset" (*BDH*, p. 98). Despite the whimsical comportment of the gods and the cuteness of their "contemporary" names (Merk Ury, Minna Erve), Lessing clearly intended the metaphysical laws they enunciate to be taken seriously. And the weight of this precontrolled and immutable system, in conjunction with a terrifying subjugation of the earth to the cold hunger of the moon, leaves little hope for the effect of purely human understanding and effort. If there seems no reason to believe in the actual existence of the gods (in either their heavenly or their earthly habitation), there also seems no reason not to, in a world in which the human will can acquiesce but never, truly, create.

Thus, while the actual vision of the future of the world passes unchanged from *The City* to *Briefing*, the particular divine context within which the story of Charles and his earthly existence is contained alters the import of particular social conditions. Although, for instance, the picture of doctors and hospitals and drugs remains much the same in *Briefing*, its significance comes not so much from what it reveals about the human condition as from the (sometimes amusing) dialectic between man's self-destructive obtuseness and the divine light within him (or within some men). Similarly, the excitement of Rosemary Baines, who attends Charles's lecture on the education of children, is not simply a result of her hopes for the evolution of humanity through preserving innate curiosity but a consequence of recognizing a fellow god. In *The Notebook* and *The City* the point of psychic flight is the return to a world lit with new knowledge of itself; in *Briefing* the descent into hell is the temporary excursion, and the landscape of hell is meaningful only insofar as it shows fitful gleams of the divinity beyond. Of course, the world is a necessary part of the divine scheme, but the value of humanity seems to consist in its potential for divinity rather than in the development of its own resources. Finally, it is not Lessing but Laing — despite the semiapocalyptic surrealism that culminates *The Politics* — who posits a relation between humans and "gods" that can save man *as* man.

Laing says true sanity involves a dissolution of the normal ego, the false self, and "the eventual re-establishment of a new kind of ego-functioning, the ego now being the servant of the divine, no longer its betrayer" (*PE*, pp. 144–45). The question that dominates Charles's conscious mind during his fantastic journey and that disturbs him subconsciously during his hospital stay — his new "descent" into the world — is precisely whether his ego will respond to the challenge of his self's divinity. In the purely psychic landscape of his journey, Charles proves his ability both to face and to transcend his own participation in the Fall of man (represented by his witnessing the slaughter of the white cattle and his eating the bloody meat with the three crazed women). Not simply acknowledging but actively accepting the fact of human evil becomes for him, as for Anna and Martha before him, the crucial intellectual, moral, and spiritual step which precedes ascent into a realm of enlightenment and peaceful ecstasy. In the favored realm — in the gods' boat, the Crystal — Charles becomes fully aware of the "cold weight" of necessity, "a sorrow bred into the essence of the race" (*BDH*, p. 92), just as Anna deep in madness recognizes "a terrible irony, a terrible shrug of the shoulders" at the root of life. As she says, "it's not a question of fighting it, or disowning it, or of right or wrong, but simply knowing it is there, always" (*GN*, p. 542). Once having recognized this necessity, Charles sees that "the eagle's cold exultation and the mouse's terror make a match in nature" (*BDH*, p. 92); the patterns that hold the substance of all that exists in a controlled dance are revealed through the Crystal walls as beautiful. Necessity and universal harmony are inextricable because, ultimately, they are the same. . . .

But attempting to survive in hell (earth) proves far more difficult than existing as a man in a morally ambivalent paradise. For on territory that is both so sickeningly familiar to his humanity and so alien to his divinity, Charles cannot bear to accept the new duality of his nature. From the accounts presented to us, mainly in the form of letters to his doctors, it is clear that Charles (presumably remembering the briefing) was deeply divided prior to his "illness." His attitudes toward the people he knew and toward his work indicated a destructive (and unexamined) tension between the needs of his true and his social selves. Thus while the lecturer on education inspires Rosemary Baines with his special quality, the private man firmly denies the otherworldly implications of her appeal.

After his psychic trip, Charles's self-division is intensified; initially he refuses to recognize the other side of his nature, denying his very presence in the hospital as well as his particular human identity. As his hospital stay lengthens he continues to preach the necessity of the inclusive view ("and

. . . and"), but his actual responses reveal that he clings to the exclusive view ("either" he is simply an ordinary person "or" he is not human at all). Finally, Charles lacks the courage, or the imagination, to *be* fully schizophrenic, to recognize his strange simultaneous existence in both worlds and to explore its meaning. Finally, under increasing pressure to conform, and consciously justifying his decision as a last-ditch effort to recover his psychic memory, Charles voluntarily submits to electroshock treatment and puts an end to the naggings of his divine conscience.

Of course, Charles is not the ideal god in human form. Rosemary Baines and her friend Frederick Larson are true servants of the divine, in Lessing's terms. Quietly and purposively—without going mad—they explore their growing sense of another world contained in and yet transcending this one and go about establishing contact with an increasing number of (apparent) fellow gods. In view of the question of hope for the world, their unobtrusive progress more than balances Charles's failure, but their goal remains the same as his, their desires are still determined by the authority of an immutable system and by their own *nonhumanity*. In *The City* human awareness is developed to such intensity that it creates, of itself, reverberations of divinity. But it is Laing, not Lessing, who introduces the idea of a psychic experience that is the ultimate extension of that conception of the human struggle toward a higher existence.

Of course, the similarities between the two Watkins' trips establish the basis for the importance of the distinctions. Both men go on journeys that involve sea and land; they find themselves in strange landscapes where they identify with (in Charles's case) or actually become (in Jesse's case) animals. The sense of evolutionary regression gives way to simple personal regression in time, and both men reexperience themselves as babies. Charles's discovery of three levels of conscious existence (human, god disguised as human, and pure god) corresponds to Jesse's belief in a "three-layered" existence: "an antechamber level [in which most people exist], a central world, and a higher world" (*PE*, p. 155). Both men feel that other people, for instance their wives, do not exist on the same plane with them; but, characteristically, Charles denies all knowledge of his wife Felicity, while Jesse feels that his wife exists in a world other than his, a world he remembers but begins to fear he cannot return to. For Charles, as for Jesse, "a greater and greater acceptance of reality and what really exists" must precede psychic advancement, but while the reward for Charles is his progression into a different order of being, Jesse envisions reaching "a higher state of evolution" (*PE*, p. 159).

This brings us to the crucial difference between Lessing's and Laing's visions of the ultimate psychic experience. While Charles struggles to cast off his humanity in order to unite himself with the Crystal, Jesse resolutely clings to his own identity. Both men are equally aware of the vast distance between their own natures and the realms they seek to enter, and both describe the breakthrough into their new existence as difficult and painful.

But the pain lessens for Charles as his being is gradually transformed into a part of the divine stuff of the Crystal, while Jesse's suffering only increases his stubborn insistence on preserving his individual human self. "It's as if something soft were dropped into a bag of nails . . . it was like a sudden blast of light, wind, or whatever you like to put it as, against you so that you feel that you're too naked and alone to be able to withstand it, you're not strong enough" (*PE*, pp. 161–62). Jesse's stark, spare evocation — more a feeling than a vision — of the source and center of existence is terrible and convincing in comparison with the smug whimsy of Lessing's gods. "Some people are equipped more for it and some are less — but he's got to have some way, some sort of sheet anchor which is holding on the present — *and to himself as he is* — to be able to experience even a little bit of what he's got to experience" (*PE*, p. 164; italics mine). Thus, for Jesse, both the internal effort of holding on to self-knowledge and the external comfort of having trusted people looking after the psychic voyager are necessary for facing and benefiting from the experience of the ultimate.

For both voyagers, prescribed drugs only impede the progress of the inner journey, render it unnaturally difficult and destructive. But while Charles finally gives in completely to the socially acceptable tyranny of electroshock "therapy," Jesse eventually stops his experience partly in order to put an end to the undermining effects of drugs. Aware, as Charles never is, of his deeply split condition, Jesse realizes that his true self might be completely destroyed ("perhaps a feeling of sudden cessation") if the doctors were tempted to use additional forms of psychiatric "treatment" (*PE*, 163). Having been true to his self, true to his humanity and the earth it inhabits, Jesse returns from his voyage not to a simple acceptance of social conformity, as Charles does, but to a greater awareness of the inner reality of the world: of the grass, the sun, the people, the good and the bad (*PE*, 166).

Faced with shipwreck, Jesse Watkins survives "this — enormity of knowing" (*PE*, p. 166), because he puts out a lifeline to his own humanity. Thus, not in Lessing's last deeply imaginative portrayal of madness but in an account of an actual schizophrenic voyage do we find the ultimate exploration of the "difficult knowledge" experienced by the young Martha Quest that evening in the African veld. Unlike Lessing, who seems to have turned away from the economic and social determinism of her early novels only to drift toward a more basic and fearful metaphysical determinism, Laing provides a vision of the limitless possibilities of psychic exploration. However, if the construction of a silly divinity and rigid fatalism suggests the failure, or perhaps the exhaustion, of Lessing's philosophical imagination, the rest of her work and other aspects of *Briefing* itself minimize the disappointments. Her most recent novel, *The Summer before the Dark*, contains no suggestion of divine fatalism although its heroine, Kate, suffers acute depression and experiences a recurrent highly symbolic dream. Furthermore, more pressing than the question of what, if anything, lies behind the order, if any, of the universe is the question of the survival of the world. Despite the divinity portrayed in *Briefing*, the question is asked as anxiously in that novel as in the others and with as little confidence in a hopeful outcome. If Charles's failure to comply with the dictates of yet another system seems irrelevant to the problem of world survival, the efforts of Anna and Martha to create from the resources of the mind and spirit a human salvation from human evil do not. Like Jesse Watkins, Anna and Martha sense a metaphysic that does not limit human dreams and human evolution but can expand with them.

Neither Lessing nor Laing is optimistic about the possibility of radically changing the society, but both are convinced that the only hope for securing our future lies in the individuals' journey "*back* and *in*" to his self (*PE*, p. 168). Clearly, the trip that involves complete loss of the ego — an ideal of the hip culture of the sixties — will solve no problems; if the individual is to emerge from his experience able to communicate or embody what he has learned, the unique self must not be submerged. As Jesse Watkins says, if we can "survive as a boat" we "can go through experiencing the storm" (*PE*, p. 164). The sheet anchor the voyager puts out into the sea enables him to suffer and survive a "sea-change" and to return to a land whose transformation, like his own, is a revelation.

Notes

1. Part of this paper — the introduction and the section on *The Four-Gated City* — were presented, in somewhat altered form, to the Doris Lessing Seminar at the 1973 MLA Convention in Chicago.

2. "The Small Personal Voice," in *Declaration*, ed. Tom Maschler (London: MacGibbon & Kee, 1957), pp. 19-20.

3. Lynn Sukenik indicates, accurately enough, the change in Lessing's focus of concern as Martha evolves from participating in "the collective conscience of communism" to "participating in the collective psyche." But it is a basic error to see Martha as a mere "vessel, a channel for all the emotions seething around her," and to negate the importance, for Lessing, of the *relation* between the individual conscience and either collective. "Feeling and Reason in Doris Lessing's Fiction," *Contemporary Literature*, 14 (1973), 532-33.

4. In a talk at the New School for Social Research (27 Sept. 1973), Lessing refers to Laing as "a peg": "All educated [sic] look for a key authority figure who will then act as a law giver. Laing became that figure." Lessing's statement (quoted by Nancy S. Hardin, *Contemporary Literature*, 14, 1973, 571-72) makes clear her awareness of Laing's importance but — somewhat unfairly and erroneously (at least for his position in the U.S.) — seems to represent him as influential primarily among academics. On the contrary, members of the American "underground" culture have revered Laing for some time, while until very recently the psychiatric and literary establishment have tended to discount his views and treat them with surprisingly undisguised disgust, skepticism, or ridicule. To quote one example among literary critics: "[Lessing] is no Laing, no touter of the void, to use Herzog's phrase, as though it were so much real estate" (Roger Sale, "Watchman, What of the Night?" review of *Briefing* in *The New York Review of Books*, 6 May 1971, p. 17).

For further opinions on Laing, expressed by American and British professionals, primarily from within the field of psychiatry, see the special issue of *Salmagundi, R. D. Laing & Anti-Psychiatry*, No. 16 (Spring 1971).

5. R. D. Laing, *The Divided Self* (1959; rpt. London: Penguin, 1965), p. 73. Hereafter page numbers from this edition will be preceded by *DS*.

6. Writing that *Briefing* "resembles the flashy insistence of R. D. Laing that the insane are the only truly sane," Sale (p. 15) presents a common and serious misinterpretation of Laing.

7. *The Four-Gated City* (New York: Knopf, 1969), p. 394. Hereafter cited as *FGC*.

8. *The Politics of Experience* (1967; rpt. New York: Ballantine, 1970), p. 90. Hereafter cited as *PE*.

9. *The Inner World of Mental Illness*, ed. Bert Kaplan (New York: Harper, 1964), pp. 4–5. True accounts of psychotic episodes provide fascinating and, perhaps, necessary supplements to understanding psychic trips in both Lessing and Laing. Lessing thinks highly of Kaplan (see her comment quoted by Hardin, p. 575, and also her review of his anthology in *The New York Times Book Review*, 23 Sept. 1973, pp. 16–18). Another compelling book, a description of one individual's 6-month experience, is Barbara O'Brien's *Operators and Things: The Inner Life of a Schizophrenic* (Cambridge, Mass: Arlington, 1958). An interesting analysis of hospitals, doctors, and drugs is provided in an otherwise rather turgid and melodramatic description of religious experience by Morag Coate, *Beyond All Reason* (Philadelphia: Lippincott, 1965). Finally, for a revelation of the process of actual Laingian therapy see Mary Barnes and Joseph Berke, *Mary Barnes, Two Accounts of a Journey through Madness* (New York: Harcourt, 1972). Mary Barnes spent 5 years at Kingsley Hall, Laing's own therapeutic community in London; her psychiatrist, Joseph Berke, contributes his perspective on her regression into infancy and her emerging self-expression through painting.

10. *Martha Quest* (1952; rpt. New York: Simon, 1964), pp. 62–63.

11. *Briefing for a Descent into Hell* (London: Cape, 1971), p. 120. Hereafter cited as *BDH*.

Doris Lessing's *Città Felice*   Ellen Cronan Rose*

In 1957, Doris Lessing called upon the responsible novelist to be "an architect of the soul,"[1] and in 1980, she acknowledged to an interviewer that buildings were a running motif in her work.[2] Susan Rawling's "room nineteen," Anna Wulf's room in *The Golden Notebook*, the various rooms and houses Martha Quest inhabits in *Children of Violence*, Kate Brown's hotel room and Maureen's flat in *The Summer Before the Dark*, the rooms behind the wall in *Memoirs of a Survivor* — all these have duly attracted critical attention, often in ways that link them to what might be called a female metaphoric tradition.

In a recent paper, Carey Kaplan has brilliantly argued that in at least one of these works, Lessing takes a conventional image of woman's enclosure and entrapment and transforms it into an image of "empowerment." In *The Four-Gated City*, Kaplan says, "the house on Radlett Street becomes a symbol of growth and fulfillment rather than a demeaning emblem of a woman's place." It is both "typologically female" and

*From the *Massachusetts Review* 24, no. 2 (Summer 1983):369–86. Reprinted from the *Massachusetts Review*. © 1983 by The Massachusetts Review, Inc.

"specifically uterine," becoming an "infinite microcosm in which Martha, like an enclosed fetus buffeted by external and internal pressures, as well as by irresistible growth processes, develops and takes form." She concedes that hers is a feminist reading of the novel, and it is certainly one which situates it within a female tradition.[3]

From Laura Ingalls Wilder's little house on the prairie to Gilbert Osmond's Palazzo Roccanera, domestic space has given women an opportunity not only to chafe at but also to explore the possibilities for moral growth afforded by the perimeters of their social identity. But although Mark's house on Radlett Street provides Martha Quest a felicitous space in which to explore and develop her unique (and uniquely female) self, at the end of *The Four-Gated City* she leaves it. While living in Mark's house has enabled Martha richly to explore the dimensions of her identity as a woman and a person, it has by the same token confined her to a social definition of her identity, of her self in relation to others. And what Martha has been yearning for, ever since she wandered aimlessly through London on her arrival from Africa, is an opportunity to explore what it might mean not to be a woman or a self-in-society, but "a soft dark receptive intelligence, that was all."[4] . . .

On either side of the house which defines Martha's identity as a woman and a unique individual, Lessing has situated another architectural metaphor which relates Martha to a reality that transcends the personal and relates Lessing to a tradition which has, so far as I know, no female exemplars. On what Lessing calls a "crucial evening," Mark tells Martha, who has been expressing discontent with her life in the Coldridge house, that what she's "really wanting" is "the mythical city, the one which appeared in legends and in fables and fairy stories" (*FGC*, p. 133). Mircea Eliade has called this city an archetype, one of "the paradigmatic models revealed to men in mythical times" by which "the Cosmos and society are periodically regenerated." He is careful to distinguish his use of archetype from Jung's who used the word to refer to "structures of the collective unconscious" with which Eliade is not specifically concerned.[5] Lessing, of course, is and I think what makes the city such a resonant metaphor for her, not only in *The Four-Gated City* but in the *Canopus in Argos* novels and in the philosophical bridge between the two, *Briefing for a Descent into Hell*, is its ability to conflate psyche and cosmos. As James Dougherty has said, what makes the city so potent an image is its standing as "the intermediate term in an isomorphic universe . . . at once the microcosm of the universe and the macrocosm of man." It is, he concludes, "essentially an image drawing its power out of the subconscious."[6]

The mythical city entered history by way of Plato and the architectural theorists of ancient Greece and Rome. Their treatises in turn influenced Italian renaissance architects, whose ideal cities were not so much practical blueprints as graphic representations of humanist philosophy. That Lessing may be aware of this architectural tradition is suggested by an otherwise inconsequential episode near the end of *The Four-Gated City*. Hearing a rumor that Mark is planning a sequel to *A City in the Desert*, a reporter asks him what he's planning to name it. Intending a joke, Mark answers "Son of the City," but the journalist hears "*The Sun City*" and so reports it in his column.

The Sun City, or *Città del Sole*, was written by Tommaso Campanella, a seventeenth-century Dominican much influenced by Giordano Bruno and the hermetic tradition whose lurking presence in renaissance humanism Frances Yates so skillfully uncovered. Although Campanella's city has certain practicable utopian features, "it is entirely misunderstood if it is viewed as a blue-print for a well-governed state," Yates insists.[7] Its significance was spiritual, cosmological, magical; its flavor a combination of mathematics and mysticism that the pragmatic Mark Coldridge might find a "nasty mixture" (*FGC*, p. 613). But Martha — and Lessing — go in for that sort of thing.

Whether or not Lessing actually knew Campanella's *City of the Sun* and its predecessors in the architectural treatises of Alberti, Filarete, Martini, and da Vinci, there are undeniable and instructive parallels between her ideal city and theirs. This should come as no surprise, since the hermeticism which forms what might be called the underside of renaissance humanism has what Idries Shah calls an "equivalence" with Sufism.[8]

As an image, therefore, which unites two systems of thought that have profoundly influenced Lessing — Sufism and Jungian psychology — the architectural metaphor that gives its name to the final volume of *Children of Violence* may prove to be for students of Lessing what it was for renaissance architects, a *città felice*. It may prove especially felicitous for readers who are, without knowing quite why, uneasy and unhappy with Doris Lessing's most recent fiction.

Since, as Lessing has recently remarked, "the whole concept of a city, four-gated or otherwise, is so archetypal, so in the mythology of all nations" (Bikman, p. 26), it is natural to confuse Martha's adolescent fantasy about an ideal city in *Martha Quest* with the four-gated city of the fifth volume of *Children of Violence*. Roberta Rubenstein, for instance, says that "though Martha Quest (and Lessing) has obviously matured and changed" from the first to the final volume of the series, the image of the city itself "has remained more or less constant,"[9] and Martha herself thinks at one point that her youthful fantasy and the one which gives birth to Mark's novel may be of "the same city" (*FGC*, p. 206). But a closer inspection shows that they are not. They differ both descriptively and in the degree to which Lessing endorses them.

In their exhaustive study of *Utopian Thought in the Western World*, Frank and Fritzie Manuel distinguish two dominant embodiments of utopian aspiration in the western tradition. One is the Judaeo-Christian myth of paradise and the other is the Hellenic myth of the ideal city. It is to this latter utopian tradition that young Martha's city belongs. In constructing a social and political order different from and superior to the one that currently prevailed, Plato's republic implicitly rebuked fifth century Athens, and More's Amaurote criticized sixteenth-century England. In the same fashion, young Martha Quest castigates Zambesian society for its inadequacies as she sees them — ethnic compartmentalization, racial segregation, and generational conflict — and rectifies them with her vision of:

> A noble city, set foursquare and colonnaded along its falling, flower-bordered terraces. There were splashing fountains, and the sound of flutes; and its citizens moved, grave and beautiful, black and white and brown together; and these groups of elders paused, and smiled with pleasure at the sight of the children — the blue-eyed, fair-skinned children of the North playing hand in hand with the bronze-skinned, dark-eyed children of the South. Yes, they smiled and approved these many-fathered children, running and playing among the flowers and the terraces, through the white pillars and tall trees of this fabulous and ancient city.[10]

Far from endorsing Martha's vision, Lessing maintains an ironic distance from her youthful protagonist. She is always careful to situate Martha's utopian reveries in a context which makes them function to characterize Martha, rather than exist as plausible visions in their own right. Repeatedly in *Martha Quest*, Lessing evokes the image of the ideal city when she is drawing attention to Martha's evasions of reality, her tendency to "distracted daydreaming" (*MQ*, pp. 27, 63), her youthful idealism with its accompanying lack of charity.[11] Lessing is especially ruthless when Martha associates the city with politics. . . .

In ridiculing Martha's utopianizing, Lessing effectively dissociates herself from it. Nowhere in the early volumes of *Children of Violence* does Lessing seriously entertain the secular utopist's belief in "a man-made paradise on earth,"[12] nor is the image of the city which dominates *The Four-Gated City* a revival of Martha's vague adolescent fantasy that there could be such a place. Instead, it is an evocation and elaboration of that golden city, "so much older than she knew," the ideal city of myth, legend, and fable, which Mark claims Martha is "really wanting." When he begins to describe it to her, she eagerly joins him "in a long, detailed fantastic reconstruction" which emphasizes certain features (*FGC*, pp. 133–135).

Physically it is much more specifically detailed than Martha's naive fantasy had been, and whereas her city had been "foursquare," this is radial:

> Great roads approached the city, from north and south, east and west. When they had fairly entered it, they divided it into arcs, making a circling street, inside which were small ones: a web of arcs intersected by streets running in to a center.

In addition to its radial design, the city is distinguished by the rationality of its construction:

> The city had been planned as a whole once, long ago: had been built as a whole. It had not grown into existence, haphazard, as we are accustomed to think of cities doing. Every house in it had been planned, and who would live in each house. Every person in the city had a function and a place: but there was nothing static about the society; people could move out and up and into other functions, if they wished to. . . . Even the trees and plants were known for their properties and qualities and grown exactly, in a relation to other plants, and to people and buildings.

Despite its radial plan, though, there is no central building:

> Yet the people maintained that somewhere in it was such a lode-place or nodal point — under the city perhaps; perhaps in some small not apparently significant room in one of the libraries, or off a market. Or it could have been that the common talk about this room was another way of putting their belief that there existed people, in this city, who formed a kind of centre, almost a variety of powerhouse, who had no particular function or title, but who kept it in existence.

Mark suggests that one day this city was destroyed by a senseless accident, like an earthquake or a meteor, but Martha protests. "Oh no, . . . Around that marvellous ordered city, another one of hungry and dirty and short-lived people [grew up]. And one day the people of the outer city overran the inner one, and destroyed it." It is this version of the ending that Mark selects for what eventually becomes a novel he writes "for Martha," which evolves through a couple of drafts into "a cool, detached account, like a history, of the existence of the city, and the principles on which it was run; and of the alien envious growth outside which eventually overran it, destroyed it, and set up the debased copy of what had been destroyed" (*FGC*, p. 175). When Mark becomes dissatisfied with *A City in the Desert*, it is Martha, as his secretary, who saves the novel from being destroyed. In every sense, she is — as Mark knows — "responsible" for it (*FGC*, p. 177). What is it about this city that appeals to Martha? Why does she make it hers? . . . Mark may be giving her a metaphor of the unified self.

As Roberta Rubenstein and Mary Ann Singleton,[13] among others, have noted, this radial city duplicates the mandala which, in Jungian psychology, represents psychic wholeness. Moreover, what Martha finds particularly "marvellous" about the city is its order, a felicitous hierarchy which allows for change and flexibility. For someone who has felt divided, compartmentalized, fragmented, such a city would be a potently appealing image.

This interpretation of the city's value to Martha as a metaphor of the unified self is corroborated by something her suggested ending to the story makes clear, that this is an ideal city, not a viable social and political blueprint. It is a genuine, not a practical, utopia — literally "no where" in time as well as space. Its special magic, its "secret," cannot be duplicated in the actual historical city it becomes when it is conquered by the shadow city.

Mark, not Martha, believes in a man-made paradise on earth. With that exasperating blend of idealism and pragmatism that characterizes the secular utopist, he rejects the novel he writes for Martha as "ivory-tower rubbish" (*FGC*, p. 175) to devote his energies to planning a "real" city in the desert for refugees of the global disaster he correctly anticipates. And then, when his dream turns out to be nothing more than "a valley filled with tents and army huts" despite all the international money that went into it, he "cannot help dreaming" — yet again — "of that perfect city, a small exquisite city with gardens and fountains that one might build somewhere with that money" (*FGC*, p. 610).

As a psychic metaphor, then, rather than a practical political model, what appeals to Martha about the "inner city" is its order, which is not a function of its design, *per se*, as her version of the city's demise reveals. According to Martha, the "marvellous ordered city" was destroyed when it was overrun by a "shadow city" that had grown up around it. Mark elaborates this idea in his novel; the people of the outer shadowy city copy "the plan of the inner city, in emulation of it. . . . But the outer city was not like the inner one, no matter how often or loudly it claimed it was" and no matter how slavishly it followed its design. What the outer city lacks, what cannot be bought or stolen, is the source of its harmony, the invisible, ineffable "powerhouse" at its center that sustains it.

The outer city is like a personality out of touch with the dynamic source of energy found in the unconscious. The inner city, on the other hand, resembles the Jungian self, "a Quantity that is supraordinate to the conscious ego [because] it embraces not only the conscious but also the unconscious psyche,"[14] which is both personal and collective. This interpretation of the psychological meaning of Martha's city is reinforced by a verbal motif that runs throughout *The Four-Gated City*.

Before Martha is "claimed" (*FGC*, p. 89) by the house on Radlett Street and its psychosocial imperatives, she wanders the streets of London incognita, trying on various aliases and roles, in an attempt to determine who she uniquely is. The answer comes to her on an evening when "the current of her ordinary thought switched off." "In this area of herself she had found," she discovers that "behind the banalities of the day" such as her social role, her clothes, her name, even her physiognomy, she is "nothing but a soft dark receptive intelligence, that was all." "Switching on" this "receiver," she discovers that she is "tuned in" to a "wavelength, a band where music jigged and niggled, with or without words" (*FGC*, pp. 35–37). She has a similar experience later that evening, making love with the sexually adept Jack. . . .

During the years when she is keeping house on Radlett Street, Martha puts this knowledge — and this area of herself — "in cold storage" (*FGC*, p. 132). Only when she is tending Lynda through one of her bad spells does Martha return to one of those places "where you could learn if you wanted to." And what she learns this time is that the jumble of sounds on the wavelength is the noise of "the human mind" and that she, or Lynda, or anyone sufficiently receptive "can choose to plug in or not" (*FGC*, pp. 472–73). Behind the "banalities of her conscious, functioning ego lies Martha's unconscious self, which contains all the potentialities for good — and for evil — of the human race. The conscious Martha can choose to plug into love or hate, just as the "citizens" of her mythical city, connected to the powerhouse at its center, can fill one function or another.

It is not selective quotation on my part, but insistence on Lessing's, that relates the powerhouse of the mythical city to Martha's discovery of her participation in the collective unconscious. And a Jungian interpretation helps us understand why the inner city has a vitality, a source of energy, that the outer city with its "rational" hierarchy lacks. But it cannot account for the "harmony, order and joy" that characterize the inner city.

For the unconscious is seething with energy, but inchoate. Decisions about how to harness this energy have to be made by a conscious ego. Who or what governs the relations of the "citizens" to the "powerhouse"?

A similar question occurs to Martha during her inward, psychological quest. When she realizes that she gets "information" from plugging into the wavelength, she starts to wonder who's programming the radio or television set: "why does he (who?) tell me that?" (*FGC*, p. 511), Martha appears finally to decide that she and the "editor" of the program or film are the same: "she directed this, but did not yet know how" (*FGC*, p. 523); but so far as I'm concerned, that answer begs the question. The very notion of editing or selecting implies the operation of a conscious ego, and Martha has presumably rejected that aspect of herself in order to plug into the wavelength. So who is in charge of the wavelength? . . .

Mary Jane Singleton would have us solve the problem by switching from Jung to the Sufis. Martha's emphasis on the secret nature of the inner city's special quality "bears a strong imprint of Sufism, with its many stories of lost or hidden knowledge — held by superior gardeners," she says, pointing out that in Martha's account of the city, "it was among the gardeners, so the stories went, that could be found, if only one could recognize them, most of the hidden people who protected and fed the city" (*FGC*, p. 134). But because Sufism "is inimical to analysis," she doesn't do much more than ask us to "keep it in mind" as we contemplate Martha's city as the model of "a state of mind."[15] Fortunately, as Idries Shah acknowledges, Sufi ideas "lay behind"[16] and infiltrated a number of systems and theories which can be analyzed, among them the hermeticism which so deeply imbued renaissance architectural theory. And while the gardeners of Martha's city remind us of the Sufis, its radial design resembles not only the Jungian mandala, but also the *città felice* of Italian renaissance architects, who "turned their backs on the formless, haphazard pile of the medieval city" and planned whole cities rationally (Manuels, p. 160).

James Dougherty discusses the sinister implications of such rational city planning; if the shape and disposition of buildings affect human beings' behavior and mentality (and Doris Lessing is on record as believing that they do [Bikman, p. 26]), architects have, at least potentially, the power to engineer human behavior to their own or a despot's ends. But few renaissance architects claimed to be interested in planning actual cities. Like Martha's, the cities depicted in such works as Alberti's *De re aedificatoria* and Filarete's *Sforzinda* — and their seventeenth-century descendant, Campanella's *Città del Sole* — are ideal. They are graphic articulations of a world view, designed not to be implemented, but contemplated.

In typical humanist fashion, when the renaissance architect sought a precedent for his endeavor, he turned to the classics. What he found was the Roman Vitruvius and his concept of *misura*, the idea that the city should draw its proportions from those of the human body. And behind Vitruvius lay a Greek tradition which provided a political rationale for *misura*. . . .

The "supreme goal" of Greek political philosophy is depicted in Plato's *Republic*. He called it Justice, but what it amounts to is unity or harmony, and a radial city plan was thought to be most conducive to achieving it.

What the philosopher-architects of the renaissance added to the idea that "a harmonious physical environment was a benign mold that would render perverse mankind more tractable, its parts more consonant one with another" was their belief that harmony was not so much a secular political desideratum as a cosmic imperative. And what they added to the Vitruvian idea of *misura* was the belief that the city of man should correspond not only to his body but to that of the heavens. "The ideal city of the Renaissance was by no means a totally secular conception," the Manuels insist. It "was not isolated or independent from the general schema of the universe [but] stood midway between the cosmic order of nature and, at the other end of the scale, corporeal man. Related to both realities, the city reflected them in its very structure, which incorporated divine and human proportions" (p. 165).

In his treatise on architecture, Alberti defined beauty as "a harmony of all the parts" he calls "congruity" and posited as a law "of Nature herself."[17] Anchored in their belief that congruity was the law of nature, renaissance artists could make man the measure of all things: the human figure with arms and legs extended, derived from Vitruvius, provided the golden ratio for renaissance architects. But although man was, mathematically, the measure according to which the architect created the "humanized" space of public buildings and communal spaces, that is not why he would feel at home in them. The ideal city of renaissance theorists would feel comfortable to its human inhabitants because its structure would put them in touch with the ground and source of their being, the "one certain Orderer" who Marsilio Ficino concluded was responsible for the "determined Harmony and rational plan" of the universe.[18]

If we align Martha's city with this renaissance tradition of ideal architecture, the problem that resulted from a purely Jungian analysis vanishes. Located at its "nodal point" or center, the city's "powerhouse" occupies what Mircea Eliade calls "the zone of the sacred" (*Myth*, p. 17). What keeps the city in existence, what sustains and feeds it, is its connection to the cosmos. As a metaphor of the unified self, what Martha's city suggests is that ontological security depends on a religious metaphysics.

If we take seriously the "clue" Lessing drops that Martha's ideal city is related to Campanella's *Città del Sole*, this conjecture becomes even more plausible. Resembling Martha's city in its general design, Campanella's is more elaborately detailed and what it amounts to, according to Frances Yates, is "a complete reflection of the world as governed by the laws of natural magic in dependence on the stars." Four roads lead from four gates, marking the points of the compass, through seven concentric circles, corresponding to the seven planets of seventeenth-century cosmology, to the center where from a circular temple a priest named Sun governs the city. Pointing out the uncanny resemblances between Campanella's city and the magical city of Adocentryn, described in a hermetic text translated into Italian by Ficino in 1463, Yates distinguishes *Città del Sole* from other utopian republics. It is, she writes, "saturated through and through with astrology; its whole way of life is directed towards achieving a beneficial relationship with the stars. . . . The City is arranged so as to be right with the stars, and thence flows all its happiness, health, and virtue."[19]

Granted, there is not much to connect Martha's four-gated city with the stars. But the cosmology of *Briefing for a Descent into Hell* is decidedly heliocentric, and the geometric cities of *Shikasta* are the "basis and foundation of the transmitting system of the Lock between Canopus and Rohanda."[20]

If the four-gated city looks in one direction forward to Lessing's cosmological space fictions, it also harks back to the earliest of the Martha Quest novels. Standing in the middle of Martha's ideal city, we can get a panoramic view of the Lessing terrain. From this vantage point, the distance from Africa to Argos doesn't look as great as it does to critics like John Leonard, who complained that on page 353 of *The Four-Gated City*, "Martha Quest went through the 'door' into mystical razzmatazz" taking Doris Lessing with her.[21]

The sustaining and nourishing power of Martha's ideal city emanates from a "lode-place" at its center. What Martha considers her "lodestone," the experience against which she measures all others, is:

> That experience (she thought of it as one, though it was the fusion of many, varying in intensity) which was the gift of her solitary childhood on the veld: that knowledge of something painful and ecstatic, something central and fixed, but flowing. It was a sense of movement, or separate things interacting and finally becoming one, but greater — it was this which was her lodestone, even her conscience (*MQ*, p. 200).

These experiences are, as it is now commonplace to say, moments of mystical illumination for Martha, revealing to her the nature of the universe and her place, as a human being, in it. As such, they provide a measure against which she can test the truth of any philosophy or ideology. When she reads, for instance, Martha accepts or rejects ideas according to whether or not they "ring true" with this "tuning fork or guide" inside her. So, I am convinced, has Lessing assembled the philosophy of *Canopus in Argos*, from a "potted library" very like the one that other writer of science fiction, Jimmy Wood, offers Martha as the source of his ideas (*FGC*, p. 486). . . .

But the outline . . . of Canopean philosophy is implicit in the structure and operation of Martha's ideal city, which is itself an extrapolation from her youthful mystical illumination, from which her (and Lessing's) adult system of belief might have been predicted. . . .

In *Martha Quest, A Proper Marriage*, and *A Ripple from the Storm*, Lessing shows Martha Quest growing painfully towards maturity by resisting imperatives to surrender her individuality to various collectively imposed identities — dutiful daughter, good time party girl, suburban wife and mother, dedicated communist. But when Lessing returned to her novel sequence after breaking off to write *The Golden Notebook*, many critics noted with alarm that the relationship between the individual and the collective "had gone inwards" (*FGC*, p. 396), manifesting itself as a conflict between a unique, idiosyncratic individual named Martha Quest and a disembodied impersonal "consciousness." Moreover, in *Landlocked* and *The Four-Gated City*, Martha's continuing development depends on her effort to reconcile her dual perceptions of herself as individual ego and as part of the collective psyche. In the novels written since *The Four-Gated City*, the individual human being comes to be seen as a "pulse" in the mind of humanity and humanity as "a pulse in the life of the sun."[22]

What this survey of the corpus fails to note is that, at the same time that Lessing was giving Martha Quest a healthy skepticism about man-made collectives, she was equipping her with a lodestone attuned to the great collective in the sky. In retrospect, Lessing's movement from *Martha Quest* to *Canopus in Argos* is so logical and appropriate that it is astonishing we didn't all see it coming. The Soviets, who inscribed the name of Tommaso Campanella on an obelisk in Moscow's Red Square (Manuels, p. 268), may have been more prescient. . . .

Describing the utopian city as "a glimpse of eternal order, a visible heaven on earth, a seat of the life abundant," Lewis Mumford conjectures that it derives not from speculative fantasy, but from the actual historical cities of ancient Mesopotamia. With an eye to ancient history, he asks "what price utopia?" and his answer puts a finger on the disturbing element in Lessing's urban symbology. "The city that first impressed the image of utopia upon the mind," says Mumford, "was made possible only by [a] daring invention of kingship: the collective human machine, the platonic model of all later machines." What made these cities possible, in the absence of machines as we know them, was the creation of a human machine, "a machine that concentrated energy in great assemblages of men, each unit shaped, graded, trained, regimented, articulated, to perform its particular function in a unified working whole." The price of utopia, he concludes, is "total submission to a central authority."[23]

At the end of *The Sirian Experiments*, we learn that Nasar — representing Canopus — is an architect.[24] As described in *Shikasta*, each city designed by Canopus "was a perfect artifact, with nothing in it uncontrolled: considered, with its inhabitants, as a functioning whole." If it is determined that an individual — a family member, say, or somebody's lover — would "function" better in another city, she or he goes gracefully, because "everybody accepted that their very existence depended on voluntary submission to the great Whole." In 1957, Doris Lessing thought there was something wrong with this attitude. Now she says it is "the source of [our] health and [our] future and [our] progress" (*S*, p. 26). . . .

It is not strange that in 1982 Doris Lessing should write a novel which imagines the end of life as we know it on our planet. What *is* strange is the rhapsodic tone of *The Making of the Representative for Planet 8*, which paradoxically celebrates in the apparent extinction of a species its ultimate, triumphant survival. The individuals who inhabit Planet 8 — Doeg and Alsi, Klin and Nonni and Marl — die, and in dying become "The Representative . . . a conglomerate of individuals — each with its little thoughts and feelings, but these shared with the others, tides of thought, of feeling, moving in and out and around, making the several one" (*M*, p. 199). Doeg, the voice of the Representative, tries to understand what has happened:

> If we had lost our old shapes, which had already disintegrated and gone into the substance of mountain and snow and wind and rock . . . if we had lost what we had been, then we were still something, and moved on together, a group of individuals, yet a unity, and had to be, *must* be, patterns of matter, matter of a kind, since everything is — webs of matter or substance or something tangible, though sliding and intermingling and always becoming smaller and smaller — matter, a substance, for we

were recognizing ourselves as existent; we were feelings, and thought, and will (*M*, p. 118. Lessing's emphasis; ellipses mine).

But ultimately the nature of such survivorship is ineffable, and Doeg can do no more than observe that "it is a strange thing . . . to feel oneself part of a whole much larger than oneself, to feel oneself vanishing as one thinks, or talks, dissolving into some core, or essence" (*M*, p. 84). So too, "it is not easy" for Eliade "to define what such a 'survival of impersonal consciousness' might mean" (*Myth*, p. 47). Nevertheless, he is convinced that "the objection that an impersonal survival is equivalent to a real death . . . is valid only from the point of view of a 'historical consciousness,' " a point of view which is only "a recent discovery in the life of humanity" (*Myth*, pp. 47–48).

In his foreword to *The Myth of the Eternal Return*, Eliade says that had he not feared to seem "overambitious," he would have subtitled his book an "introduction to a philosophy of history." I should conclude this essay with a similar admission, for I think an analysis of Lessing's use of the trope of the mythic city constitutes at least a prologomena to a more ambitious inquiry into her attitude towards history.

Eliade's study of archaic societies left him convinced that we "have something to learn from the valorization that pre-Socratic man (in other words, traditional man) accorded to his situation in the universe. Better yet: that the cardinal problems of metaphysics could be renewed through a knowledge of archaic ontology" (*Myth*, p. x). In the final analysis, it seems to me that Lessing does not demand that we "believe" her space fiction, only that we renew our discussion of ultimate questions by refusing to "dismiss" archaic cosmology as a "quaint fossil from a dead past" (*S*, p. x).

Notes

1. "The Small Personal Voice," in Doris Lessing, *A Small Personal Voice*, ed. Paul Schlueter (New York: Alfred A. Knopf, 1974), p. 7. Hereafter cited parenthetically as *SPV*.

2. Minda Bikman, "A Talk with Doris Lessing," *NYTBR* (Mar. 30, 1980), p. 26. Hereafter cited parenthetically as Bikman.

3. I want to thank Carey Kaplan for allowing me to quote from her unpublished paper, "The House on Radlett Street in Doris Lessing's *The Four-Gated City*."

4. Doris Lessing, *The Four-Gated City* (New York: Alfred A. Knopf, 1969), p. 38. Hereafter cited parenthetically as *FGC*.

5. *The Myth of the Eternal Return or, Cosmos and History*, ed. Willard Trask (1954; rpt. Princeton: Princeton Univ. Press, 1971), pp. xiv–xv. Hereafter cited parenthetically as *Myth*.

6. *The Fivesquare City: The City in the Religious Imagination* (Notre Dame: Univ. of Notre Dame Press, 1980), pp. 4–5.

7. *Giordano Bruno and the Hermetic Tradition* (Chicago: Univ. of Chicago Press, 1964), p. 369.

8. *The Way of the Sufi* (London: Jonathan Cape, 1968), p. 15.

9. *The Novelistic Vision of Doris Lessing* (Urbana: Univ. of Illinois Press, 1979), p. 127.

10. Doris Lessing, *Martha Quest* (1952; rpt. New York: New American Library, 1970), p. 11. Hereafter cited parenthetically as *MQ*.

11. Martha mentally excludes "her parents, the Van Rensbergs, in fact most of the people of the district" from her golden city "because of their pettiness of vision and small understanding" (*MQ*, p. 11), thereby inadvertently revealing her own. In her 1979 article, "Dialectic and Counter-Dialectic in the Martha Quest Novels," Claire Sprague aptly defines young Martha's image of the ideal city as "little more than a revenge fantasy" (*Journal of Commonwealth Literature*, Vol. 14, No. 1 [Aug. 1979], 44). I am greatly indebted to Claire Sprague for early pointing out the central importance of the city metaphor in Lessing's evolving world view and for continuing to discuss it with me.

12. Frank E. and Fritzie P. Manuel, *Utopian Thought in the Western World* (Cambridge: Harvard Univ. Press, 1979), p. 112. Hereafter cited parenthetically as Manuels.

13. In addition to Rubenstein's book, already cited, see Mary Ann Singleton, *The City and the Veld* (Lewisburg: Bucknell Univ. Press, 1977), especially her chapter on "The Ideal City."

14. C. G. Jung, "The Relations Between the Ego and the Unconscious," *Collected Works*, Vol. 7 (New York: Pantheon Books, 1953), p. 175.

15. Singleton, *The City and the Veld*, pp. 11, 199.

16. *The Way of the Sufi*, p. 17.

17. Quoted in Wylie Sypher, *Four Stages of Renaissance Style* (Garden City: Doubleday, 1955), pp. 57, 62.

18. Quoted in Sypher, p. 55.

19. Yates, *Giordano Bruno and the Hermetic Tradition*, pp. 369–70.

20. Doris Lessing, *Re: Colonised Planet 5, Shikasta* (New York: Alfred A. Knopf, 1979), p. 25. Hereafter cited parenthetically as *S*.

21. John Leonard, "The Spacing Out of Doris Lessing," *NYTBR* (Feb. 7, 1982), p. 34.

22. Doris Lessing, *Briefing for a Descent into Hell* (New York: Alfred A. Knopf, 1971), pp. 112, 116.

23. Lewis Mumford, "Utopia, the City and the Machine," in *Utopias and Utopian Thought*, ed. Frank E. Manuel (Boston: Houghton Mifflin, 1966), pp. 13–17.

24. Doris Lessing, *The Sirian Experiments* (New York: Alfred A. Knopf, 1981), p. 283.

Competing Codes in *Shikasta*   Betsy Draine*

Lessing has always produced her most exciting work when struggling to integrate seemingly incompatible perceptions, ideologies, and styles. The works in which she most comfortably rests in a single attitude and genre (for example, the socialist realism of *Retreat to Innocence* or "Hunger") are literary pygmies by comparison with the giant works (*The Four-Gated City*, for example, or *The Golden Notebook*), in which competing attitudes, warring styles, wage a fierce battle, first to last.[1] The

*This essay was presented at a Modern Language Association meeting in 1982 and is now published in *Substance under Pressure: Artistic Coherence and Evolving Form* (Madison: University of Wisconsin Press, 1982), 143–61. Reprinted with permission of University of Wisconsin Press.

Canopus in Argos series promises to be another of those giants — a work at odds with itself philosophically, stylistically, generically.

In *Shikasta* (1979), the first volume of the series, one can clearly trace what Roland Barthes calls the "braid of codes," the stereophony, the "triumphant plural" of the rich text.[2] On the one hand, Lessing uses many of the tropes of science fiction (flight to the stars, "the rivalries and interactions of great galactic Empires,"[3] extraterrestrial visitors to and influences on earth, the report of the alien to superiors in a higher galaxy) and generates her narrative according to the basic rules of the genre: First, one extrapolates from present earthly conditions to a scientifically plausible future, or para-reality, and, second, one estranges one's readers from their former view of earth's place in the universe so that they may be tutored to evaluate history from an alien perspective. On the other hand, in the same novel Lessing violates utterly some of the essential elements of the science fiction code. She downplays the scientific and technological aspects of her story, while emphasizing magical and supernatural elements; she overlays the more fantastic sections of the narrative with allegorical significance; she bases the whole of the fiction on a mystical vision of the cosmos and often stops the narrative in order to sermonize on the necessity to accept and live by mystic knowledge. Each of these narrative maneuvers has been identified in the past as a cardinal sin against the integrity of science fiction. Lessing commits these "sins," moreover, in order better to perform some of the functions of sacred literature, a genre that many writers of science fiction declare to be diametrically opposed to their own. In *Shikasta*, the code of extrapolative logic is confronted by the code of belief — and against all predictions, they coexist without destroying each other. Nonetheless, the reader continually feels a sense of scandal at the incursion of religious imperatives onto essentially agnostic ground, the territory of science fiction. The resulting threat of the reader's disaffection gives a special tension to the narrative, which ultimately is positive, because it involves the reader in a constant evaluation of an initial reaction to the narrative and the premises behind it. . . .

Lessing opens the series with "Some Remarks" that suggest the plural nature of her project:

> *Shikasta* was started in the belief that it would be a single self-contained book, and that when it was finished I would be done with the subject. But as I wrote I was invaded with ideas for other books, other stories, and the exhilaration that comes from being set free into a larger scope, with more capacious possibilities and themes. It was clear I had made — or found — a new world for myself, a realm where the petty fates of planets, let alone individuals, are only aspects of cosmic evolution expressed in the rivalries and interactions of great galactic Empires: Canopus, Sirius, and their enemy, the Empire Puttiora, with its criminal planet Shammat. I feel as if I have been set free both to be as

experimental as I like, and as traditional: the next volume in this series,
The Marriages Between Zones Three, Four, and Five, has turned out to
be a fable, or myth. Also, oddly enough, to be more realistic. (p. ix)

Lessing here identifies the experimental with science fiction, the traditional with myth, fable, and realism (itself an odd combination, as she
notes). These several impulses converge in *Shikasta*.

In her pluralism of conception and technique, Lessing feels herself to
be in the mainstream of science fiction. However, she claims for science
fiction a scope much wider than many of its own practitioners and
theoreticians would grant. She praises not only the predictive accuracy of
much early science fiction but also the eclecticism of those science fiction
writers who "have also explored the sacred literatures of the world in the
same bold way they take scientific and social possibilities to their logical
conclusions so that we may examine them" (p. *x*). For her, predictions that
science fiction writers make about "scientific and social possibilities" are
on a par with the prophecies of sacred literatures concerning man's
spiritual destiny — and the two kinds of future-projection may be mixed in
a single work. Most writers on science fiction vigorously oppose this view
and exclude from the canons of science fiction those works which give
prominent place to mystical or spiritual concerns.[4]

For all those critics who have attempted to set limits between science
fiction and surrounding genres, a fundamental distinction is that science
fiction, as its name implies, grounds itself in *science*. All forms of fantasy
posit conditions that the reader recognizes as untrue to present-day reality.
Science fiction is that form of fantasy which extrapolates logically from
accepted *scientific* facts and theories to hitherto unknown but plausible
conditions as the basis for a narrative. The demands of scientific logic
control the conditions and give direction to the incidents in science fiction;
in other forms of fantasy, narrative premises and their development are
controlled by the demands of religious or philosophical belief or by the
pressure of irrational fears or desires. Science fiction is at pains to be
natural, not supernatural; secular, not sacred; rational, not irrational;
empirical, not philosophical, religious, or mystical; turned outward to the
tangible realities of the cosmos, not turned inward toward the personal
psyche or "upward" toward God or any other spiritual reality. . . .

Lessing therefore strikes a special kind of reading contract with her
audience when, in the preface to the first volume of *Canopus in Argos*, she
so prominently identifies herself with science fiction and with a specific
subgenre, the tales of the galactic empires. The epic of galactic civilization
has its roots in early works of space travel, such as Jules Verne's *From the
Earth to the Moon* (1865) or H. G. Wells's *The War of the Worlds* (1897)
and *The First Men in the Moon* (1901), but it did not achieve its own
integrity until 1929 when Edmond Hamilton's stories began to appear in
the American magazine *Weird Tales*. Hamilton imagined an Interstellar

Patrol, headquartered "on a planet of the mighty sun *Canopus*."[5] The task of the Canopean patrol was to rescue stars from destruction and to protect the civilizations of the Canopean galaxy from hostile invaders. The parallels with Lessing's *Canopus in Argos* series are extraordinary. The first volume, *Shikasta*, is offered as a compilation of documents relating to the missions of Johor, who calls himself an emissary in the Colonial Service of the Canopean galactic empire. Johor, like the members of Hamilton's Interstellar Patrol, reports to his superiors on the astronomical threats to stars and planets; his main function, however, is to help human beings on the planet Shikasta overcome the pernicious influences of the invading "Empire Puttiora, with its criminal planet Shammat" (p. *ix*). With these parallels of plot and the borrowing of the name Canopus, Lessing situates her narrative in the context of not only Hamilton's stories but also the running saga by many hands which it helped to generate — the story of the rise, decline, fall, and restoration of the Galactic Empire.[6]

In her preface to *Shikasta*, Lessing speaks of her admiration for Olaf Stapledon's *Last and First Men* (1930), the first major chronicle of the Galactic Empire. *Shikasta* is in many ways an extension of Stapledon's novel. His is a future history, beginning with his own time and extending two thousand years to the destruction of our galaxy. Lessing's is a retrospective history, moving from the founding of the human race to just a few years beyond our own time. Together, Lessing's and Stapledon's works trace the evolution of human consciousness from the first stirrings of practical intelligence to the achievement of a universal overmind and cosmic harmony. To Stapledon's "cosmogony of the future,"[7] Lessing appends her cosmogony of the past and present. . . .

To a large extent, Lessing's *Shikasta* fits comfortably within the genre. The novel chronicles a crisis in the affairs of the Canopean Empire. The reports by the Canopean Johor, diary entries by humans, and letters between the officials of the evil Puttioran Empire all refer to Colonised Planet 5, Shikasta (obviously our Earth). Having the conditions for rapid evolution of species, Shikasta is a key location in the Galactic Empire and, as Johor notes, always an important item on "the cosmic agenda" (p. 4). As in other fiction of the Galactic Empire, the force of evolution is a prime mover of plot and theme. The whole genre is built on the belief that life in the cosmos is in a constant process of change according to the dictates of the "cosmic agenda" — and predominantly this is a progressive movement. A basic supposition is that just as we have developed from primitive tool-using animals into intelligent beings capable of philosophic inquiry and complex technological accomplishment, so we shall further develop into beings capable of establishing contact with forces and with lives situated beyond Earth. Lessing has always held a progressivist faith, even at the darkest moments of her vision of apocalypse. . . . In *Shikasta*, Lessing's faith in the beneficent power of evolution is emphasized more definitely than ever before. The mission of Johor is to assist in the evolutionary progress of life on Shikasta:

> The planet was for millions of years one of a category of hundreds that we kept a watch on. It was regarded as having potential because its history has always been one of sudden changes, rapid developments, as rapid degradations, periods of stagnation. Anything could be expected of it. . . . We wanted the northern hemisphere, because it was chiefly here that a subgroup of the former "monkeys" had established themselves and were developing. . . . They showed rapid increases in intelligence. Our experts told us that these creatures would continue a fast evolution and could be expected to become a Grade A species in, probably, fifty thousand years. (Provided of course there were no more accidents of the cosmic type.) (pp. 14, 15)

It is in terms of the science of genetic management (of our race by Canopus) that Lessing explains the extraordinary evolution of human life. The faults of the human race—its stubbornness, selfishness, arrogance, and ultimately disastrous belligerence—she renders in terms of the effects of one of those dreaded "accidents of the cosmic type," a "shift in stellar alignments" (p. 21) that leads to disruptions of the lines of force between Canopus and its colonial charges. In the tradition of science fiction, she re-imagines human history from a cosmic, rather than an earth-centered, perspective. In so doing, Lessing rewrites both the secular Darwinian history of evolution and the sacred history of the Fall.

As is typical in science fiction, a de-mythologizing impulse runs through the text, at the same time as the narrative itself establishes a new mythology. We might call this a process of re-mythologizing, except that the constant reinterpretation of old myths points the reader toward the conclusion that all myths are provisional models of understanding and that none is to be taken literally. This highly modern attitude toward myth is frequently stressed by the messenger Johor, who continually admits the partial nature of his own perceptions and the inadequacies of his images and fables to the depiction of the reality he is trying to express. Nonetheless, Johor's overturning of our past scientific theories and, more especially, his wrenching of Biblical history and Western myth into Canopean perspective constitute the major sources of interest in that part of the narrative which operates under the science fiction code. For example, the giants and "little people" of Celtic and European legend prove (after "scientific" blood, tissue and bone tests) to be species from planets of faraway galaxies, placed on earth by the Canopeans to tutor the rather slow-thinking natives in art, sciences, and "Higher Powers" (which seem to be equivalent to what science fiction writers call "psi powers"—e.g., mental telepathy and precognition). The dual image of these beings in our myths—their benevolence in some tales and their malevolence in others— is explained by the story of their degeneration after the break in the lines of communication with Canopus. Like all other creatures of the once-Edenic planet, the giants and little people could not remain good after they were deprived of Canopean energy, the *sine qua non* of right perception and moral judgment. . . .

Shikasta is full of such readjustments of context. We are made to see the Biblical Flood and the inundation of Atlantis as results of a shift in Earth's axis—one of the many misalignments of a confused time in our galaxy. The rescue of Noah and his crew is carried out by a Canopean messenger, mistaken as a god by the ignorant patriarch. Likewise the covenant of the ark, the songs of King David, the wanderings of Moses, the delivery of the Commandments, the fall of the tower of Babel, the destruction of the cities of the plain, the birth of Ishmael and Isaac to the elderly Abraham—even the modern worship of the Infant of Prague—all make "scientific" sense in the story of Canopean interference in human history for the purpose of fostering a stronger line of communication (called "the Lock") between the sun Canopus, source of health, and the morally weak inhabitants of Shikasta. In the course of these revisions of Biblical history, the messenger Johor often indulges in antireligious diatribes worthy of the purest science fiction, which always works to secularize knowledge. Johor declares woefully primitive the humans' tendency to speak of the messengers as Lords, Gods, and Masters. He bitterly decries the organized religions, which "distorted what was left of our envoys' instruction" (p. 111) and which often acted as the agents of the evil planet Shammat, encouraging militarism, self-righteousness, and bigotry.

At the heart of Lessing's reconception of earth's history and destiny is a Golden Age myth, made fit for science fiction by the supposition that all human good depends on a physical force which is not native to earth, but which must be supplied by a beneficient power beyond us. The messenger Johor stumbles in his efforts to describe this substance: It is "a rich and vigorous air, which kept everyone safe and healthy, and above all made them love one another." Again, it is the "substance-of-life" or "SOWF—the substance-of-we-feeling" (p. 73). The poignance of the Shikastan dependence on this foreign substance and the horror of their degeneration when the supply of the substance dwindles are powerfully rendered from the alien perspective of the Canopean Johor. . . .

The alien perspective enormously facilitates the reader's participation in a simultaneous act of self-distancing and self-understanding. In the opinion of Darko Suvin, the chief academic critic of science fiction, such an estranging device is essential to successful science fiction. The attitude of estrangement creates the opportunity for a fresh and penetrating consideration of subjects that are normally approached with the glazed eye of habitual perception. "SF, then, is a literary genre whose necessary and sufficient conditions are the presence and interaction of *estrangement* and *cognition*, and whose main formal device is an imaginative frame-work alternative to the author's empirical environment."[8]

The estranging device in this case is built with the narrative structure of the work. *Shikasta* is a compilation of documents from the Canopus in Argos Archives, "selected to offer a very general picture of Shikasta for the use of first-year students of Canopean Colonial Rule" (p. 2). Apparently in order that the selections may be readily comprehensible, the documents all relate to the visits of emissary Johor, although there have been thousands of other emissaries over the centuries. The majority of the documents are his own reports to his superiors, but the authorities also have included reports by emissaries whose work relates to Johor's, relevant selections from the official *History of Shikasta*, letters written by Johor in human incarnation as George Sherban, letters and diary entries by Sherban's friends and relatives, and communications between world leaders whose actions impinge on Sherban's fate. Thus the reader experiences not only Johor's compassionate viewpoint, but also a variety of other extraterrestrial and human perspectives.

Johor himself varies in his degree of empathy with human beings. While he seems deeply and even painfully moved by those people with whom he forms relationships, he gives terse, distanced reports of a large number of individuals who are due to plays parts in the Canopean plan for Shikasta's salvation. These reports read like a sociologist's case histories: We have reports titled "Individual Three (Worker's Leader)," "Individual Four (Terrorist Type 3)," etc. These reports differ tonally from Johor's more personal responses, but in their own way they too serve both to estrange the reader from familiar material (one recognizes some of the models for these reports—Patty Hearst, the Baader-Meinhof gang, even Doris Lessing herself) and to encourage a more original and probing consideration of the depicted sociological phenomena than a contemporary familiarity with the data would tend to promote. . . .

The only character who appears continually in the narrative is Johor; however, because he focuses his attention outward on his assignment (the development of Shikastan potential from prehistoric times to a near future), we never have the sense of following a single character's story through the narrative. . . . *Shikasta* does not really have a central character, though it does have in Johor a presiding presence.

In this respect, again, the novel operates according to the code of science fiction. Concerned as it is with the fate not only of a world but of a cosmos, the literature of the Galactic Empire focuses its attention on the grand sweep of history, not on individual experience. Science fiction writers are concerned with those conditions of existence which transcend, while determining, the individual case. Their task is a difficult one—to expand the reader's consciousness so that it can grasp events from the alien perspective of huge vistas of time and space. . . . This has been the conscious agenda of Galactic Empire fiction since Olaf Stapledon's *Last and First Men*, one of Lessing's acknowledged models.[9] . . .

Johor and the impersonal historical documents give a bird's-eye view of Shikasta's history—the genetic experiments that led to human life, the establishment of the Canopean Bond, the leaking of the SOWF line, the interference of Shammat with even "the little trickle of SOWF that reached this place" (p. 73), the gradual decline of the human race, and finally, the history of "The Century of Destruction," our own. The *History of Shikasta* disposes of this century in eleven succinct pages, noting our wars, our ideologies, our living conditions, and our disasters, which include chemical poisoning, epidemics, famine, and finally nuclear war.

By contrast, the journals and letters of the Sherban family (relatives of Johor, incarnate as George Sherban) provide a more detailed and emotionally charged account, from the human angle—from the viewpoint of those who, lacking Canopean perspective, are astonished by both the calamities of the apocalyptic decade and the marvels of their last-minute deliverance into peace and harmony. In the last pages of the novel, Kassim, the stepson of George Sherban, writes to Suzannah, George's wife:

> The first houses are already up, and the central circular place is paved, and the basin of the fountain is made. As we build, wonderful patterns appear as if our hands were being taught in a way we know nothing about. . . . George left after a few days. I walked with him a little way. I said to him, What is happening, why are things so different? . . .

Everything in this passage is explicable in terms of the science fiction motifs developed throughout the novel. For example, Kassim's description of the newly built town echoes Johor's descriptions of the geometric cities that he visited many thousands of years before, at the time of the first threat to the SOWF line. The geometric town, with a fountain and circular plaza at its center, is Lessing's architectural ideal (present also in the utopian fantasies of *The Four-Gated City*, *The Memoirs of a Survivor*, and *Briefing for a Descent into Hell*). Johor's early reports prepared us to understand that this architectural imperative is physically (that is, empirically, scientifically) determined by lines of Canopean force in the earth, a grid structure no more mysterious than a magnetic field. . . .

Yet Kassim's awe-struck tone creates an atmosphere more appropriate to religious legend than to science fiction, and the passage is thick with allusions to messianic literature. Kassim walks a little way with George, in the same cadences as many a Christian hymn has asked the faithful to walk a little way with Jesus, in imitation of the Apostles.[10] This allusion is only the culmination of a whole string of passages that equate George Sherban (Johor) with the redeemer-god of the New Testament, Gnostic legend, and ancient myth. George is the keeper of the esoteric knowledge toward which parables may hint but which must be kept protected from the prying eyes of the populace. Here we have the first statement in the novel suggesting that Johor ever shared his Canopean vision of earthly history with any human being, and it is passed over quickly, as if to keep "the veil" over the ultimate Truth. As if this were a Gnostic text, we next read that the savior must die when his work—the spreading of the divine Knowledge—is finished. Finally, Kassim's words suggest that humankind has been released from limitations of spiritual vision, as the New Testament has predicted: Before our deliverance we saw as through a glass, darkly—"all stumbling about in a thick dark"—but now we begin to see the Canopean truth face to face; then we, like David and Sais, knew that truth only in part, but now we begin to know that truth even as also Johor and Canopus knew us (see I Cor. 13:12). . . . Like divine grace, the Canopean substance-of-life washes away the human tendency toward error and provides the strength for conduct and belief in harmony with Canopean law. The Fall is redeemed.

The compatibility of the scientific and the spiritual perspectives in this passage may offend the arbiters of the science fiction genre, but it is there to be accounted for. Moreover, this intertwining—or as Barthes calls it, this "braiding"—of codes is a constant feature of the text. The set piece of this braiding is the treatment of Johor's mission from Canopus to Earth. On the one hand, Johor is little different in conception from the many benevolent messengers in science fiction who are sent from a superior to a lesser civilization in order to teach the skills of survival and the rules of galactic cooperation: LeGuin's Genly Ai (*The Left Hand of Darkness*). Arthur C. Clarke's Karellan (*Childhood's End*), or even Stapledon's Last Man (*Last and First Men*). On the other hand, rarely, if ever, has an extraterrestrial messenger been depicted with such consistently messianic overtones. Just as the Messiah is the servant of God, Johor is the servant of Canopus; Canopus, as a star, is one of the gods, the creators and sustainers of life (p. 40). Johor's mission to earth also parallels Christ's, both in intention and in practice. He comes to "save" (p. 107) or to "redeem" (pp. 107, 113, 168) human beings from the consequences of their fall into "disobedience to the Master Plan" (p. 47). It will be his work to re-establish the flow of the substance-of-we-feeling (SOWF), a gift from Canopus that is constantly equated with the grace of Christian theology. In order to perform the act of redemption, Johor must, like Christ, become incarnate; although his essence is incorporeal, he must take on bodily form, being born to human parents selected, like Joseph and Mary, for their saintly attributes.

Much of the interest in the messianic parallel comes from contrasting the story of Johor's redemptive mission with the version of Christian scripture and tradition. The first departure is that Johor's incarnation is a multiple event. He records three visits before his embodiment as George Sherban—one about 35,000 years ago when the fall from grace had just begun and Earth was beginning to decline from its Edenic state, one at the time of Abraham, and one in the recent past (perhaps in the 1970s) when he scouted around for proper parents for his most important incarnation, as George Sherban. Moreover, these manifestations on Earth are not Johor's only missions; in between visits to Earth, he undertakes missions on other planets. Unlike the coming of the Messiah in Judeo-Christian tradition, Johor's incarnation is not the unique and all-important event in salvation-history. Indeed, Earth is by no means the center of the Canopean "Master Plan"; here, Lessing's braiding of the messianic story with the cosmic viewpoint of science fiction has salutary effects on the implied theology. Humanity may no longer see itself as the only child of an alternately doting and punitive Father; now human beings must democratically share their position with myriad brothers and sisters, the planets of all the galaxies: "We are *all* creatures of the stars and their forces, they make us, we make them, we are part of a dance from which we by no means and not ever may consider ourselves separate" (p. 40). This attitude involves a radical departure from Judeo-Christian cosmology, and in turn a major alteration in the role of the messiah.

As one among many Canopean emissaries, Johor must be much more independent and enterprising than his Biblical counterpart. Unlike Christ, Johor must negotiate his own entryway into the flesh, choosing his parents and arranging his passageway through the dangerous Zone Six, the waystation of souls seeking reincarnation. The constant counterpointing with the Biblical version provides a wry sort of humor, as we watch Johor struggling, scheming, and sweating his way to a messianic incarnation. No doubt, such touches of light irony are largely responsible for Lessing's success in combining the interests of science fiction and sacred literature in her representation of Johor's mission to Shikasta.

With the depiction of Zone Six, however, Lessing sorely tests the reader's confidence in her delicate generic balance. For Zone Six is a truly fantastic invention . . . wholly unconnected to the empirical code of the space fiction. . . . Zone Six stands alone, nearly completely sealed off from the rest of the fiction, as the sanctuary of the purely fantastic imagination.

The structure of six Zones, each lying concentric to earth's surface in an ordered hierarchy of levels, is established in the first pages of *Shikasta* and then largely forgotten — except for the important Zone Six. However, the next novel explores at length the allegorical and fantastic implications of these Zones. Shikasta itself, the earthly level of existence at the center of the Zones, is depicted as both geographically and spiritually the lowest level of existence. As in dualistic Christian heresies and Sufi mystical tradition, the earth itself is a dangerous snare, a "drag and pull" (p. 6) on the soul aspiring to Canopean harmony. As in some Sufi lore, "the world" is a "place to be visited only in case of need," like a latrine.[11] For human beings, the common necessity is the obligation to earn deliverance into a higher order of being—or Zone—by living one good life in "the world" of Shikasta. If one fails, one is returned to Zone Six, the first level of spiritual existence.

In *The Marriages Between Zones Three, Four, and Five*, Zone Six takes its place in a spiritual allegory, based on the mystical tradition of "stages" or "stations"[12] of enlightenment. In Sufism, the mystic tradition that Lessing knows best, various Sufi masters count the number of stages differently, but all lists start with the stage of repentance. . . . The genuineness of one's entry into this first stage is tested by whether one does in the new life abandon one's sins. Likewise, the soul who enters Zone Six expresses the repentance proper to this "station" by recognizing the failures in a past life in Shikasta and repentantly getting in line for a new life in which to prove a sincere resolve to sin no more.

When, in *Marriages*, the six ascending orders of being are developed in the context of a fabulous fantasy, complete with kingdoms, queens, magic wishes, and talking animals, the allegory (elaborated much more fully than in *Shikasta*) succeeds brilliantly, largely because it never arouses and thus never violates the expectations proper to realism. Here, in *Shikasta*, realism and fantasy meet in a major confrontation. In the depiction of Zone Six, there is no attempt to use extrapolative logic to justify affronts to the reader's sense of the plausible. Most outrageously, there is no discussion of how six layers of being, each with an earthly geography, can be said to be "in concentric shells around the planet" (p. 5). Obviously, if she were writing this section in the science fiction mode, Lessing would have to answer such elementary questions as how people on Shikasta see the stars, if there are six physical shells of matter between the earth and the universe beyond. Lessing does not address the issue. If the six zones were to be viewed as wholly immaterial and yet somehow existent, a science fiction writer would feel obligated to suggest a scientific or pseudoscientific theory under which such an anomalous state could obtain. Lessing supplies such a theory, for example, in regard to SOWF, and again in regard to Shammat's interference with SOWF (see the description of the invention Effluon 3 and its SOWF-deflecting properties, p. 66). Yet in her trips into Zone Six, Lessing seems to feel no such obligation. For these sections, she wholly abandons the rules of extrapolation and adopts the much looser rules of analogy. As in allegory, conditions and episodes are invented in *parallel* to the author's perceived reality, without the need for the parallel world to be tied to the "real world" by any logic but analogic.

It requires the most skillful sleight of hand for Lessing to convince her reader to accept the coexistence—indeed, the interrelationship—of two fictional worlds that operate on such different principles. First, she makes sure that the short and infrequent visits to Zone Six, the sections that are most out of alignment with the science fiction mode, are the most brilliantly conceived and stylishly written passages in the book. The Zone

Six sections are thick with metaphor and alive with startling descriptions of the wondrous phenomena of the special locale. In these descriptions, too, Lessing's sentence style is conspicuously more direct and her vocabulary more emphatic than in the rest of the novel. For example, the brief, intense description of Johor's descent into throbbing, fermenting flesh contrasts sharply with the prolixity of the sections dealing with Shikasta — Johor's prosaic reports on social conditions, the historians' flat summaries of aeons, or Rachel Sherban's adolescently chatty diary. The Zone Six sections are, simply, both beautiful and gripping. As such they gain a special status with the reader that no amount of conceptual or generic incongruity can undo.

Second, Lessing provides compelling characters who bridge the distance between Zone Six and Shikasta. At about the middle of the book, not only Johor himself, but also two lost souls named Rilla and Ben, pass from Zone Six into human flesh — as George, Rachel, and Ben Sherban, respectively. By this point in the narrative, we are starved for characters to follow consistently. Ben and Rilla in their new incarnations feed this hunger. We are ready to grasp at Rachel's diaries and Ben's letters for a sense of the personal texture of Shikastan life. As we become attached to their stories, which fill the second half of the book, we become seduced into accepting the linkage of Zone Six and Shikasta — for at every turn of Ben's and Rachel's narratives we are made to recall the terms under which they have entered Shikasta and confront the questions of whether either is passing the test of true repentance that passage from Zone Six into Shikasta represents.

The third way in which Lessing allows for a plural text — a text that accommodates separate and very different systems of meaning — is by using typography, headings, and spacing to signal shifts from one kind of narrative to another. For example, the sections of this book that most boldly represent the extraterrestrial perspective of the space fiction — the official Canopean histories — are set in a boldface version of Electra type. The sections written by Johor, an ordinary emissary of Canopus, are set in normal Electra type. His sections are further divided by headings and line spaces that demarcate his reports on Shikasta from his reports on the fantastical Zone Six. The letters written by Johor, Rilla, and Ben in their Shikastan incarnations are distinguished by an italic version of the Electra that had described them in Zone Six. Finally, the very few documents written by officials of the power that rivals Canopus and all its emissaries are set in a completely distinct, Spartan type; this emphasizes the likeness in difference of all Canopean perspectives (normal, boldface, and italic Electra) as against the radically opposed perspective of Shammat (Spartan).

Most important, the fact that the novel is a compilation of documents from different sources gives the reader an early signal that the reading of this text will involve frequent shifts of perspective. The most significant of these shifts is perhaps the most subtly handled. In the secular mode of science fiction, the bulk of the text makes a brief for cooperation among the races, laying down of arms, respect for the environment, for animals, for human life — all under the rubric of harmony with the rule of the great star Canopus. Threaded through this basically secular fabulation is a spiritual message which finds its greatest concentration in the allegory of the six Zones: the belief that a divine Master Plan, not individual will, directs the course of this planet and its inhabitants and that submission to that will is the swiftest — indeed, the only — road to deliverance from worldly suffering. In the Edenic period before the diminution of contact between Canopus and Shikasta, "everybody accepted that their very existence depended on voluntary submission to the great Whole, and that this submission, this obedience, was not serfdom or slavery . . . but the source of their health and their future and their progress" (p. 26). Individual human will becomes irrelevant under these conditions: "There could not be disharmony, because they *were* harmony" (p. 288). In Johor's spiritual vision of the cosmos, all earthly creatures, all nations, all planets in the universe are the "ever-evolving Sons and Daughters of the Purpose" (p. 35). But, Johor admits, even the Gods err in their service to the Purpose, and when they do — when stars explode or wander in their courses — then sickness of spirit occurs, the Degenerative Disease become epidemic, and creatures lose the ability to act in accordance with the Master Plan. That is what happened to the creatures of Shikasta, when "the misalignment" sapped their supply of SOWF, the substance designed to keep the inhabitants aware of "how they stood in relations to stars, planets, the dance of the heavens, the forces of the earth, the moon, our sun" (p. 288). Johor bemoans the fate of the Shikastans, which he depicts both as an accident of the stars (the secular version) and as an error of the Gods (the sacred version) — but in neither case as a fault of the doomed themselves:

> Creatures infinitely damaged, reduced and dwindled from their origins, degenerate, almost lost — animals far removed from what was first envisaged for them by their designers, they are being driven back and away from everything they had and held and now can take a stand nowhere but in the most outrageous extremities of — patience. . . . Shikastans are, in their awful and ignoble end, . . . reaching out with their minds to heights of courage and . . . I am putting the word *faith* here. After thought. With caution. With an exact and hopeful respect. (p. 203)

In this passage, we see how even the spiritual vision of the novel is itself a mediation between two seemingly contradictory views — the Christian myth and a more fatalistic cosmic vision. On the one hand, the story of Shikasta echoes continually the essentials of Christian belief — the existence of one omnipotent, benevolent Creator, the fall of his creatures from grace, their redemption from sin by a messiah, and finally their individual salvation by means of an act of faith in that redemption. Yet, in fact, Johor's story subtracts from the Christian system two of its essential elements. First, the God of Shikasta is neither unique nor omnipotent. According to Johor there are many Gods — the stars — and they are neither faultless nor eternal. The divine liability to error is, in fact, the key to the plot, since the fall of Shikasta directly results from an error in Canopean alignment with other celestial bodies. With that error, the second essential element of Christian theology goes by the board: there is no free will for creatures who are designed to depend on grace (SOWF) for their moral health but who, through no fault of their own — indeed through the fault of their God — are denied it.

Still, Johor in awestruck tones praises the Shikastans' courage and faith, as if the thoroughly fated human beings could somehow be credited with strength of personal will in "reaching out with their minds to heights" of courage and faith. Johor makes this illogical judgment "with caution," for it contradicts everything he has said about the absolute dependence of human moral judgment on SOWF. This passage is not an anomaly. It is typical of the logically inconsistent but imaginatively potent plurality of the text as a whole. The voice that denies free will is countered by a voice that affirms it. Likewise, the terse voice that respects the empirical bias of science fiction at times is overtaken by the impassioned voice that speaks in wildly fantastic or reverently spiritual tones. No matter that the contrary voices often issue from the same person, Johor — they are voices of different moods, different moments, different sections of the book. . . .

The text traces a movement without end, an action without climax. There *is* tension in the narrative, most notably between the science fiction and spiritual strands of the work. In fact, the reader is often curious, puzzled, even at times frustrated, because of the refusal of the terms of the text to resolve into unity. However, we come to realize that the terms that create the tension are in a continual process of being pulled and twisted into the form of an endless braid. The viewer of this braid focuses on the twistings of the separate strands against each other and wonders at the long line of strength that they build together, without ever losing their separate identities in the "gestalt" of a fully transcendent form.

Arranged as an archive, a repository of diverse perspectives, *Shikasta* is both open to multiple interpretations and readable in various modes. As the book drifts to an end, with an instruction to consult other volumes of the archive, the reader is implicitly asked not to conclude, not to settle on a single perspective, but to sustain tentatively and simultaneously the appreciation of both the science fiction saga still in progress and the spiritual fable that has only begun to be developed. The former will be continued in *The Sirian Experiments*,[13] while the latter is the business of volumes that precede and follow it. At the same time, the reader is asked to have the patience of the Shikastans in awaiting a time when apparent contradictions of theme, such as the conflict between free will and determinism in Johor's cosmic vision, will become comprehensible to our cleared and expanded imaginations. . . .

Notes

1. *Briefing for a Descent into Hell* and *The Summer Before the Dark* are two special cases in this regard. In *Briefing*, the incongruities of the surface elements of the text, which initially seem at war, are ultimately so firmly fixed into the metaphysical scheme of the work that the narrative falls flat; the didactic force straight-jackets the fantasy, leaving the reader with a feeling of stultification rather than excitement. In *The Summer Before the Dark*, Lessing interweaves the opposing elements — quest allegory and novel of character — so carefully that the effect is one of harmony and fruitful cooperation; the novel pleases and illuminates, but it is hardly exciting.

2. Roland Barthes, *S/Z*, trans. Richard Miller (New York: Hill and Wang, 1974), pp. 160, 15, 30, 5, 263.

3. Doris Lessing, "Some Remarks," preface to *Shikasta* (New York: Alfred A. Knopf, 1979), p. ix. The full title of this first volume of the series *Canopus in Argos: Archives* is *Re: Colonised Planet 5, Shikasta; Personal, Psychological, Historical Documents Relating to Visit by Johor (George Sherban), Emissary (Grade 9), 87th of the Period of the Last Days.*

4. See the definitions of science fiction by Kingsley Amis, *New Maps of Hell: A Survey of Science Fiction* (New York: Harcourt, Brace & Co., 1960), p. 18; Darko Suvin, *Metamorphoses of Science Fiction: On the Poetics and History of a Literary Genre* (New Haven: Yale Univ. Press, 1979), pp. 4, 7–8; Donald A. Wollheim, *The Universe Makers: Science Fiction Today* (New York: Harper & Row, 1971), p. 10; Sam Moskowitz, *Explorers of the Infinite: Shapers of Science Fiction* (Westport, Conn.: Hyperion Press, 1974), p. 11; and David Ketterer, *New Worlds for Old: The Apocalyptic Imagination, Science Fiction, and American Literature* (Bloomington: Indiana Univ. Press, 1974), pp. 15–18.

5. Donald Wollheim, *The Universe Makers*, pp. 30–31.

6. Much of this developing saga was recorded in short stories in the early magazines *Weird Tales, Argosy,* and *Amazing Stories,* and most notably in the 1950s in *Astounding* (later titled *Analog*), *The Magazine of Fantasy and Science Fiction,* and *Galaxy Science Fiction.* Some of the major works in the Galactic Empire mode are Bradbury's *The Martian Chronicles* (1950), Isaac Asimov's *The Foundation Trilogy* (1942–1966), Robert Heinlein's *Double Star* (1956), *Starship Troopers* (1960) and *Stranger in a Strange Land* (1962), Frank Hebert's *Dune* (1966), and Ursula Le Guin's *The Left Hand of Darkness* (1970).

7. See "The Cosmogony of the Future," in Donald A. Wollheim, *The Universe Makers*, pp. 42–44.

8. Darko Suvin, *Metamorphoses of Science Fiction*, pp. 7–8; emphasis mine.

9. Olaf Stapledon, *Last and First Men: A Story of the Near and Far Future* (1930; rpt. Hammondsworth, Middlesex: Penguin Books, 1963), p. 17.

10. Lessing's phrasing echoes hymns such as "Walk daily with your Savior," "Walk with the Lord along the Road," "Walking, Savior, close to thee," and "Walking with Jesus day by day." See Katherine Smith-Diehl, *Hymns and Tunes — An Index* (New York: Scarecrow Press, 1966), p. 329.

11. Annemarie Schimmel, *Mystical Dimensions of Islam* (Chapel Hill: Univ. of North Carolina Press, 1975), p. 109.

12. Ibid., pp. 109–130, chapter section titled "Stations and Stages."

13. *The Sirian Experiments* (New York: Alfred A. Knopf, 1981). Lessing describes the book in her March 1980 interview with Minda Bikman for *The New York Times Book Review*, cited above.

RECEPTION AND
REPUTATION

The Grass Is Singing

Some Recent Fiction
Ernest Jones*

. . . *The Grass is Singing*, a first novel, abounds in local color, a South African farm—but does examine carefully the eclipse of a dim soul, a townswoman whom a bad marriage and years in the veld drive to madness and death. Mrs. Lessing is preoccupied with the racial problem, but her rather pat analyses do not, fortunately, obscure the disintegration of her central figure. The prose is unadorned; the book is too long for the subject—at least as Mrs. Lessing has conceived it. . . .

The Grass Is Singing
Klad.**

"The Grass Is Singing," based on the novel by Doris Lessing, proves to be a thoughtful film adaptation which should find some success in the marketplace.

The co-production between England and Sweden was filmed in Zambia and deals with a woman who cannot come to terms with life in the African bush. As played by Karen Black, the central character accepts a marriage proposal from farmer John Thaw rather than face the prospect of being alone and single in the big city.

Her new home and surroundings are less than she bargained for from constant hard work with little return to insects and black natives. Black leaves once only to discover she no longer fits in the urban community and returns with new demands on her husband.

Things get better momentarily, then a turnaround drives Black deeper into depression and finally, breakdown.

Black is particularly good in the central role of Mary Turner. Difficult part calls for edgy quality as Mary succumbs gradually to the bush.

---

*From the *Nation* 171 (23 September 1950): 273.

**From *Variety*, 3 June 1981, p. 20. Reprinted with permission.

her paranoia and tension toward her black employee [sic]. She avoids the obvious cliches and steers away from an hysterical interpretation.

Location footage in Zambia is stunning in this handsome production. Director Michal Raeburn has taken great pains to adapt the Doris Lessing story and may have erred in being too reverential. At times, the story unfolds much too slowly. Another round at the editing table could do a lot to quicken the pace of the film.

High-quality production of "The Grass is Singing" and lack of obvious commercial hooks will probably mean the art house and festival circuit for the film. In some overseas markets the film could have broader appeal on large and small screens.

Children of Violence

Frustration on the Veldt

C. P. Snow*

. . . A good example of . . . a natural writer is Miss Doris Lessing and confronted with her harsh, living books we do not know quite what to praise or (which is just as much a sign of insecurity) what to blame. In *Martha Quest* Miss Lessing has begun her most ambitious work so far, which is to be a series of novels called "Children of Violence." Of this series *Martha Quest* is the first and tells us the story of the eponymous heroine, living in Miss Lessing's native Rhodesia, through adolescence to marriage: the marriage is a foolish one and the author intends us to realise that in the next volume it will break.

The story, then, is very simple, a few years in a girl's life, her antagonisms with her parents on the veldt farm, her job in the local city, her first love affair, her political faith opening out to her through the crises of the thirties, her lost, pathetic marriage; and the fundamental merit of Miss Lessing's writing is that you believe every act and every thought. It happened thus, and not otherwise.

You may not like what happens or what Martha thought; in fact, you won't, for much of it is displeasing. But the book lives, and to a considerable extent succeeds through the steady pressure of truth. It is the truth of a girl's temperament; a girl clever, compassionate, suspicious, shot through with resentment, so avid for wonder that she is disappointed before she gets it, so longing to worship a man that as soon as she meets one she feels he is a poor fish. . . .

Despite the brilliant power with which Martha's feelings are entered into, the reader has to supply much for himself in order to work out what she is really like. That was also true, if you changed the sex, of D. H. Lawrence, the writer with whom Miss Lessing has most affinity. It gives a certain monotony of vision, and at times a rancour, that Miss Lessing ought to guard against as she proceeds with Martha Quest. But this volume confirms my opinion that she is one of the most powerfully equipped young novelists now writing.

*From the *Sunday Times* (London), 4 November 1953, p. 11.

173

New Novels   Kingsley Amis*

. . . Mrs. Doris Lessing, whose earlier work has attracted important attention, offers in *A Proper Marriage* the second in a series of five novels. In this volume the heroine, Martha Quest, has just got married to a man she seems not to like much. She has a baby and he goes off to war. After a time he comes back from the war and she still doesn't like him much. Then she gets mixed up in left-wing politics and leaves him. Now, it is always hard to summarise a story without seeming to be offensively implying that almost nothing happens, especially when, as here, almost nothing happens. Anyone with so little to narrate should, I feel, make more concessions to her readers than Mrs. Lessing does with her preference for description and *oratio obliquoas* against scene-drawing and *oratio recta*, her thousand-word paragraphs, and her tissues of abstract commentary doing duty for characterisation: character, I also feel, is what people do, not what they think or in what terms they can be generalised about. There are, of course, some excellent bits of South African background, some minor figures are well grasped, the episode about the husband in the services is a remarkable feat for a woman writer. Martha quarrelling with her mother is always good value, there is some shrewd observation and attractive irony. But the observation remains marginal, the irony parenthetical, and the author's obvious intelligence only increases one's fury at finding half a novel puffed up into a piece of stodge as long as two novels. Even the author of *The Bostonians* (whom, alas the day, I suspect Mrs. Lessing of admiring) might have been expected to get a situation or two under way in 150,000 words.

I need hardly say that Mrs. Lessing is a whole network of streets ahead of the "average" novelist. . . .

Last Children of Violence   Joyce Carol Oates*

. . . The concluding "novel" of the five-volume *Children of Violence*, this powerful, prophetic, mysterious work takes the heroine, Martha Quest, from her young womanhood in London just after the conclusion of World War II to a contaminated island off the coast of Scotland sometime around 1997. Miss Lessing says in her Author's Notes that the book is "what the Germans call a *Bildungsroman*. We don't have a word for it. This kind of novel has been out of fashion for some time."

*From the *Spectator*, 8 October 1954, p. 450. Reprinted with permission of the *Spectator*.

*From the *Saturday Review of Literature* 52 (17 May 1969):48. Reprinted with permission of Joyce Carol Oates.

We certainly do not have a word for what Miss Lessing has done, and I doubt that the Germans do either. *The Four-Gated City* seems to me a truly extraordinary novel, an experimental work in the very best sense— and I am conscious of "experimental" works everywhere, most of them unreadable—that audaciously combines a traditional technique (the most scrupulous, authentic realism) with a fantastic theme (the prophecy of the catastrophe of England and the attendant madness of most of the world). One begins with *Martha Quest*, published in 1952, a perfectly competent novel about Martha's girlhood in "Zambia [sic]," Miss Lessing's fictional equivalent of Northern [sic] Rhodesia. In subsequent volumes one is taken slowly, with meticulous detail, through Martha's marriages, love affairs, and experiences in politics—only to find oneself, bewildered in the highly complex world of *The Four-Gated City*, which treats the future with exactly the same naturalistic scrupulosity as the past. Has any other novel attempted this fusion of naturalism and fantasy, and with such success?

Miss Lessing's main themes are two: the mystery of the self, explored brilliantly here as it is in her other masterpiece, *The Golden Notebook*, and the insanity of the twentieth century. Martha, like Anna of *The Golden Notebook*, probes her own personality for weeks—months—in what must be the most fastidious self-analysis in literature, if not life. . . . Like other Lessing characters, though far more advanced than they, Martha Quest deliberately brings herself to the edge of madness, and past the edge in order to live out the potentialities in herself for hatred, for "evil," for whatever truer and more deadly insanity has infected the modern world.

Turning from individuals who have approached or crossed the border into madness (and *The Four-Gated City* is filled with "neurotics" and "psychotics"), Miss Lessing makes a most convincing and depressing argument for the madness of the entire world. Gradually the novel becomes prophetic: we move unobtrusively into the future. The "history" of violence begins with a consideration of what we already know and progresses reasonably into another dimension, the logical development of what we already have. "Sometimes it was gangs of young men . . . who might decide to go off in cars or even running in a pack like wolves to smash up some other place. Or it was men and women together . . . Sometimes it was students. Sometimes it was the semi-organized militia employed by a big farm of industry. . . . From the early Seventies onwards individuals or groups or, even whole cities might succumb to a condition like a child's promising to be good.". . . And there are, of course, race riots, crimes, self-administered "justice," etc. "People kept taking leave of their senses," says a man whose record of his experiences is included in the long Appendix to the novel.

Growing apace are the insanity of weapons—newer and bigger and more weapons—and the insanity of man's mismanagement of his own power over nature and himself. "We were poisoned. Our nervous systems

were shot to pieces — from the noise we had to endure from traffic and . . .
aircraft; the air we breathed was foul, and full of toxic substances; we
were ill because of the drugs we filled ourselves with . . . and purgatives of
all kinds and sedatives and sleeping drugs. Our food was poisoned by
preservatives and the toxic substances we used on crops, and the atomic
wastes dumped in the sea. . . ."

It will probably be objected to that Miss Lessing has began a fairly
traditional work and taken it to unusual, even perverse, extremes. When
Martha Quest appears in London and seeks a job, she is a typical young
woman, an intellectual, politically conscious, but not terribly brilliant or
artistic person. She accepts a job as secretary to a writer. From that point
onward the novel is a sometimes exasperating series of anecdotes, dramatic
interludes, dogmatic passages, meticulous analyses of the states of mind of
quite a few people, most of them what we would call, conventionally,
mentally ill; and we keep waiting for Martha, the "heroine," to become
central again and to move on to new adventures. We particularly wait for
her to fall in love or to somehow shape her shapeless, peculiar life. . . .
She does not. Indeed, the novel concerns itself with Martha only as a point
of view, a consistent consciousness, rather than as a dramatic character.
For all the ups and downs, the domestic and international crises, this is a
strangely undramatic novel, and it is certainly Miss Lessing's intention
that it be so. . . .

The Golden Notebook

Neither Compromise nor Happiness

Irving Howe*

". . . Personal relations" as the very substance and sufficient end of our existence; "personal relations" as a surrogate for transcendence through religion, fulfillment through work, satisfaction through community: "personal relations" as a fragile shelter for sensitive men, a bulwark against the nihilist void, an ideology of privacy to replace the lapsed ideologies of public action—all this has become a style of life in New York and Moscow, London and Warsaw, accepted by some intellectuals with a tiresome literalness and by others with a skeptical grin. Among ourselves the devotion to "personal relations" seems at times like a malaise eating away at personal life; in the Communist countries it can serve as a rallying call for marginal freedoms. But in both parts of the world, psychological man begins to replace social man.

Hundreds of novels have been written in the last few decades reflecting this concern with "personal relations." Some are works of distinction, but many suffer from a narrowness of perspective that approaches claustrophobia. Just as Marxist writers will too often apply the corrosive test of the "sociology of knowledge" to everyone but themselves, so the novelists of sensibility too often see no need to question their own assumptions. . . .

It is a particular distinction of *The Golden Notebook*, a long and ambitious novel by the gifted English writer Doris Lessing, that while dealing with some of the materials favored by novelists of sensibility, it escapes their constrictions of tone and outlook. . . . She understands that the idea of "personal relations" has been shaped by the catastrophes of our time and, in the form we know it, is not to be taken as an absolute or uncontaminated value.

It is a further distinction of Miss Lessing's novel that its action is carried mainly by that rarity in modern fiction: a heroine, Anna Wulf, who is a mature intellectual woman. A writer with a sophisticated mind, sharp tongue and an abundance of emotional troubles, Anna Wulf is

*From the *New Republic* 147 (15 December 1962):17–20. Reprinted by permission of the *New Republic*. © 1962 by The New Republic, Inc.

sufficiently representative of a certain kind of modern woman to persuade us that her troubles have a relevance beyond their immediate setting; she is also an intelligence keen enough to support the public combativeness and personal introspectiveness that Miss Lessing has given her. At the very least, Anna Wulf is someone who has measured the price for being what she chooses to be—"a free woman," she would say with pride and irony—and who is prepared, no matter how much she groans, to pay it.

Miss Lessing has a voice and a mind of her own. She is radically different from other women writers who have dealt with the problems of their sex, first in that she grasps the connection between Anna Wulf's neuroses and the public disorders of the day, and second in that she has no use either for the quaverings of the feminist writers or the aggressions of those female novelists whose every sentence leads a charge in the war of the sexes. The feminine element in *The Golden Notebook* does not become a self-contained universe of being as in some of Virginia Wolf's novels. . . . And Miss Lessing is far too serious for those displays of virtuoso bitchiness which are the blood and joy of certain American lady writers.

Anna Wulf and her old friend Molly understand perfectly well that modern women do face crippling difficulties when they choose one or another role of freedom. But they do not fall back upon their charm, wit or headaches; they take their beatings, they ask no quarter, they spin and bear it. They are tough-minded, generous and battered—descriptives one is tempted to apply to the author herself, formerly close to the English Communist movement and still a lively radical, a woman whose youth in southern Africa had shaken her into a sense of how brutal human beings can become, a novelist who has published extensively and taken the risks of her craft. One feels about Miss Lessing that she works from so complex and copious a fund of experience that among women writers her English predecessors seem pale and her American contemporaries parochial.

At the center of *The Golden Notebook* is a series of remarkable conversations between Anna Wulf and Molly. Meeting in one another's London homes, they talk again and again about "personal relations," but always with a muted irony, an impatience with the very topics they know to concern them most. They are alternately open and guarded, sometimes wounding but usually honest. Simply as precise and nuanced dialogue, this is the best writing in a novel that never stoops to verbal display and is always directed toward establishing a complete and visible world.

When they discuss their failures in love, their problems as divorced women with children to raise, their disillusionments as former Communists who would still like to needle the Establishment, their inability to talk with the passionless and apolitical young, their contempt for the new gentility of intellectual London, their difficulties in reconciling the image they hold of a self-sufficient human being with the needs they feel as anything but self-sufficient women—when these conversations between Anna and Molly recur throughout the book, one turns to them with the delight of encountering something real and fresh. My own curiosity, as a masculine outsider, was enormous, for here, I felt, was the way intellectual women really talk to one another when they feel free and unobserved. It makes the Bloomsbury writers seem a little quaint.

Though their interest in politics has lessened, both Anna and Molly feel themselves to be voices of a baffled generation, those people who gave their youth to radicalism and ended not knowing how to live. This could be, it so often has been, a sticky self-pitying kind of subject; but not in *The Golden Notebook*, for it is a virtue of these deeply interesting women that even while suffering neurotic torments they can still regard themselves as objects of laughter. And also, as figures of hope. History, they feel, has left them stranded, but on the beaches of disillusion there must still be other stranded ones, there must be men of strength, to help them.

For both women remain interested in men with a curiosity that is almost archaelogical: as if there were so few good ones left that it is necessary to hunt for them amid the ruins. Both Anna and Molly, in a wry and pleasing way, are frank about their sexuality; both are ready to have affairs when their emotions are stirred. Yet, as they feel it, men somehow "fail" them. Their men do not "come through," and the more pliant they seem, the less dependable they prove. . .

In temperament the two women are sharply different: Anna morose and burrowing, Molly cheerful and extrovert; but they share problems, needs, failures. Both try hard to preserve their independence, which means not a refusal of relationships but a hard decision not to delude themselves when they do take up with second-raters and even more, a strict watch, mostly within themselves, against the mediocre, the resigned, the merely comfortable. At the end Molly does give in to a marriage of convenience, though with a characteristic quip: "There's nothing like knowing the exact dimensions of the bed you're going to fit yourself into." Anna, reduced to hysteria by a disasterous affair with an egomaniacal American writer, still keeps pushing ahead, deciding to go into Labour Party work and—a nice touch of irony—to take a job as a marriage counsellor ("I'm very good at other people's marriages.") She remains loyal to that refusal to compromise which had bound the two women in friendship.

Refusal to compromise with what? It is not easy to say, since the answer depends at least as much upon Anna's visceral reactions as her conscious ideas. Miss Lessing, with the patience of a true novelist, keeps returning to the problem, not explicitly but through a series of narrative variations. Sick as Anna is, trapped as she often finds herself in a pit of anxiety, she still commands a burning sense of the possibilities of life. That this very restlessness of hers may itself be a function of neurosis, she also knows; for she has undergone the inevitable analytic bout, with a spiderish lady doctor she calls "Mother Sugar." . . .

Anna is the kind of woman who would send D. H. Lawrence into a sputter of rage: so much the worse for him. To be sure, many of the complaints he might make of her would be accurate. She whines, she is a bit of a drag, she often drives her men crazy. She does not inquire closely enough as to her own responsibility for the failures of her men or why she seems so gifted at picking losers. In her steady groaning about her writer's block, she does not ask herself whether it is caused by a deep contempt for the whole idea of the intellectual life — like many women of her sort, she has fitful passions for cooking and domesticity — or whether it is caused by overweening ambition — at times one suspects her of wanting to write a novel as good as *The Golden Notebook*. More can be said against her. Indeed, she is open to almost every judgment except that of having died before her death.

In its structure *The Golden Notebook* is original but not entirely successful. Miss Lessing has wanted to show the relation between Anna's past and her present, as well as between both of these and her fantasies, but she has wanted to show them not simply through the usual juxtaposition of narrative strands which might, for her purposes, lack tension and the effect of simultaneity. She therefore hit upon the ingenious device of carrying her narrative line forward in the present while inserting long excerpts from several notebooks Anna keeps, each a different color and representing a distinct part of her life. The advantage of this scheme is that Miss Lessing can isolate the main elements of Anna's experience with a sharpness that might not be possible in a traditional kind of novel; the disadvantage, that she has had to force large chunks of narrative into a discursive context.

In a black notebook Anna returns to her youth, sketching a group of English radicals astray in a provisional African town and preying on each other's nerves. This is the least vivid section of the book, and one that does not justify the length given it. In a red notebook Anna looks back upon her political life, drawing a number of amusing vignettes of left-wing intellectual circles in the London of the fifties. In a yellow notebook she writes a fictional version of her own experience, focusing on a love affair which has, in the narrative present, already reached its end. And in a blue notebook she keeps an objective record of her daily life, which comes to a brilliant climax in a detailed account of a single day. Bit by bit she builds up the mosaic of her anxiety: how she must face early in the morning the conflicting needs of her lively child and sleepy lover; how she copes with the irritations of work in a fellow-travelling publishing house; how she gives way to the compulsion of repeatedly washing her body for fear that her period causes her to have a bad smell; how she returns home at night to the nagging of her thoughts.

Finally there comes the golden notebook which is to record the reintegration of the various Annas who appear in the other notebooks. But as the love affair on which she stakes her hopes begins to crumble, the golden notebook turns into a record of collapse, and in pages of nightmarish power Anna is shown entering a psychotic episode, locking herself into her bedroom where she pastes alarming newspaper items on the walls and slowly tastes the progress from despair, in which she abandons herself to the vividness of remembering what she has lost, to desolation, in which the image of loss becomes dim but the pain, feeding on itself, lives on.

Doris Lessing is a natural writer: she has the prime novelistic gift of involving one so deeply in the desires and frustrations of her characters that one reads with a positive yearning to spend more time with them. Some of her failures, however, I found disturbing. The cumbersome structure of the novel allows for a rich interweaving of complexities but does not fully encourage the free flow of emotion which her story demands. She writes about Americans with the astigmatism peculiar to certain English leftists: she has no ear for American speech nor eye for American manners. More important, at the end of the book she fails to keep a sufficient distance from her heroine, so that Anna's hysteria comes dangerously close to taking over the narrative. Perhaps Miss Lessing faced an insoluble problem at this point: she achieves enormous intensity through surrendering herself to Anna's suffering, but the price she pays is a loss of the critical objectivity she had maintained in earlier pages. It is a feat of evocation, but not matched by steadiness of control.

By any final reckoning *The Golden Notebook* is a work of high seriousness. That I have omitted to mention important characters and elements of plot hardly matters, for this novel will be discussed repeatedly in the years to come. It is the most absorbing and exciting piece of new fiction I have read in a decade: it moves with the beat of our time, and it is true.

"An Interview with Adrienne Rich"

Elly Bulkin[*]

AR: I remember reading *The Golden Notebook*, Doris Lessing, in 1962 when it first came out, and again I keep associating things that I've read with periods in my life. It was a period in my life when I was very much in love with a woman and not calling it by that name and *The Golden Notebook* at that time seemed like a very radical book. It doesn't anymore, but it was a radical book because it did focus on women, even if on women who, although they were writers or professionals in some way, seemed to have no real center to their lives apart from trying to relate to men and to male politics. But it talked about things that had not been talked about in literature before, you know, what happens when you're

[*]From *Conditions* April 1977, 60 (Part 1). Reprinted with permission of Adrienne Rich and Elly Bulkin.

having your period and your lover's coming to sleep over, what happens if you're a single woman with a child and there's a conflict between your loyalty to the child and your loyalty to your lover.

So it seemed like a very radical, very feminist book, and I remember distinctly, at one point in that book, the woman is getting fed up with her relationships with men, none of them have come off well, and then she begins to worry and she thinks, women like me become "man-haters or bitter or lesbian." The implication of course was that it's only from being jaded with too many unsuccessful encounters with men that you would ever turn to women, and that stereotype too still holds. Lessing has been enormously important as a quasi-feminist writer, a writer centering on women's lives, and the failure of her novels, because in many ways she's a very brilliant political novelist, but the failure of *The Four-Gated City* and of what has come after is a real failure to envisage any kind of political bonding of women and any kind of really powerful central bonding of women, even though individual women get together in her novels and go through intense things together. In some ways I feel it goes back to that notion which she evidently has, that women become lesbians — bitter and full of hatred — not because there is a fulfillment in loving women, but because there is this terrible battle of the sexes going on and men just get to be too much to deal with. . . .

On Several Novels

Doris Lessing: Cassandra in a World under Siege

Margaret Drabble*

Doris Lessing is a prophet who prophesies the end of the world. She is much read but not perhaps much heeded, for there is very little that can be done, in her view, to avert catastrophe. Why, then, does she continue to write for a posterity that does not exist? Because, she says, we must continue to write and live *as if*. She is used by now to living on the edge of destruction, though her conception of it has changed over the years: now she foresees a world polluted and ruined by nerve gas and fallout, with England "poisoned, looking like a dead mouse in a corner, injected with a deathly glittering dew," whereas she used to foresee revolution. One of her characters, contemplating her miserable marriage in the war years, comforts herself in these terms: "I'm caught for life, she thought: but the words, 'for life,' released her from anxiety. They all of them saw the future as something short and violent. Somewhere just before them was a dark gulf or chasm, into which they must all disappear. A communist is a dead man on leave, she thought." And that is how she continues to write, though no longer a communist: a dead man on leave.

If her prophecies are listened to, it is with helplessness. Her literary prestige in England could not be higher, though she cares little for the literary world. She also has real readers. She is the kind of writer who changes people's lives: her novel *The Golden Notebook* has been described as "the Bible of the young," and although I don't think she'd care much for the portentousness of the phrase, it certainly catches the feeling of converted emotion that she arouses.

In a new, as yet unpublished preface to *The Golden Notebook*, she says that like all writers she is constantly besieged by letters from students who want to write theses and essays about her work, and who ask for "a thousand details of total irrelevance which they have been taught to consider important, amounting to a dossier, like an immigration department's." To these students, she replies, "why don't you read what I have written and make your own mind up about what you think, testing it

*From *Ramparts* 10 (February 1972):50–54. Reprinted with permission of Margaret Drabble.

against your own life, your own experience. Never mind about Professors White and Black."

Her attitude to interviewers is much the same. She is interviewed occasionally, and sometimes lectures, but usually for practical reasons — to finance travel, to oblige publishers who believe that interviews promote sales. But she has very little faith in the value of what she says in such circumstances and insists that what she does want to say is written down in her novels. (Two of her books contain accounts of lecturers who have been unable to continue lecturing through fits of stammering, caused by a lack of faith in the generalizations they are delivering from the platform of authority. Finding themselves in false positions, they become physically unable to speak.) I invited her to lunch, but found myself unable to ask her the usual interviewer's questions, knowing as I did her views on the subject. We discussed these views a little and then talked about our dentists and the price of meat, lecture tours, psychoanalysts and dreams, and why people take so many pills these days. She is a great dreamer, a creative dreamer, but one doesn't have to ask her to know it, because they are all there in her novels and short stories, Jungian dreams, prophetic dreams what she describes as "bad B picture dreams." It is only fair to say that for a writer who consistently foresees and confronts the worst, she is neither depressing nor apparently depressed. We talked about cooking and exchanged recipes. One can tell (again from her novels) that she is a good cook, that she notices what she eats. She is an organized person: when working on a novel, she cuts herself off, doesn't go out, doesn't see people. She has learned to say no, though she doubtless learned the hard way; she is not a hard person.

Doris Lessing was not brought up in England. She came here in 1950 at the age of 30 with the manuscript of her first novel, *The Grass is Singing*, which was accepted, published and became an immediate success. So for over twenty years she's been a courted, successful, even popular novelist. Part of her initial impact came from the subject matter of her work; she wrote about Africa and racialism, topics which in the '50s could hardly have been more in the news. She was born in Persia, where her father ran a bank: the family moved to Rhodesia when she was five, because her father fancied that he could make a fortune growing maize. They were out, she told me, "with very little money, a governess, a piano, clothes from Liberty's, visiting cards," and there they all sat "in an elongated thatched hut, while the farm did not succeed." She received hardly any proper education, she says, and that together with "wandering about in the veld by myself, on foot or by bicycle" were the two things that she thinks most formed her. She worked in Salisbury for a time, married twice, had three children, and then left everything to come to England.

The evidence of not-having-any-education is easy enough to see in her work, and it manifests itself in several ways, not least in her distrust of the academic establishment, with its generalizations, fashions and categories.

She's found things out for herself, and she thinks other people should do the same. In *The Four-Gated City*, she writes about the heroine whose life she chronicles in the *Children of Violence* series. "Somewhere in Martha's life it had been instilled into her, or she knew by instinct, that one should never read anything until one wanted to, or learn anything until one needed it. . . ." It is Freud and Jung that fill her baskets on this occasion; earlier, it had been the Marxists; later, more esoteric authors. But the point is, Martha doesn't read because she thinks she ought to, or because she wants to keep up with things; she reads because she needs to, for living.

Doris Lessing is an experimental novelist, perhaps, but it's misleading to see her in those terms, because most experimental writers deliberately, provocatively, depart from the old in order to create the new. Novelty is not her aim: on the contrary, she harks back frequently and nostalgically, to the "old-fashioned novel," to the philosophic novel of Thomas Mann. She is not obsessed with form but with content, and she does not care whether the form she finds is new or old, fashionable or unfashionable, as long as it serves her purpose. Her discontent with the traditional novel, as expressed in *The Golden Notebook*, is not with its conventional ingredients, with its plot and its characters and its chronology, with its reading public: she is dissatisfied with it *because she can't get enough into it*. It is too simple for the enormous number of things that she has to say. *The Golden Notebook* (and her later novel, *The Four-Gated City*) bulge with information, with abundance, with characters, ideas, locations; their very forms express complexity, profusion, excitement.

And yet it took her some time to reach this freedom and boldness. Her early novels and stories are conventional, often showing the marks of clumsiness. *The Grass is Singing* is sensational: it opens, dramatically, with the account of a white woman murdered by her houseboy. The first novels of her *Children of Violence* sequence, though less melodramatic, are commonplace in theme and style: we see Martha Quest, first as an adolescent on the farm struggling against her extremely unsympathetic mother, then as a young married women fighting against the expectations of Rhodesian society, producing a child, abandoning it, having affairs, joining a communist group. The writing is ordinary, and the lack of education shows itself in split infinitives, dangling prepositions, home-made words like "abolishment." And yet the momentum is powerful, it presses forward, it is compulsively readable: one reads on for all those wrong reasons, to find out what is going to happen to the characters, to the political group, to find out if one agrees with the heroine and ought therefore to go and do likewise. The first three volumes of Children of Violence — *Martha Quest* (1952), *A Proper Marriage* (1954) and *A Ripple From the Storm* (1958) — have been variously claimed as works about the status of women, works about Marxism or African nationalism, and as novels of social protest in the vein of the Angry Young Men of the '50s.

Children of Violence must be one of the oddest novel sequences ever written, and its oddity, as a structure, is symptomatic of Doris Lessing's disrespect for consistency, categories, style as a-thing-in-itself. Most authors who embark on novel sequences claim to have planned the thing as a whole, and repudiate any suggestion that they might have changed their minds as they went along. As we know, Proust wrote the beginning and end of his work at the same time, and one cannot imagine Anthony Powell, his admirer, adding a volume to the *Music of Time* that would depart radically from the tone and format of its predecessors. But if one thinks about it, why on earth not? Surely, if one is going to write a work that will be more than seventeen years in the making, it is more than likely that as the world changes, so will one's conceptions. Doris Lessing could certainly not have plotted the amazing last volume of her sequence, *The Four-Gated City*, seventeen years ago, for the simple reason that most of the events in it had not happened; some of them have not happened yet, for it is a prophetic book, but Doris Lessing does draw a line between prophecy and history. At the end of it she says, in the Author's Notes, "This book is what the Germans call a *Bildungsroman*. This kind of novel has been out of fashion for some time: which does not mean that there is anything wrong with this kind of novel."

The point is, *The Four-Gated City* is littered with sentences that begin, bluntly, desperately, with the words "The point is . . ." And the point follows. Most writers feel compelled to write bridging passages, to plane down the surface, to conceal their points. But Doris Lessing is too urgently involved in getting to the end of her seven hundred pages (for this novel is not only utterly different in style from its predecessors, it is also several times as long) — and she must grasp the point before she goes on. The flexibility of her writing is by now amazing: she changes tense, tone, place, she skips decades, moves from the past to the future, documents, speculates, describes, with relentless urgency. The world of *The Four-Gated City* is a different world from the world of *Martha Quest*, though its protagonist is the same, and has endured the same history. The shape of the sequence is the shape of the exploration and widening which is experience. And she gets everything into one book.

The Four-Gated City was written after *The Golden Notebook*, which was a watershed. *The Golden Notebook* is a transforming work. There is nothing at all like it. It was published in 1962, and the depth and scope of its preoccupations mark a major development; they are territory gained forever. It marks a dissatisfaction with the confines of the ordinary novel, with the telling of stories and a new concept of the spirit. The protagonist this time is Anna Wulf, who is suffering from a writer's block: she is trying to write a book about Ella (the third, She, the Other) who is trying to write a book about a suicide. It is easy to speculate that Doris Lessing could not have written this book if she had not become deeply involved in the regions of madness, psychoanalysis, Jungian and Freudian thought: and her later books follow through this concern. . . . But *The Golden*

Notebook is not about madness, though it uses its terminology. Though Doris Lessing points out, obsessively, the parallels between her life and Anna's, though she dwells much on the use of fiction and analogy, the purpose of fiction, the need for truth, one can never safely identify her with Anna, any more than Anna identifies herself with her shadow, Ella.

Anna, like Doris Lessing, is from Africa. She too has left a husband, has written a best-selling novel which she thinks of as banal. She wishes to put the record straight. Also, she knows that if she wishes to go on writing she cannot go on writing in the old way: there must be a new way. Like Martha Quest, she is a disaffected member of the Communist Party. Anna / Ella has had a long affair with a working class British / European refugee psychiatrist, and is undergoing psychotherapy herself with a Jungian analyst. Ella's lover was named Paul, her son Michael. Anna's lover was called Michael, and she has a daughter, not a son. It is not surprising that she feels it fair to point to "that game that writers play with themselves, the psychological game—that written incident came from that real incident, that character was transposed from that one in life, this relationship was the psychological twin of that." Not that it is such a game: one of the points that she makes is that this search for analogy is not merely a search for equivalence, an evasion of libel actions, a polite form of presentation: it is also at the heart of the creative process, for in writing novels we create not only a book but a future, we draw up through our characters "our beautiful, impossible blueprints," and bring into being what we need to be.

The Golden Notebook contains five recurring sections: one a conventional novel called "Free Women," with archaic chapter headings such as "Anna meets her friend Molly," "Two visits, some telephone calls, and a Tragedy," and the other four as the notebooks. The Black Notebook deals with the past, with the secretions of nostalgia, and the problems of turning material into fiction; the Red deals with Anna's involvement in the Communist Party, of which she was a member during the unfavorable cold years 1950–54. The Yellow "looks like the manuscript of a novel" and it is about Ella, her life and writing. The Blue Notebook is the realist notebook, in which Anna aims to set down the facts of daily life, in painstaking detail, but three quarters of the way through, she concludes that it is the worst failure of all, it is even less truthful than the others. She says, "I expected a terse record of facts to present some sort of pattern when I read it over, but this sort of record is as false as the account of what happened on 15 September 1954, which I read now embarrassed because of its emotionalism and because of its assumption that if I wrote 'at nine-thirty I went to the lavatory to shit and at two to pee and at four I sweated,' this would be more real than if I simply wrote what I thought. And yet I still don't understand why." Finally, Anna writes the Golden Notebook, because she refuses to allow herself to be fragmented by literary styles, by roles, by life styles: she is going to bring them all together. She says "I'll pack away the four notebooks. I'll start a new notebook, all of myself in one book."

In her unpublished preface, Doris Lessing describes the writer's dissatisfaction with any finished book: "How little I have managed to say of the truth, how little I have caught of all that complexity: how can this small neat thing be true when what I experienced was so rough and apparently formless and unshaped." In *The Golden Notebook*, she catches at least some of the complexity. Inevitably, a discussion of it makes it sound like a formal exploration, but how can one convey its richness, its characters (actresses, doctors, Africans, politicians, African politicians, housewives, children, media men, journalists, writers, lorry drivers, business men, all known, all seen first hand), its dense profusion of human interest? Intellectually, it is a masterpiece: but is has none of the aridity of an intellectual construction. It grows out of life.

The Golden Notebook has, of course, been seen as a book about Women's Liberation, and with good cause. The title of the novel-within-a-novel, "Free Women," indicates that this is at least one of her subjects. How could it not be? It goes without saying that Doris Lessing is in favor of the liberation of women and thinks that it has not yet come about. She has worked hard for her own liberty, and says that women who allow themselves to be bullied by men who call them "unfeminine" and "castrating" deserve all they get. She is politically aware of the implications of being a woman writer: one of the reasons why Martha Quest is drawn to Marxism is because it, at least in theory, gives the woman a serious role, attacks the nuclear family, and allows Martha to act. Anna, similarly, at one point is described as "living on behalf of all women." And she insists to her analyst that she is living the kind of life women have never lived before: she rejects the view that she is one of a great line of women stretching into the past, who have insisted on sexual freedom, who have been artist-women. She feels herself to be new, to be in a new situation. *The Golden Notebook*, with its insistence on freedom, its moments of aggression, its attacks on the masculine world — there is a fine scene where all the women leave a lecture on the orgasm of the swan, another where they listen incredulously to a man trying to explain a sexual failure in terms of the size of the sexual organ — is inevitably a document in the history of liberation, but it was in a sense published too early, for its tone is not at all explanatory: it assumes its readers will know what is meant. The movement came later. Doris Lessing says, "Some books are not read in the right way because they have skipped a stage of opinion, assume a crystallization of information in society which had not yet taken place. This book was written as if the attitudes that have been created by the Women's Liberation movements already existed. . . . Things have changed very fast."

In fact, what happened was that she got there first, once more prophetic, but this time didn't realize it. (She does now see the subject as relatively unimportant: The doom she prophesies is so general that when it arrives it won't matter much which sex one happens to be.) She knew it was new, but thought that other people were more with her than they were. From 1950 onwards, she has been successful, courted, attractive, free: and therefore she has been able to report on an area of life that is largely unrecorded. She writes about men, about the con-men of the art world, the film men, the journalists, with wit and hatred; she destroys their sexual dignity, their unspoken assumptions, their maneuvers, with an entirely justifiable indignation. Perhaps few women had been exposed as she had to such solicitations, but if they had, they had politely kept their mouths shut. She tells the truth, and I remember the sense of shock I felt when I first read *The Golden Notebook*, and found a description of Anna, courted by a film man, professionally and of course along with the package deal, sexually: Anna rejects him, firmly but civilly, and there is a moment of "pure hatred" between them. Yes, exactly so: what a liberating realization, to know that it is, precisely, hatred that one feels, and that one feels it rightly. . . .

The next novel, after *The Golden Notebook*, was Book Four of *Children of Violence*, *Landlocked*, which is perhaps the least satisfactory volume of the sequence, for its traditional narrative seems to hamper the direction of the power in the book. Or maybe one feels that more with hindsight, after reading *The Four-Gated City*. As already described, this is a very curious genre of book, and an extremely long one. On one level, it is a documentary account of English life from 1945 to the end of the '60s, and it records everything: political movements, fashions, educational theories, trends in food and books and psychoanalysis. Historically, everything is placed and accurate: for instance, Doris Lessing describes the nuances of behavior of journalists towards the people they interview in terms of whether the interview took place before or after the creation of the Press Council (1953). This is the kind of realism, the type of observation of which Angus Wilson or Arnold Bennett or Flaubert would have been proud. And yet what would they make of the other regions of her novel?

Most of the characters in this volume are new, though a few visit from the past, and of the new ones, the most important are Mark, the writer, and his wife, Lynda. They represent the old world, Bloomsbury, and live in an old house which is the past. Martha becomes Mark's secretary, Lynda, Mark's wife, is mad: she has been ruined by drugs and doctors. She lives in the basement with a mad friend, and moves into and out of madness. Martha at times sleeps with Mark, at times not. They are a sort of *ménage à trois*, and there are children which come and go, and grow up during the thirty year time-span of the action. Martha has stopped shaking herself free, she has settled, she has become loyal. But she has not settled into security, for like Lynda she too voyages into madness. She and Lynda become very close, they exchange thoughts. They can read what other people are thinking. They dabble in the esoteric, in science fiction: they believe in extra-sensory perception (if one can put it like that). And it emerges that Lynda is not mad at all, that on the contrary she has always been able to hear too much, and that doctors have been for years destroying and immobilizing the most gifted people, labelling them as schizoids and paranoids. . . .

It is clear that she had moved into dangerous territory in more ways than one. There are few writers who would dare to risk such subject matter. Science fiction is all right now: it has become respectable: Vonnegut is chic. And it is perfectly all right for R. D. Laing to criticize the conventional means of treating schizophrenics. It is also all right for those young people who choose to reject Western science and technology to read Oriental mystics and reject the processes of rational thought, because everybody knows that most of them are not serious. What is really alarming is Doris Lessing's combination of mental qualities. On one level, she describes mystical experience, spiritual experience, never drug-induced, but natural. (Martha and Lynda see drugs as the weapon of the enemy.) On another level, she criticizes with very high practical intelligence the way that doctors manipulate their sick patients, the organization of hospitals, the social attitudes towards the sick. Martha and Lynda give dinner parties and attend political rallies: they also spend weeks in the basement beating their heads and scrabbling with bloody fingertips along the wall. They worry about the education of the children, they feed their cats, they run a large household, they are sometimes interested in clothes and sometimes not, they search, they wait, they foresee the end of England. They are, though mad, complete.

Doris Lessing's vision of the future can be rejected, but not for lacking credibility or documentation. She has read books and newspapers and has known well several sections of society; she has recorded the facts and has not missed out the evidence for her case. Her political experience shows in everything she writes. Mary Ellman, in her book, *Thinking About Women*, says that nowadays we expect poets and novelists to be personal, ignorant, intimate, self-confessing, though occasionally a writer (more often a poet) will adopt the prophetic stance. But, she says, nobody wants to play Prime Minister. And this is precisely what is so important and significant about Doris Lessing. She is personal: she was one of the first women to write truthfully about sex. (Her description of why Martha feels unhappy sleeping with a man she loves while married to a husband she does not love, and whom she married for his political convenience, is masterly and unprecedented.) She is also prophetic, but not in a vague, exhortatory, passionate mode. Her judgments are practical, based on sound observation, and her grasp of what is actually happening in the world is ministerial. She is one of the very few novelists who have refused to believe that the world is too complicated to understand. She sees the Catastrophe in technological terms, pointing to various accidental prece-

dents off the South Coast of Spain, and in the Porton nerve gas laborato-
ries. She offers explanations for the final breakdown of Britain, describing
in all too plausible detail the growth of violence, the breakdown in
communications, the gradual collapse of machinery, the increasing vacil-
lations and dictatorial spasms of government, the declining health of the
population, the computerized data banks. The true explanation for the
poisoning of Britain is never given: some believe it was caused by
radioactive material from a sunk Russian submarine, some say a Chinese
pilot in a plane full of nuclear devices crashlanded in Britain, some think a
wing of Porton caught fire, or that Aldenmaston had been blown up, or
that vandals were releasing gas from the North Sea. The point is that we
never see these as the speculation of a writer sunk in mysticism, turning
her back upon the world. Nor are any of her suggestions, alas, inherently
implausible. Her devoted application to the understanding of life is not
likely to produce improbable or irrelevant conclusions.

What needs to be said, in short, is that we cannot afford to write off
the things that Doris Lessing has to say. Like Cassandra, she is probably
right and like Cassandra there is a risk that she will be ignored.

And They All Lived Unhappily
Ever After
Rebecca West*

. . . This splendid figure [Doris Lessing] may be styled the English
George Sand. Like her, Mrs. Lessing would try anything twice, and her
strength is as the strength of ten. . . . She is not as elegant a writer as her
counterpart . . . But both women have the same Mississippian flow of
being which it is hardly possible to separate into the intellectual and the
physical; this forceful tide bears with it whatever useful material happens
to be lying about on the territory it washes, and bears it on to the wide
estuary and shoreless sea of our general culture. . . .

It is a culminating disappointment that such a formidable woman,
who can carry about with her such a heavy intellectual satchel and has
conquered the difficulties of self-support, plainly cannot believe that
women can hope for satisfactory sexual lives. That, indeed, she seems to
regard as the most depressing feature of the modern world. The general
impression given in most of her books is that men reject women for reasons
they cannot understand, terminating sexual relationships which appeared
to be satisfactory and companionship which they appeared to enjoy. It is
not that all of these women expected to be given financial support or a
place in society, for many could provide those requirements for them-

*From the Times Literary Supplement 3777 (26 July 1974):779.

selves, and it might be apparent to all of them that some men could provide neither. It is not even that all of the women expected the commitment of the man to a permanent relationship. Rather is it that a certain scene is re-enacted, which might take this form: The man comes into the kitchen, suffused for her by a delightful atmosphere caused by recent embraces and continuing friendship, and says, "Please cut me some bread and butter, remembering that I like the bread very thin and the butter very thick." But he gives her no time to sharpen the bread knife, so the bread is rather thick, and he comments on this though he is silent about the abundance of butter. The only explanation of this behavior (irrational if only because of his declared liking for butter) is that men do not like women. But perhaps the last phrase should be written "that men do not like." It is possible that men are deficient in the capacity for love, and that women too suffer from the same deficiency, but had to hide it in the days of their subordination, and would in any case be least likely to exercise it in their times of sexual flowering, when things were going best for them. But there are account-books which can never be balanced. All we can do to dam this source of suffering is to love more and hate less. . . .

Briefing for a Descent into Hell
Joan Didion*

To read a great deal of Doris Lessing over a short span of time is to feel the original hound of heaven has commandeered the attic. She holds the mind's other guests in ardent contempt. She appears for meals only to dismiss the household's own preoccupations with writing well as decadent. For more than twenty years now she has been registering, in a torrent of fiction that increasingly seems conceived in a stubborn rage against the very idea of fiction, every tremor along her emotional fault system, every slippage in her self-education. *Look here*, she is forever demanding, a missionary devoid of any but the most didactic irony: *the Communist party is not the answer. There is a life beyond vaginal orgasm. St. John of the Cross was not as dotty as certain Anglicans would have had you believe.* She comes hard to ideas, and, once she has collared one, worries it with Victorian doggedness.

That she is a writer of considerable native power, a "natural" writer in the Dreiserian mold, someone who can close her eyes and "give" a situation by the sheer force of her emotional energy, seems almost a stain on her conscience. She views her real gift for fiction much as she views her

*From the *New York Times*, 14 March 1971, pp. 1, 38, 39. © 1971 by the New York Times Co. Reprinted by permission.

own biology, another trick to entrap her. She does not want to "write well." Her leaden disregard for even the simplest rhythms of language, her arrogantly bad ear for dialogue — all of that is beside her own point. More and more Mrs. Lessing writes exclusively in the service of immediate cosmic reform: she wants to write, as the writer Anna in *The Golden Notebook* wanted to write, only to "create a new way of looking at life."

Her new novel, *Briefing for a Descent Into Hell,* is entirely a novel of "ideas," not a novel about the play of ideas in the lives of certain characters but a novel in which the characters exist only as markers in the presentation of an idea. The situation is this: a well-dressed but disheveled man is found wandering, an amnesiac, on the embankment near the Waterloo Bridge in London. He is taken by the police to a psychiatric hospital where, in the face of total indifference on his part, attempts are made to identify him. He is Charles Watkins, a professor of classics at Cambridge. Husband to Felicity, once his student. Father of Felicity's two sons. Father of a third son by Constance, again his student. An authority in his field, an occasional lecturer on more general topics. Lately a stammerer. Lately prone to bad evenings during which he condemns not only his own but all academic disciplines as "pigswill." A 50-year-old man who finally cracks, and in cracking personifies Mrs. Lessing's conviction that "the millions who have cracked" are "making cracks where the light could shine through at last." For of course the "nonsense" that Charles Watkins talks in the hospital makes, to the reader although not to the doctors, unmistakable "sense."

In fact so pronounced is his acumen about the inner reality of those around him that much of the time *Briefing for a Descent Into Hell* reads like a selective case study from an R. D. Laing book. The reality Charles Watkins describes is familiar to anyone who has ever had a high fever, or been exhausted to the point of breaking, or is just on the whole only marginally engaged in the dailiness of life. He experiences the loss of ego, the apprehension of the cellular nature of all matter, the "oneness" of things that seems always to lie just past the edge of controlled conscious thought. He hallucinates, or "remembers," the nature of the universe. He "remembers" — or is on the verge of remembering, before electroshock obliterates the memory and returns him to "sanity" — something very like a "briefing" for life on earth.

The details of this briefing are filled in by Mrs. Lessing, only too relieved to abandon the strain of creating character and slip into her own rather more exhortative voice. Imagine an interplanetary conference, convened on Venus to discuss once again the problem of the self-destructive planet Earth. (The fancy that extraterrestrial life is by definition of a higher order than our own is one that soothes all children, and many writers.) The procedure is this: certain superior beings descend to earth brainprinted with the task of arousing the planet to its folly. These emissaries have, once on Earth, no memory of their more enlightened life.

They wake slowly to their mission. They recognize one another only vaguely, and do not remember why. We are to understand, of course, that Charles Watkins is among those who have made the Descent, whether literal or metaphorical, and is now, for just so long as he can resist therapy, awake. This is the initial revelation in the book, and it is also the only one.

Even given Mrs. Lessing's tendency to confront all ideas tabula rasa, we are dealing here with less than astonishing stuff. The idea that there is sanity in insanity, that truth lies somewhere on the far side of madness, informs not only a considerable spread of Western literature but also, so commonly is it now held, an entire generation's experiment with hallucinogens. Most of Mrs. Lessing's thoughts about the cultural definition of insanity reflect or run parallel to those of Laing, and yet the idea was already so prevalent that Laing cannot even be said to have popularized it: his innovation was only to have taken it out of the realm of instinctive knowledge and into the limited context of psychiatric therapy. Although Mrs. Lessing apparently thought the content of *Briefing for a Descent Into Hell* so startling that she was impelled to add an explanatory afterword, a two-page parable about the ignorance of certain psychiatrists at large London teaching hospitals, she has herself dealt before with this very material. In *The Golden Notebook* Anna makes this note for a story: "A man whose 'sense of reality' has gone; and because of it, has a deeper sense of reality than 'normal' people." By the time Mrs. Lessing finished *The Four-Gated City* she had refined the proposition: Lynda Coldridge's deeper sense of reality is not the result of but the definition of her madness. So laboriously is this notion developed in the closing three hundred pages of *The Four-Gated City* that one would have thought Mrs. Lessing had more or less exhausted its literary possibilities.

But she is no longer interested in literary possibilities, which is where we strike the faultline. "If I saw it in terms of an artistic problem, then it'd be easy, wouldn't it," Anna tells her friend Molly in *The Golden Notebook* as explanation of her disinclination to write another book. "We could have ever such intelligent chats about the modern novel." This strikes one as a little on the easy side, even if one is willing to overlook Anna's later assertion that she cannot write because "a Chinese peasant" is looking over her shoulder. ("Or one of Castro's guerrilla fighters. Or an Algerian fighting in the F.L.N.") *Madame Bovary* told us more about bourgeois life than several generations of Marxists have, but there does not seem much doubt that Flaubert saw it as an artistic problem.

That Mrs. Lessing does not suggests her particular dilemma. What we are witnessing here is a writer undergoing a profound and continuing culture shock, a woman of determinedly utopian and distinctly teleological bent assaulted at every turn by fresh evidence that the world is not exactly any closer to a happy ending. And, because such is the particular quality of her mind, she is compelled in the face of this evidence to look even more frantically for the final cause, the unambiguous answer.

In the beginning her search was less frenzied. She came out of Southern Rhodesia imprinted ineradicably by precisely the kind of rigid agrarian world that most easily makes storytellers of its exiled children. What British Africa gave her, beside those images of a sky so empty and a society so inflexible as to make the slightest tremor in either worth remarking upon, was a way of perceiving the rest of her life: for a long time to come she could interpret all she saw in terms of "injustice," not merely the injustice of white man to black, of colonizer to colonized, but the more general injustices of class and most particularly of sex. She grew up knowing not only what hard frontiers do to women but what women then do to the men who keep them there. She could hear in all her memories that "voice of the suffering female" passed on from mothers to daughters in a chain broken only at great cost.

Of those memories she wrote a first novel *The Grass is Singing*, entirely traditional in its conventions. Reality was *there*, waiting to be observed by an omniscient third person. *The Grass is Singing* was neat in its construction, relatively scrupulous in its maintenance of tone, predicated upon a world of constants. Its characters moved through that world unconscious of knowledge shared by author and reader. The novel was, in brief and not surprisingly, everything Mrs. Lessing was to reject as "false" and "evasive" by the time she wrote *The Golden Notebook*. . .

The sheer will, the granitic ambitiousness of *The Golden Notebook* overrides everything else about it. Great raw hunks of undigested experience, unedited transcripts of what happened between Molly and her son today, overwhelming memories and rejections of those memories as sentimental, the fracturing of a sensibility beginning for the first time to doubt its perceptions: all of it runs out of the teller's mind and into the reader's with deliberate disregard for the nature of the words in between. The teller creates "characters" and "scenes" only to deny their validity. She berates herself for clinging to the "certainty" of her memories in the face of the general uncertainty. Mrs. Lessing looms through *The Golden Notebook* as a woman driven by doubts not only about what to tell but about the validity of telling it at all.

Yet she continued to write, and to write fiction. Not until towards the end of the five-volume "Children of Violence" series did one sense a weakening of that compulsion to remember, and a metastasis of that cognitive frenzy for answers. She had seen, by then, a great deal go, had seized a great many answers and lost them. Organized politics went early. Freudian determinism seemed incompatible. The Africa of her memory was another country. The voice she felt most deeply, that of women trying to define their relationships to each other and to men, first went shrill and then, appropriated by and reduced to a "Movement," slipped below the range of her attention. She has been betrayed by all those answers and more, and yet, increasingly possessed, her only response is to look for another. That she is scarcely alone in this possession is what lends her quest its great interest: the impulse to final solutions has been not only her dilemma but the guiding delusion of her time. It is not an impulse I hold high, but there is something finally very moving about Mrs. Lessing's tenacity.

The Summer before the Dark

Everywoman out of Love?

Erica Jong*

A really good book resists reviewing, and *The Summer Before the Dark* is a really good book. . . . For all her occasional polemicism, Doris Lessing has no program for womankind nor for civilization. Her characters are not "little engines of cause and effect"; "they wander in the dark woods of their destiny"—to borrow two of my favorite phrases from D. H. Lawrence's "The Novel and the Feelings." Lessing has, in fact, a great deal in common with Lawrence. The same rigorously moral preoccupations, the same understanding that sexual and political revolution are inseparable, the same concern for the masks women wear in a male-dominated culture. She also has certain faults in common with Lawrence, particularly her tendencies toward didacticism and overwriting. Yet it is always clear while reading her that one is in contact with a first-rate mind. . . .

The Summer Before the Dark has been compared to *The Golden Notebook* because the ostensible subjects of both books are the same: the dilemmas of intelligent women in a world made by and for men. Yet, in the straightforwardness of its narrative, *The Summer Before the Dark* reminds me much more of Lessing's earlier Martha Quest novels. *The Golden Notebook* and *The Four-Gated City* are dense, long, layered books: books within books. *The Summer Before the Dark* whizzes by in a mere 273 pages. Similarly, its heroine, Kate Brown, seems far plainer and less obsessive than either Anna Wulf or Martha Quest. She is a "serviceable woman"; a machine for translation; "a skilled parrot"; "a fluent parrot with maternal inclinations"; a woman with "the sympathetic eyes of a loving spaniel." Above all, she is a mother, a wife, a nurse, a nanny. So it is, in a way, even more astonishing when this women becomes ill, enraged, wasted, and is stripped of her masks. One expects such existential extremes from an Anna Wulf or a Martha Quest. One does not expect them from pretty, "serviceable" Kate Brown.

And perhaps that is exactly Lessing's point. Or one of them.

It is clear from the very start of the book that Kate Brown is a kind of

*From *Partisan Review*, 40 (1973):500–503. Reprinted with permission of *Partisan Review*.

mid-twentieth-century Everywoman. "A woman stood. . . ." the book begins; and that phrase is echoed at crucial times throughout the narrative. Kate Brown is "a woman." Her very name is faceless, universal, blank. Lessing intends her as Everywoman . . . and a main point of hers seems to be that at this moment in history, even the pretty, serviceable Kate Browns of this world are cracking up. Even they cannot make sense of all the contradictions of their lives.

Raised to be maternal, they have to face the flight of their grown children. Raised to believe in love as a kind of substitute religion, they have to face its disintegration. Raised to be nurturant, they have to face the fact that most of the world's children are starving. Raised to believe in progress, reform, socialism, they have to face the resurgence of authoritarianism. Raised to give their lives to their families, they have to face the fact that families are obsolete.

Most of the action of the novel is depicted in a detached third person narrative which resembles the telling of a fable or parable. The writing is graceful (especially compared to *The Golden Notebook*), slightly ironic, and from Kate's point of view. She is a tireless and precise observer of everyone, including herself. Yet during the first part of the book, she seemed such a universal type that she was slightly unreal to me. . . . The power of the story became irresistible toward the end, however, when Kate, back in London and living with a young woman named Maureen, engages in endless conversations about marriage, motherhood, growing older. These seemed to me the most convincing scenes in the book: the dialogue not only accurate but profound; not only convincing for these two particular characters but for all of us. . . . And in these dialogues, Lessing succeeds brilliantly at stating the dilemmas of contemporary humanity. They are not resolved, of course. Whether Kate's choice of a quarter century of childbearing and wifehood was "right" or "wrong" is something neither Kate nor Lessing can tell us. Whether Maureen ought to imitate Kate or rebel is also not resolved — either by the characters or the author. Kate does not know whether her choice was "right" and so she cannot tell Maureen. Lessing certainly does not know, though she implies, by the resolution of Kate's recurrent dream about a dying seal, that the maternal virtues Kate exemplifies have some life-giving power after all. But the very value of life-giving is uncertain in a world where too many babies are born and many must die. The maternal gifts which Kate has built her life around are obsolete, and Lessing knows this. Kate also knows it at the end; but what is she to do? She has been prepared for nothing else. Her needs and the world's needs are out of step. And Maureen, though twenty-five years younger, suffers the same discontinuity between her emotions and the outer reality. Maureen's habit of wearing old clothes ("putting on the clothes of the circumscribed women of the past") is a perfect metaphor for this. A twentieth-century girl who loathes the idea of being like her mother, she nevertheless longs for the clothes of a Jane

Austen heroine and the emotions which go with them. Maureen is no less obsolete than Kate.

It would be easy and glib for a reviewer to see this as "the dilemma of modern woman" and thus put all Lessing's disturbing observations about contemporary society at arm's length. "Woman's novel," like "Black novel," is simply one more way of saying, "That doesn't apply to me." And certainly many reviewers (even those who raved about this book) put the limiting adjective "woman's" around it and tried to slink away. But, of course, Lessing is smarter than they are. She is no more talking only about women than Ralph Ellison is talking only about blacks in *Invisible Man*. Lessing knows that in women, the conditions of alienation, waste of resources, discontinuity between emotions and "reality," are simply more visible and painful. But the problems themselves are those of all of us. Overpopulation and starvation, the obsolescence of the family and the resurgence of authoritarianism are not "women's problems" — comfortable though it may be to see them that way.

The feminist publishing boom has provided its own built-in evasions. That freak show of women over there, that fad, that gaggle of geese — is not simply fifty-three percent of humanity and not simply a passing fancy. When having and raising babies is no longer honorific and necessary, then both sexes have to change. A book that considers such changes is not "women's fiction" but people's fiction. Kate Brown is not Everywoman; she is everyone.

Canopus in Argos: Archives

Paradise Regained

Gore Vidal*

. . . Although Doris Lessing has more in common with George Eliot than she has with any contemporary serious-novelist, she is not always above solemnity, as opposed to mere seriousness. Somewhat solemnly, Lessing tells us in the preface to her new novel *Shikasta* that there may indeed be something wrong with the way that novels are currently being written. She appears not to be drawn to the autonomous word-structure. On the other hand, she is an old-fashioned moralist. This means that she is inclined to take very seriously the quotidian. The deep — as opposed to strip — mining of the truly moral relationship seems to me to be her territory. I say seems because I have come to Lessing's work late. I began to read her with *Memoirs of a Survivor*, and now, with *Shikasta*, I have followed her into the realms of science fiction where she is making a continuum all her own somewhere between John Milton and L. Ron Hubbard.

Lessing tells us that, originally, she thought that she might make a single volume out of certain themes from the Old Testament (source of so much of our dreaming and bad behavior) but that she is now launched on a series of fables about interplanetary dominations and powers. "I feel as if I have been set free both to be as experimental as I like, and as traditional." I'm not sure what she means by "experimental" and "traditional." At best, Lessing's prose is solid and slow and a bit flat-footed. She is an entirely "traditional" prose writer. I suspect that she did not want to use the word "imaginative," a taboo word nowadays, and so she wrote "experimental."

In any case, like the splendid *Memoirs of a Survivor*, *Shikasta* is the work of a formidable imagination. Lessing can make up things that appear to be real, which is what storytelling is all about. But she has been sufficiently influenced by serious-writing to feel a need to apologize. "It is by now commonplace to say that novelists everywhere are breaking the bonds of the realistic novel because what we all see around us becomes daily wilder, more fantastic, incredible. . . . The old 'realistic' novel is

*From the *New York Review of Books*, 30 December 1979, pp. 3–4. Reprinted with permission from the *New York Review of Books*. © 1979 by Nyrev, Inc.

being changed, too, because of influences from that genre loosely described as space fiction." Actually, I have seen no very vivid sign of this
influence and I don't suppose that she has either. But it is not unusual for a
writer to regard his own new turning as a highway suddenly perceived by
all, and soon to be crowded with other pilgrims en route to the City on
the Hill.

If this book has any recent precursor, it is Kurt Vonnegut, Jr. Lessing
has praised him elsewhere: "Vonnegut is moral in an old-fashioned way
. . . he has made nonsense of the little categories, the unnatural divisions
into 'real' literature and the rest, because he is comic and sad at once,
because his painful seriousness is never solemn. Vonnegut is unique among
us; and these same qualities account for the way a few academics still try
to patronize him. . . ."

Lessing is even more influenced by the Old Testament. "It is our habit
to dismiss the Old Testament altogether because Jehovah, or Jahve, does
not think or behave like a social worker." So much for JC, doer of good and
eventual scientist. But Lessing's point is well taken. Because the Old
Testament's lurid tales of a furious god form a background to Jesus' "good
news," to Mohammed's "recitations," to the Jewish ethical sense, those
bloody tales still retain an extraordinary mythic power, last demonstrated
in full force by Milton.

In a sense, Lessing's *Shikasta* is a return more to the spirit (not, alas,
the language) of Milton than to that of Genesis. But Lessing goes Milton
one better, or worse. Milton was a dualist. Lucifer blazes as the son of
morning; and the Godhead blazes, too. Their agon is terrific. Although
Lessing deals with opposites, she tends to unitarianism. She is filled with
the spirit of the Sufis, and if there is one thing that makes me more nervous
than a Jungian it is a Sufi. Lessing believes that it is possible "to 'plug in' to
an overmind, or Ur-mind, or unconscious, or what you will, and that this
accounts for a great many improbabilities and "coincidences." She does
indeed plug in; and *Shikasta* is certainly rich with improbabilities and
"coincidences." Elsewhere ("In the World, Not of It"),[1] Lessing has
expressed her admiration for one Idries Shah, a busy contemporary
purveyor of Sufism (from the Arab word *suf*, meaning wool . . . the
costume for ascetics).

Idries Shah has been characterized in the pages of this journal[2] as the
author of works that are replete with "constant errors of fact, slovenly and
inaccurate translations, even the misspelling of Oriental names and words.
In place of scholarship we are asked to accept a muddle of platitudes,
irrelevancies, and plain mumbo-jumbo." Lessing very much admires Idries
Shah and the woolly ones, and she quotes with approval from Idries Shah's
The Dermis Probe in which *he* quotes from M. Gauquelin's *The Cosmic
Clocks*. "An astonishing parallel to the Sufi insistence on the relatively
greater power of subtle communication to affect man, is found in scientific
work which shows that all living things, including man, are 'incredibly

sensitive to waves of extraordinarily weak energy — when more robust influences are excluded.' " This last quotation within a quotation is the theme of *Shikasta*.

It is Lessing's conceit that a benign and highly advanced galactic civilization, centered on Canopus, is sending out harmonious waves hither and yon, rather like Milton's god before Lucifer got bored. Canopus lives in harmony with another galactic empire named Sirius. Once upon a time warp, the two fought a Great War but now all is serene between the galaxies. I can't come up with the Old Testament parallel on that one. Is Canopus Heaven versus Sirius's Chaos? Anyway, the evil planet Shammat in the galactic empire of Puttiora turns out to be our old friend Lucifer or Satan or Lord of the Flies, and the planet Shikasta (that's us) is a battleground between the harmonious vibes of Canopus and the wicked vibes of Shammat which are constantly bombarding our planet. In the end, Lucifer is hurled howling into that place where he prefers to reign and all is harmony with god's chilluns. Lessing rather lacks negative capability. Where Milton's Lucifer is a joy to contemplate, Lessing's Shammat is a drag whose planetary agents sound like a cross between Tolkien's monster and Sir Lew Grade.

Lessing' narrative devices are nothing if not elaborate. Apparently, the Canopian harmonious future resembles nothing so much as an English Department that has somehow made an accommodation to share its "facilities" with the Bureau of Indian Affairs. The book's title page is daunting: "Canopus in Argos: Archives" at the top. Then "Re: Colonised Planet 5" (as I type this, I realize that I've been misreading "Re: Colonised" as recolonised); then "Shikasta"; then "Personal, Psychological, Historical Documents Relating to Visit by JOHOR (George Sherban) Emissary (Grade 9) 87th of the Period of the Last Days." At the bottom of the page, one's eye is suddenly delighted by the homely phrase "Alfred A. Knopf New York 1979." There is not much music in Lessing spheres.

Like the Archangel Raphael, Johor travels through Shikasta's time. The planet's first cities were so constructed that transmitters on Canopus could send out benign waves of force; as a result, the local population (trained by kindly giants) were happy and frolicsome. "Canopus was able to feed Shikasta with a rich and vigorous air, which kept everyone safe and healthy, and above all, made them love each other. . . . This supply of finer air had a name. It was called SOWF — the substance-of-we-feeling — I had of course spent time and effort in working out an easily memorable syllable." Of course. But the SOWF is cut off. The cities of the plain are blasted. The Degenerative Disease begins and the race suffers from "grandiosities and pomps," short life spans, bad temper. The Degenerative Disease is Lessing's equivalent for that original sin which befell man when Eve bit on the apple.

There is a certain amount of fun to be had in Johor's tour of human history. He is busy as a bee trying to contain the evil influence of

Shammat, and Lessing not only brings us up to date but beyond: the Chinese will occupy Europe fairly soon. Lessing is a master of the eschatological style and *Memoirs of a Survivor* is a masterpiece of that genre. But where the earlier book dealt with a very real London in a most credible terminal state, *Shikasta* is never quite real enough. At times the plodding style does make things believable, but then reality slips away . . . too little SOWF, perhaps. Nevertheless, Lessing is plainly enjoying herself and the reader can share in that enjoyment a good deal of the time. But, finally, she lacks the peculiar ability to create alternative worlds. For instance, she invents for the human dead a limbo she calls Zone 6. This shadowy place is a cross between Homer's Hades and the Zoroastrian concept of that place where eternal souls hover about, waiting to be born. Lessing's descriptions of the undead dead are often very fine but when one compares her invention with Ursula Le Guin's somewhat similar land of the dead in the *Earthsea* trilogy, one is aware that Le Guin's darkness is darker, her coldness colder, her shadows more dense and stranger.

Lessing's affinity for the Old Testament combined with the woolliness of latter-day Sufism has got her into something of a philosophical muddle. Without the idea of free will, the human race is of no interest at all; certainly, without the idea of free will there can be no literature. To watch Milton's Lucifer serenely overthrow the controlling intelligence of his writerly creator is an awesome thing. But nothing like this happens in Lessing's work. From the moment of creation, Lessing's Shikastans are programmed by outside forces — sometimes benign, sometimes malign. They themselves are entirely passive. There is no Prometheus; there is not even an Eve. The fact that in the course of a very long book Lessing has not managed to create a character of the slightest interest is the result not so much of any failure in her considerable art as it is a sign that she has surrendered her mind to SOWF, or to the woollies, or to the Jealous God.

Obviously, there is a case to be made for predetermination or predestination or let-us-now-praise B. F. Skinner. Lessing herself might well argue that the seemingly inexorable DNA code is a form of genetic programming that could well be equated with Canopus's intervention and that, in either case, our puny lives are so many interchangeable tropisms, responding to outside stimuli. But I think that the human case is more interesting than that. The fact that no religion has been able to give a satisfactory reason for the existence of evil has certainly kept human beings on their toes during the brief respites that we are allowed between those ages of faith which can always be counted upon to create that we-state which seems so much to intrigue Lessing and her woollies, a condition best described by the most sinister of all Latin tags, *e pluribus unum.*

Ultimately, *Shikasta* is not so much a fable of the human will in opposition to a god who has wronged the fire-seeker as it is a fairy tale about good and bad extraterrestrial forces who take some obscure pleasure in manipulating a passive ant-like human race. Needless to say, Doris

Lessing is not the first to incline to this "religion." In fact, she has considerable competition from a living prophet whose powerful mind has envisaged a race of god-like Thetans who once lived among us; they, too, overflowed with SOWF; then they went away. But all is not lost. The living prophet has told us their story. At first he wrote a science fiction novel, and bad people scoffed. But he was not dismayed. He knew that he could save us, bring back the wisdom of the Thetans, "clear" us of badness. He created a second holy book, *Dianetics*. Today he is the sole proprietor of the Church of Scientology. Doris Lessing would do well to abandon the woolly Idries Shah in favor of Mr. L. Ron Hubbard, who has already blazed that trail where now she trods — treads? — trods.

Notes

1. Reprinted in *A Small Personal Voice* (Knopf, 1974).
2. L. P. Elwell-Sutton, *The New York Review of Books*, July 2, 1970.

The Spacing Out of Doris Lessing John Leonard*

The question: Why does Doris Lessing — one of the half-dozen most interesting minds to have chosen to write fiction in English in this century — insist on propagating books that confound and dismay her loyal readers? The answer: She intends to confound and dismay.

The Making of the Representative for Planet 8, the fourth in her cycle of "visionary novels," is about a glacier. The glacier eats up Planet 8. Until the coming of the glacier, the brown-skinned, black-eyed vegetarian peoples of Planet 8 had known nothing but color and warmth, "the many blues of the sky, the infinite greens of the foliage, the reds and browns of our earth, mountains shining with pyrites and quartz, the dazzle of water and of sun." Then the water slows with cold, "and on its surface it wrinkles as it moves, or even, sometimes, makes plates," and the sun goes blind in the wind-whipped snow. It is closing time in the gardens of Arcady. The horned beasts will turn north to die, icy meat.

As a sort of ecological thriller, *The Making* is splendid. If the sun in Mrs. Lessing's African stories was fixed on emptiness, the ice on Planet 8 is intimate. It numbs and consoles. It presses and smothers. It is prism and preservative. It cracks the black wall and stoppers the sacred lake. (Mrs. Lessing has been partial to the symbolic ever since she abandoned realism

*From the *New York Times Book Review*, 7 February 1982, pp 1; 34; 35. © 1982 by The New York Times Co. Reprinted by permission.

on page 353 of *The Four Gated City*, when Martha Quest went through the "door" into mystical razzmatazz.) And who wouldn't be saddened by the new ponderous beasts that evolve and die in such a winter palace? . . .

Unfortunately, the people on Planet 8 — gray-faced from meat eating, stuporous from cold, estranged from "congruity," huddled half hibernating and half homicidal under the hides of behemoths — are less compelling than the weather. They do not mate, they don't much talk, and Mrs. Lessing can't be bothered to differentiate among them except by pointing to the roles they play in a hazy, clan-based social order: the teacher, the healer, the keeper of the orchards, and the teller of stories and singer of songs, who is Doeg, the "representative."

Mrs. Lessing is no longer very interested in people. She has come to feel that individuality is a "degenerative disease." The "archeologist" of human relations, so celebrated by Irving Howe in his review of *The Golden Notebook*, has gone intergalactic. The "seismograph" that registered, according to Joan Didion in her review of *Briefing for a Descent Into Hell*, every tremor along our "emotional fault-system" wants now to be an ear on evolution. Nor are we likely to hear any more from her on racism, capitalism, colonialism, Marxism, sexism, psychoanalysis, science and technology. Having eaten too many *-isms*, she is still hungry. She has gone *beyond* — and transcended.

She explains some of herself in an afterword to *The Making*. (Ever since she gave up on realism, she has been explaining herself in prefaces and afterwords, as if to bully the reader.) She first heard about Robert Falcon Scott's two expeditions to Antarctica when she was a child. Scott's second party froze to death, and she said to her mother, "Anyway, they were all in the dying business." Fifty years later, she wonders how extreme situations — the bad weather of the mind — alter "social processes." What is the glacier trying to teach the garden?

This, as we shall see, is a little disingenuous, but to understand what happens to Planet 8 we must first consult the cosmology Mrs. Lessing has elaborated in *Shikasta, The Marriages of* [sic] *Zones Three, Four, and Five"* and *The Sirian Experiments*, the previous three volumes of her cycle. We are asked by this cosmology to believe that earthlings have been watched over and trifled with for millions of years by three separate galactic empires. (In a preface to *The Sirian Experiments*, Mrs. Lessing declared her faith in Unidentified Flying Objects.) The benign and androgynous Canopeans, the imperialistic and anxiety-ridden Sirians and the brutish Shammats all muck around in our gene pool.

We used to be a garden, named Rohanda. Then, by a tilt of the axis, we went out of "alignment," turning off the faucet of SOWF, or "substance-of-the[sic]-we-feeling," and became Shikasta, after which famine, pestilence, nuclear destruction and unkindness to animals ensued. The Canopeans, your basic Greeks without the dualism, fiddle to bring us back into line with the harmonious and the necessary. The Sirians, technologically savvy but afflicted with "the existentials," breed to enlarge their industrial base and expand their market economy. The Shammats, who are into evil, specialize in Mongols, Aztecs and Hitlers.

As well as empires, there are zones in this busy space through which the imperial agents must pass. These zones may constitute a parallel time-dimension or the ages of the past or the stages of political and economic development. More probably, they represent spiritual states, like the Seven Valleys over which the lapwing is obliged to flap in Sufi mysticism. (We shall return to the Sufis.) Certainly Zone Two — beyond art and apples, wherein an unspecified cavorting goes on with blue air and flames — suggests the cosmic song and dance of the Persian poet Rumi.

All right: Planet 8 gets out of line before Rohanda. The Canopeans, to whom everybody listens as if to E. F. Hutton, advise Doeg that there are evolutionary advantages to being iced. If his people learn their lesson, they may be worthy of a spacelift to Rohanda and warm times again. Alas, while they are being taught to freeze to death with a Bergsonian *élan vital*, Rohanda degenerates into Shikasta. Bad luck. The next chariot of the gods has been canceled by the Canopeans.

What is Planet 8, an entire world of displaced persons, supposed to learn? About bad luck, of course, and taking the long view. Nobody takes a longer view than Mrs. Lessing since she went into space; she winks in light-years and the Olduvai Gorge is a pimple. Doeg and his colleagues are encouraged to grow up from "me" to "we." They lose their innocence, which was a kind of stupid sleepwalking. (Justice needs grief for season-ing.) They are nudged into understanding the inadequacy of reason, the futility of guilt, the terror of choice, the community of dreams, the flavor of death and the duplicity of gods. This is a lot to know, but it is not enough.

Doeg, before Mrs. Lessing is done with him, will dance with the atoms. He will ride "the wind that blows through the immense spaces that lie between electron and electron, proton and its attendants, space that cannot be filled with *nothing*, since nothing is *nothing*." He will "earn" his appreciation of all that vibrates and dazzles, the mote in the eye and the ghost in the machine, "a lattice, a grid, a mesh, a mist, where particles or movements so small we cannot observe them are held in a strict and accurate web." He will look, listen, warp and woof before spinning free of his magnetic pole, as if to swim in a gravitation as variable as chance, no longer Doeg but one of those archetypes for which Carl Jung is properly blamed.

These pages dance on our head. Anyone acquainted with the litera-ture knows that mystical passages, like detective stories and nucleic acids, follow a formula. The soul, propelled by gymnastics or mushrooms, begins a journey, usually poetic, through Enlightenment, Detachment, Amaze-ment and so on until, after some blue cavorting, it is devoured by God.

Behind the veil or under the Sephiroth Tree, "me" and "we" are All and One, a harp on which to thumb the ineffable.

It is Mrs. Lessing's fancy to press us by glacier through a microscopic web. The passage is *inside*. The atom agitating in a vacuum speaks for itself. Mrs. Lessing has spoken elsewhere for Idries Shah, the pedagogue of Sufism. We need not be experts on the conservation of energy and mass or the protocol of self-annihilation in the Absolute to realize that she marries, metaphorically, Rumi's dervish to the whirl of modern molecular physics. Idries Shah meets Erich Von Daniken, and Werner Heisenberg skyjacks a lapwing. The mind is blown.

Like, wow! This is not the Mrs. Lessing who told us everything we didn't want to know about sex and history in her African stories, her Martha on a Quest, her Anny crying Wulf; nor the commonsensical and tenacious Mrs. Lessing who was determined to pin the century down and break its arm, to make the *-isms* cry uncle; that Mrs. Lessing who grew up under empty skies in Rhodesia and lived in a London full of cats. It is not even the Mrs. Lessing who managed to pause in her mystifying to imagine a Kate Brown in *The Summer Before the Dark* and a Rachel in *Shikasta* and the wonderful Queen of Zone Three.

This is some Ur-Lessing, born in Persia and arrived at, via the disintegration of Anna's personality, at the end of *The Golden Notebook*; tempered by Mark Coldridge's dream in *The Four-Gated City* of an ancient metropolis, a clairvoyant priesthood and emancipating mutants; on the dark side of R. D. Laing with the Charles Watkins of *Briefing* for a Descent Into Hell, who knew himself to be a fragment of the consciousness of superior beings sent down from Venus to save our garden. The truth and grace of madness, the existence of a saving remnant of an Elect, the Canopean agent and the dizzy spin in and out of space and time are ideas that have been steadily gaining on her since Clancy Sigal. She seems on her trip to be in the process of junking not only traditional narrative and conventional characters but the details of feeling as well, the hard-won integrity of an "I" that suffers and conspires and is culpable. She would substitute, in her moral economy of the cosmos, states of undeveloped being.

One imagines this Ur-Lessing, androgynous like her Canopeans, listening to the whistle of the ether. One also imagines her hungry, rising like Rumi in a dervish whirl to eat zones and find God, going around the bend with Einstein. It won't do to shrug off her reinventing of biology, to comfort ourselves by thinking that Yeats believed in faeries, and Pound in funny money, and Bellow in Anthroposophy, so why not Doris Lessing and flying saucers? She has already insisted, in yet another preface, on her right to invent a universe at least as problematic as the one the physicists have tricked up with black holes, white dwarves and charmed quarks.

Besides, inside all this machinery, she is free to be as wise about evolution, agriculture, matriarchy, myth, war, slavery, decadence, human sacrifice and whales as, once upon a time, she was on contemplating the dialectic of men and women and the botch they made of their appointed days — remember that Anna was "very good at other people's marriages" — and their culture. According to Mark Coldridge: "I don't see any point in writing any more — what point has there ever been? To whom? What for?"

Nor will it do to complain that the Johors and the Ambiens of her "vision," choked up on good intentions and blank uneasiness, are "unreal." Ur-Lessing would reply, "What is real?" Or she would explain impatiently, "I've used up those realities," and type another dream.

She wants out. She is tired of our modernist mewling. One of the many sins for which the 20th century will be held accountable is that it has discouraged Mrs. Lessing. She will transport herself, no longer writing novels like a Balzac with brains but, instead, Books of Revelation, charts of the elements and their valences. I don't happen to like any of her clairvoyant priests, genetic engineers, secret agents of the orchidaceous and the condign, failed gods and certified loons, perhaps because I am lacking in the substance-of-the-we-feeling and perhaps because they remind me of a Leninist vanguard, after which the ice had a flavor of shame. That, however, may be her message. Marx and Freud, and Jesus too, let her down. Shuck determinism (the dead skin of ideas, all those minutes in a neat pile) and personality (a fabrication, infantile) and the world itself (that fist in the night).

Arthur Koestler occurs to me, although he wouldn't to Mrs. Lessing. Mr. Koestler's autobiography — *Arrow in the Blue* and *The Invisible Writing* — is, like *The Golden Notebook*, one of the sacred texts of our time. After a career which took him from Budapest to Vienna to Berlin to the Mount of Olives and Montparnasse, as an engineering student, a foreign correspondent, a science editor, a Zionist, a novelist and a Comintern agent, he discovered, in one of France's prisons during the Spanish Civil War, a "reality of the third order" and the "oceanic feeling." He now propagandizes on behalf of parapsychology.

Mrs. Lessing, after Persia and Rhodesia and the England she finished off in *The Four-Gated City*, after the Communist cell and the analyst's couch and the children of violence and the death of love, after all those poems and plays and novels on which the century was written as if on bandages at the bloody front, discovered the Sufi lapwing. She now propagandizes on behalf of our insignificance in the cosmic razzmatazz.

Mr. Koestler went by Zeppelin to the North Pole. Mrs. Lessing goes south, by dreamy door to Antarctica. Both, for a period, took Stalin, that glacier, seriously and were dismayed. Both live now in an imaginary London, outside of calendar time, bending spoons. History is, as usual, the nightmare from which they woke up, and at its wake — the death of the Enlightenment, the lie of progress — they would waltz.

With respect, I'll sit this one out. The spoon benders — and no apology is necessary to the likes of Uri Geller—let us off the hook. If "I" am not to blame for the failures of character of the individual and the culture and the species in this time and this place, and the family is not to blame, and neither is history, then nobody needs to feel guilty about the bad weather. Superior beings, dropped from a star to fish in our gene pool, will take the rap. They are the ice in our hearts.

But we bleed on the hook. Freud, behind his cigar, knew this. A year before he died, Freud was asked by Mr. Koestler whether he had ever experienced the "oceanic feeling." Freud said no, and Mr. Koestler felt sorry for him. The impudence of Koestler! Freud felt sorry for all of us and, like Marx, tried to do something about it. The despair of Mrs. Lessing is equally impudent. History is our dance. She leaves too early, and we miss her.

Galactic Orthodoxies   Claire Sprague*

The Canopus in Argos series has reached its fifth volume with the publication of *The Sentimental Agents* (1983). This latest volume invites a number of speculations about the Canopus series itself and about the series novel as a genre. It also invites comparison with Lessing's earlier series, the Children of Violence[1952–1969]. . . . The current series has reached five in only four years (1979–1983). It is still going—though not going strong. Those readers who had hoped for a fifth novel with the impact and originality of that earlier fifth, *The Four-Gated City* (1969), must be disappointed, for this one is the weakest in the series.

Its attack on political rhetoric was done with greater power and point in earlier novels, especially in *A Ripple from the Storm* (1958) and *The Golden Notebook* (1962). As a novel it is finally more interesting for its presence in an unconventional series than for itself.

It is only in part about the young Canopean agent, Incent (innocent), whom the seasoned and orthodox Klorathy rescues and watches and reports on to his superior Johor throughout the novel. Suffering from a bad case of Undulant Rhetoric, Incent is drying out in the Hospital for Rhetorical Diseases where Klorathy visits him. The treatment is severe: Total Immersion in a Paris Commune simulation. Imagine another, more benign treatment in a "wonderful, all-artificial cool, stimulus-free room," to use Klorathy's description of the stark white room no earlier Lessing character called mad could agree with. In that room, Incent watches projections of curative geometrical shapes. Klorathy twice voluntarily commits himself to Restorative Detention to enjoy "the dance of the

*From the *American Book Review* 6, nos. 5–6 (1984):9–10. Reprinted with permission of the *American Book Review*.

polyhedrons." His orthodoxy can turn pedantic in nuggets of wisdom like, "A governing class that are victims of their Rhetoric are not likely to survive for long." . . . Sometimes he tries for a joke; to the also ailing Governor Grice of Volyen he says, "I'm afraid you're far from cured. But it isn't going to be Sirius."

Incent's cyclical states of illness, partial recovery, relapse are an approximate or parodic mirror of the pattern of rise and fall, fall and rise that governs the movement of empires which is the real subject of the book—as it is of the other Canopean novels. In fact, Incent and his disease are a comic sub-plot that also foreshadow the graver relapse of Governor Grice of Volyen. The trial of Grice vs. Volyen, which climaxes the novel, indicts Volyen for having failed to deliver to its citizens what its constitution promises; the trial thus turns on accountability, to use new jargon. It is difficult to know if this trial, a parallel to the trial against the white race in *Shikasta* (the name for our planet after catastrophe), is meant to be taken seriously. The Chief Peer at the trial, Arithamea, is one of the new leaders who will bring about a long reign of peace and prosperity. The historical summary of Volygen's future which follows develops another general law: that at the height of its prosperity, each nation is open to invasion and deterioration which begins the next cycle downward, and so on and on. Probably intended to celebrate process, these so-called laws are simplistic as history and uninteresting as fiction. Dialectical materialism had more teeth and more complexity.

By the end of the novel three planets have changed direction: Volygen, Volyendesta, and Volyenadna, while a fourth, Sirius, never directly onstage, has been changing in the background. Canopus, in the game of Harmonic Cosmic Development, is interfering beneficently (of course) on all three planets. The new Volygen leadership may avoid or turn to advantage the expected Sirian invasion. The hunger-ridden Volyenadnans have been given the magic plant Rocknosh (Yiddish gone galactic?); the occupying Makens on Volyendesta will mix their uniform gene pools with the remarkably varied gene pools of the Volyendestans. This last interchange is the final exemplum in the novel. It subverts invasion and war and mixes two peoples.

Only women escape the general attack on all things Shikastan, as Lessing continues to admonish us through her transparent Canopean framework. . . . Like the women in earlier Lessing works, the women here refuse rhetoric and are connected with pragmatic ends. Arithamea, the "strong and competent" Chief Peer who forces the *he* of court discourse to become *she* and threatens to knit if the men continue to posture with their pipes provides genuine comic insight into language and role bias. That a society could justify the burning of the women called witches becomes an example of pseudo-logic Grice must study as part of his cure. (Surely Lessing is indebted to recent feminist scholarship about witches.) The single other woman is the nameless archetypal wife of

Calder of Volyenadna who immediately recognizes the usefulness of the Rocknosh which will make her planet self-sufficient and so propel it toward higher evolution. Her husband, at first skeptical, "speaks in the kindly, fatherly way they use with their females when the females are playing their allotted role, which is to work harder than their men." "Like all their females," Calder's wife is "all strength and ability to withstand." For her, ordinary things are real things, like the tomatoes and the tea Anna Wulf presents to Tommy as reality in *The Golden Notebook*. Rhetorical disease may be a male affliction

Women in our culture remain, as Lessing noted in a 1980 interview, "usually tucked away, generally in a subordinate position" within the "dominantly male structures." The women in her series are generally still "tucked away," though influential, as they are on Shikasta / Earth. Lessing wants to record this reality as much as she wants to imagine women as full participants and leaders which she does so well through characters like Al·lth in *Marriages*, Ambien in *The Sirian Experiments*, and Arithamea in *The Sentimental Agents*.

Lies seem to be male and religious in origin. Krolgul, the agent of Shammat or Evil, is called "the Father of Lies" as he is in Christian texts. . . . Christianity, which never interested Lessing before, is both used and abused in the Canopus volumes. As "one of the most savage and long lasting tyrannies ever known," it "allowed no opposition of any kind, and kept power by killing, burning, torturing its opponents, when not able to do so by . . . indoctrination and brainwashing." The secular religions in their various guises are described as inheriting the methods of the church. The Thoughts of President Motz, the Churchillian "We shall fight them on the beaches," the civil rights song, "We shall overcome," even the "They shall not pass," which I take to be a translation of the Spanish Loyalist slogan, "No pasarán," are mocked in *The Sentimental Agents*.

The Lessing who would not play the ex-communist turned rabid anti-communist seems indiscriminately rabid now. In this novel she takes cheap shots at almost everything in sight. "Fascist" and "history" are dirty words; "disinterested," "magnaminity," "detached" are clean words. But these words, belonging as they do to an Arnoldian world, are unlikely to command belief, especially in the over-generalized context in which they appear. Readers will have to go to earlier works to hear the Lessing ear report at its savage best the excesses of left wing or other rhetoric. Nothing in *The Sentimental Agents* comes close to Anton Hesse's "fresh analysis of the class forces" in every situation, or the cruel parodies in Anna Wulf's notebooks. Anna's lament about "the thinning of language against the density of experience" contains an anguish inconceivable in this novel.

So Lessing is still political but in often cranky and hectoring ways. Her permanent obsession with the group mind and group actions of the human animal is in the current novel reduced to conventionalized comment. Compare the brilliant, painful analyses of group behavior in the

Children of Violence series or in *The Golden Notebook*. In *Agents* nothing hurts or bites. Particularity has disappeared. There is only the tendentious Klorathy advising Incent, playing up to Johor.

The series is running down.

Yet the series as a whole does mark a radical and provocative departure from the simpler chronological novel of development with a single protagonist familiar in the Martha Quest novels and in male-centered English examples. Feminists and modernists may, for very different reasons, find any comparison between Lessing and Faulkner heretical, yet it ought to be made. In his Yoknapatawpha series Faulkner has so loosened the patterns of interrelationship in the series novel as to have created something new. His example may be said to both destroy and re-validate the form of the multiple novel originated by Balzac and Zola. Lessing, who once felt "caged" by the demands of the Martha Quest series, obviously feels freer in her current conception of the multiple novel. And well she should in a series that can use multiple narrative forms, protagonists and time frames. The problems in the series are, therefore, less methodological than conceptual. Lessing's galactic orthodoxies represent a new kind of cage. The irony may be that the series will be most remembered for its feminist parable, *The Marriages between Zones Three, Four, and Five*, the novel least dependent on the Canopus framework.

When is the multiple novel finished? Potentially never. That must be one of the attractions of the form. However, this volume in the Canopus series calls for a breather, if not for a dead halt. When Lessing last interrupted a series, she produced *The Golden Notebook*. Let us hope for another interruption.

The Diaries of Jane Somers

The Doris Lessing Hoax

Ellen Goodman*

In the annals of publishing, it will go down as the Doris Lessing hoax. Not once, but twice, the much-acclaimed, praised and "bankable" British author wrote novels under a pseudonym.

As Doris Lessing, she had known "success" for decades with 25 books to her credit. *The Golden Notebook* alone sold 900,000 copies. But as Jane Somers she was a modest "failure." And that, she said, was the point.

"I wanted to highlight that whole dreadful process in book publishing that 'nothing succeeds like success,' " said the author, who finally confessed that she dunnit. "If the books had come out in my name, they would have sold a lot of copies and reviewers would have said, 'Oh, Doris Lessing, how wonderful,' As it is, there were almost no reviews, and the books sold about 1,500 copies here [Britain] and 3,000 in the United States."

So we are told that the ruse was devised as a monument to the unknown writer—to salve 10,000 egos bloodied by the paper cuts of rejection slips, to vindicate all the paranoia about the publishing world. After all, Doris Lessing's own British publisher rejected Jane Somers' novel. After all, not one reviewer recognized the real writer. After all, if Doris Lessing couldn't sell unless she was Doris Lessing, well. . . .

It was a wonderful scam that produced a rash of embarrassment in the book world. But I suspect that her motives were more complex than that. Here is a woman who has spent her life wrestling with questions of who-am-I. It's unlikely that she would throw her name away for a cause. If she was toying with the book industry, I suspect that she was playing a more intriguing game with her own identity.

Indeed, the Lessing Hoax reminded me of a passage in her novel, *The Summer Before the Dark*, when a 45-year-old woman named Kate, freed from her family for the summer, lets go of every role that propped up her female life. In a powerful scene, Kate, inches of gray hair showing at her roots, body covered by a shapeless jacket, crossed a construction site full of workers who paid absolutely no attention to her.

*From the *Washington Post*, 27 September 1984, p. 31. © 1984, The Boston Globe Newspaper Company / Washington Post Writers group, reprinted with permission.

Out of their sight, she took off the jacket to reveal her slim dress, wrapped her hair dramatically with a scarf, altered her body language then crossed the same space. This time, she was greeted by "a storm of whistles, calls, invitations." It was a moving costume drama, in which a woman was covered and stripped of her identity.

Now, in real life, Lessing subjected herself to a different experiment in identity. She left her name at the edge of the public square. Her words were anonymously paraded before the publishers and the critics. If Kate Brown was invisible without her "looks," would Lessing be invisible without her "name"?

There is in all this a simple desire to masquerade, an intrigue as old as the prince and the pauper. People born with names such as Kennedy or Rockefeller must sometimes wish they were called Smith. But Lessing is one of those people who "made a name for themselves." She is not the only one to then worry if she is just valued for the name.

We all know, or know of, people like that. People who cannot introduce themselves without sounding as if they are name-dropping. The superstar who wonders whether he is getting work on his talent or his celebrity. The Nobel Prize winner who wonders if it's the title gathering attention.

There is, in many successful people the fear that they are frauds protected by fame. Many wonder whether they could do it again, remake it on their own. In the preface to these novels now being published under her own name, Doris Lessing says she wanted to know how she would fare "as a new writer without benefit of a name."

There is the more profound motive for this ruse. It's familiar to any successful person who has ever watched the television ads for the American Express card, who ever stared at a shopping-bag lady in the park and wondered what separates one life from another. Who am I without a name? Would those who claim kinship and offer praise still know me?

Doris Lessing is too world-wise to be victimized by vanity. The point of her experiment was, I am convinced, to address in public a theme that haunts her writing: life is too fragile if your identity is solely defined by others; it is hard, a life-long task to go on defining and redefining yourself. This extraordinary, vulnerable piece of personal risk-taking, this profound hoax carries the unmistakable byline of Doris Lessing.

Lessing Is More: An "Unknown" Author and the Success Syndrome

Jonathan Yardley*

In the matter of Doris Lessing and her two pseudonymous novels there are several points to be made, not all of them quite as flattering to Lessing as she apparently would like us to believe. She says she published the novels under the name of Jane Somers "to dramatize the plight of unknown writers," as one wire-service report put it, but on the evidence presented there seems to be a good deal more to the story than that.

"I wanted to highlight that whole dreadful process in book publishing that 'nothing succeeds like success,' " Lessing said. "If the books had come out in my name, they would have sold a lot of copies and reviewers would have said, 'Oh, Doris Lessing, how wonderful.' As it is, there were almost no reviews, and the books sold about 1,500 copies here (in England] and scarcely 3,000 copies each in the United States." But Lessing also says that she pulled her little trick for a "frankly, if faintly malicious" reason: To settle scores with reviewers who had disliked her "Canopus" quintet of science-fiction novels.

There's an obvious contradiction here. If Lessing's first point about famous authors is correct, then it stands to reason that when reviewers saw the "Canopus" novels with her name on them they would have said, "Oh, Doris Lessing, how wonderful" and given them favorable notices regardless of their actual merit. But that did not happen. Instead, after reading the novels a great many reviewers said, in effect, "Oh, Doris Lessing, how terrible." One can't help but wonder: Is it the success syndrome that really bothers Lessing, or is it that reviewers refused to be seduced by her name on the "Canopus" novels and picked them to pieces?

Certainly a success syndrome exists in the book industry, and reviewers are susceptible to it as well as publishers. But it also exists in the minds of writers, an aspect of the situation that is conveniently ignored in Lessing's argument. If it is true that famous authors too often get free rides from publishers and critics, then it is equally true that famous authors *expect* free rides. The ego of an author can be a monumental thing — especially, need it be said, that of a famous one — and it can lead the author to believe that everything he or she writes is a work of genius. This, as it happens, is not always true, but one constant remains: Famous authors expect all their books to be published, to be praised and to sell.

This expectation is entirely human, as is the publishers' desire to make more money off authors whose names assure substantial sales. But the results is that a great many bad books get published under the names of famous writers. When the first of the "Canopus" novels crossed my desk a number of years ago, I scanned it for a while and concluded that had

*From the *Washington Post*, 1 October 1984, pp. B1 and B4. Reprinted with permission.

Lessing's name not been on it, it never would have been published. Ditto for *Deadeye Dick*, by Kurt Vonnegut, *Good as Gold*, by Joseph Heller, *God's Grace*, by Bernard Malamud, and any number of works by Norman Mailer, Anthony Burgess and Ernest Hemingway.

Not merely do these bad books get published, they get reviewed. The reviewers have no choice; these authors have large followings, and their readers want to know how their new books stack up against their old ones. Since judgments of that sort can't be described very informatively in a couple of dozen words, it follows that a fair amount of review space is devoted to what even Lessing describes as "not very good books by established writers." This is not a matter of willfulness on the part of book-review editors, or of hostility to the work of new and unknown writers, but of simple journalistic necessity.

If anything, the Lessing case proves that the unknown but serious writer stands a reasonable chance of getting review attention, if not vast sales. The Jane Somers novels were reviewed by all three major American newspaper book-review supplements, which hardly justifies her complaint that "there were almost no reviews." The editors of those supplements obviously were able to spot the work of the unknown Jane Somers on their shelves, to recognize that it deserved a thoughtful reading, and to assign it for review. Jane Somers got pretty much the same treatment as any unknown novelist receives, and that treatment is neither as unfair nor as indifferent as Lessing imagines it to be. Her contention that book-review editors spend insufficient time looking for good books, regardless of the identity of their authors, is simply without foundation; the search for good but undiscovered books is what keeps many people in a business that too often presents them only with bad or mediocre ones.

Lessing's American editor, Robert Gottlieb of Knopf, was right when he told the *New York Times*: "My view . . . is that what's worthy sooner or later surfaces. If a writer is really good and keeps on writing, it doesn't stay secret." Which raises the obvious and interesting question: What would have happened had Doris Lessing kept on writing as Jane Somers? Rather than spill the beans all over the newspapers and television, what if Lessing had given real weight to her experiment by carrying it to the end? To publish two pseudonymous novels and then almost immediately declare one's authorship is no genuine test of any thing except the public's appetite for literary tempests; but to have kept plugging away as Jane Somers, *that* would have been a real test.

But for Lessing to continue to write as Jane Somers would be less a test of whether an unknown writer can make it in the cold, cruel world than of whether Doris Lessing herself is still capable of work equal to that upon which her reputation rests. Surely Lessing knows that anything with her name on it will find an eager publisher; but to remove her name from it and subject it to the clinical, objective scrutiny of editors and reviewers — that is another matter entirely, and one that any established writer would be loath to risk for fear of considerable, if private, embarrassment.

That Lessing chose not to follow this course is understandable and she deserves no criticism for failing to do so. But with a paperback edition of the two novels under the title *The Diaries of Jane Somers* now about to appear, bearing Lessing's name on the cover and including a new introduction by her, the sight of Lessing chasing after newspaper reporters and television interviewers to leak her story is something less than becoming. Were it not for her unsullied reputation for high solemnity and ideological rectitude, it would look for all the world as if the woman were staging a publicity stunt.

Doris Lessing in New York: 1969 and 1984

"Best Battles Are Fought by Men and Women Together"

Susan Brownmiller*

When a cult writer is introduced to his / her cult, is it necessarily a painful encounter? An encounter full of surprise and misunderstanding took place last Thursday evening at the Lexington YMHA when Doris Lessing met some vociferous Doris Lessing fans at her first New York public appearance. The expectations of fan and writer collided in a drama that was not without irony. Irony being a Lessing virtue, the writer emerged with her virtue, if not her aplomb intact. Some of her fans were sent reeling. Prepared to crown a leader, a delegation from the women's liberation movement was thrice refused. The writer was shaken, moderately. She has no use for True Believers.

To set the scene, let it be noted that before Mrs. Lessing walked hesitantly on stage to read from her latest work, *The Four-Gated City*, there was a lively discussion in a few rows of the auditorium over the probable length of the writer's skirt. The giddy discussion was, in its harmless way, an indication of what a writer who is also a woman is up against. It seemed to matter what Lessing looked like, how she stacked up in the fashionability scale. The heavy betting was on "just below the knee." No money was actually seen to have exchanged hands, but the heavy betters lost. Mrs. Lessing's hemline, now it can be told, was just above the knee.

Those who speculated on Lessing's skirt length, however, were not those who call themselves radical women. Their moment came during the discussion period after the reading. In three separate attempts, an effort was made to have the writer declare herself as a champion of feminism. Lessing, who had previously declared that she was not Martha Quest (the heroine of her quintet of novels, "The Children of Violence," of which the new book is the final volume), was having none of it. Perplexity gave way to exasperation and then to irony as the women questioners pursued their theme. When an intense young girl demanded, "Mrs. Lessing, will you

*The *Village Voice*, 22 May 1969, pp. 5–6. Reprinted with permission of the *Village Voice*. © 1969.

give us your definition of a free woman?" Lessing responded, straight-faced, "Freedom is the recognition of necessity, isn't it?"

It was a small in-joke, this use of a Marxist slogan, and a joke that only a Martha Quest, at age 50, could make. It went over dully, not understood by those without an acquaintance with Marx, and misunderstood by others who still hoped for a commitment. The flippancy was later apologized for, but the apology made matters worse. "I'm sorry," Lessing said to the next questioner. "I'm sorry there are so many unhappy women. But there are a lot more important battles than the sex war."

The next afternoon, in her hotel room, Lessing was still feeling the unsettling effects of the previous night's encounter. "What are these things?" she said earnestly. "I don't understand." The writer held out some mimeographed pamphlets. They had been handed to her by the radical women as she left the auditorium. "I've read them all through," she said in a plaintive little voice. "I'm so far away from it, I don't know where to begin."

The hotel room was in a fine state of chaos. Lessing was packing for a trip to San Francisco and then on to Oregon and the Midwest. "I'm hungry for emptiness, emptiness of the land," she explained. "I come from Africa, and England is so full." She offered water from the bathroom tap, apologized for the lack of room service, and haphazardly shoved a panty girdle and stockings into a bulging shopping bag. "Belongings," she sighed as she surveyed the room. "I have too many things."

The writer twisted her long graying hair through her fingertips. "If there's one war that no one can win it's the sex war. There isn't anyone in my generation who hasn't fought it. Of course I think women should have equal pay for equal work and day nurseries and things like that, but I don't see — I don't understand what they want from me. In England I'm not considered a woman's writer. This same thing happened to me two years ago in Sweden. My hotel room was besieged from 8 in the morning until midnight. I was accosted as a champion of the sex war. I'd be interviewed by these women journalists, I'd talk for three hours from A to zed and all they'd write about was the sex war. Now I won't give any interviews to any Swedish woman journalist. Look, I would support a women's trade union in a factory, but the rest is bad political thinking. Is one-half of the human race equating itself with a minority? Do they think of themselves as a minority? I should feel extremely nervous in a battle where there are no men around."

The telephone rang, and Lessing moved with slow grace to answer it. Fred McDarrah coming up. The writer picked up a brush and began to work at her long hair in earnest. "It's 10 years since I wrote *The Golden Notebook* and six years since it's come out. *The Golden Notebook* is not the only thing I've written and 'The Golden Notebook' is not even a feminist book. The book said that people shouldn't put things into compartments."

The writer faced a mirror above a dressing table adorned with a bottle of Desert Flower Sparkling Cologne. She deftly pinned her hair into a bun at the back of her head. "I've always suffered from a violent conflict," she laughed gently. "I hate organizations, I hate rhetoric, I hate slogans. My idea of hell is a committee meeting. But I'm eternally fascinated by politics. Oh yes, I'm full of passion for the good and the fair and the true. I'm 50 years old. I don't participate. I'm at the stage where I get put on the letterheads."

Fred McDarrah, in the room, nosed about with the lighting, opened windows, and clicked his shutter. McDarrah does not just take photographs. He participates. The photographer asked the novelist what she thought of Kenneth Tynan's nude show, *Oh, Calcutta*. Lessing gave him a demure look: "May a hundred flowers bloom."

When McDarrah departed, Lessing resumed the unfinished conversation. "If I've learned nothing else in my life, I've learned that you don't fight a bad thing head-on. I'm afraid there's nothing I can say to you about men and women that won't sound terribly reactionary. The truth is, I have sympathy for men. Men ought to be horizon-bashing, challenging and raising hell, full-stretch all the time. A woman would be perfectly happy with that sort of man. But what's happened is that the poor bastards are spending all their time earning a living in cages, offices. Some of the best battles have been fought by men and women together." She twisted a long hairpin in her hands. "Nude shows and sex wars are not the most important battles, are they? And the sex war is not the only battle I've fought. My contribution to the current scene is what I think about mental illness. I've gone rather far on a limb on that one. You haven't read the new book?"

Resigning herself to the lack of preparedness of the interviewer, Lessing went on. "For me, now, is the top priority. The danger is worse now. We've just gotten used to it. Every time we fight a war we give up further liberties. I see things as getting worse and worse. Nasty authoritarian governments here and in England. I attended an SDS meeting in Stony Brook. It broke my heart. The students are innocent as baby lambs. They are so idealistic, they don't know what they're up against. I think they'll be defeated. Raids at 3 o'clock in the morning terrify me. This clamping down on pot smoking is nothing but anti-youth. I'm not very optimistic about the future."

The telephone rang again, more urgently. Doris Lessing's dinner companion was waiting in the downstairs lobby. The writer mechanically applied a red lipstick and hurriedly brushed some black mascara on her short, honest eyelashes. "If you want to give me a good mark, say I don't believe in getting married, unless you have children. I don't like marriage at all. I've had two of them. People expect too much from marriage — long term romance, financial security. I like living with men, however. But having to stick to one forever is a bit much, isn't it? Also, assure those women that it's very pleasant to be middle-aged. One can take everything or leave it. It doesn't become a question of principle." Doris Lessing laughed a faint laugh.

Candid Shot: Lessing in New
York City, April 1 and 2, 1984   Virginia Tiger*

"When I jest with my publishers that I've become part of their sales department, I think they find the remark in bad taste," Doris Lessing observed toward the end of her second lecture at the 92nd Street Y in New York last April. The wry response was occasioned by one among many comfortable questions asked that evening by the sellout audience. Why — it was asked — had she decided on this North American tour, after so long a period of relative reclusiveness. For it had been fifteen years since last she stood (then, as now, hands combing hair tendrils back from her brow) before this same auditorium, a talk I vividly recall — as do others — for its audience's alternately baffled and vociferous response to Lessing's apparent rejection of feminism. (Yet, to our dismay, we were once again to hear her dismiss its politics as being too parochial, too class-bound, too emotional. "I've never agreed that the women's movement should be restricted to women," she observed. And summarily concluded: "I didn't expect much to arise out of it, and nothing much has.")

"This lecture giving is all very jolly, but it has *nothing*, nothing to do with my writing," Lessing continued. And the candor of this comment, given today's hype when too many writers fatten literary reputations by offering fans all manner of fare from talk-show confessions to product endorsements, had the crispness one certainly expected from the author of *The Four-Gated City*. Here (as *DLN* readers will remember) Martha Quest observes in one of her "Signs of the Times" bulletins: "It has literally become impossible for anyone to read a work of fiction except in terms of the author's life. Since they learned to read at all, the 'lives' of the artists, the experience of the artists, the opinions of the artists, have been offered side by side with the work of the artists, which has been infinitely less important."

What *is* important to Doris Lessing, then? At least, on that cool April night when she so charmed us all by walking hesitatingly on stage to read "Homage to Isaac Babel," a story she described (with glee) as being "*very autobiographical*" and whose humor appeared to delight her as much as her audience.

*From the *Doris Lessing Newsletter* 8 (Fall 1984). 5–6. Reprinted with permission of the *Doris Lessing Newsletter*.

"Literature of the Fantastic," the brief lecture which followed, not only gave the clue, but amounted to an apologia for her *Canopus* series. Born in magic and religion, fantastic literature has a long tradition, she argued; fables and parables have always run beside the realistic novel and now that stream is growing stronger and stronger, since technology has laid the basis for "a rebirth of fantastic literature." Devotees of the realistic novel who reject the fantastic mode are myopic, even "resentful," she insisted. "My readers under thirty enjoy what is their idiom, speculative fantasy. My readers over thirty are appalled by my move into this realm."

Of course, readers of Doris Lessing are familiar with this stance. What may most interest readers of the *DLN*, however, are Lessing's incidental remarks in the question period which followed. For example, she said that — since she couldn't get the sixth *Canopus* fable to "jell" — she was now writing a realistic novel. The new book is set in London in 1981: "It's about a girl — rather loosely based on something I've seen — who drifts into becoming a terrorist out of sheer stupidity or lack of imagination." The idea for the novel evidently began "cooking" in 1979 when Lord Mountbatten was killed and Lessing, in Ireland at the time, saw disaffected kids running around cheering.

"Cooking," "jelling," "simmering," these domestic words were often used when Lessing described the process of working through a novel's recipe. Her explanation of how *Marriages* evolved, for example, is worth a lengthy quote:

> This novel came into existence in the following way. When I was in my forties I went through a phase that women often do, thinking that if they're not married they might as well be dead — which is luckily a very passing phase.
>
> While it was going on . . . I invented for myself imaginary landscapes, a technique used by certain schools of therapy, though I did not know this at the time.
>
> I created two ideal landscapes, male and female, somewhat exemplary in both ways. They were equally strong, very different, operating from strength. This was a very beneficial fantasy that I then forgot all about. I just lost interest.
>
> When I fished that story out of my unconscious and looked at it, it had become different. The two original landscapes were both my favorite landscapes — which happens to be because of my childhood: high, dry, mountainous, cool with a clear sky.
>
> What came out of my unconscious was that the male realm, which is a highly exaggerated sort of Prussian realm or British public school, had become low, flat and watery. This was not any conscious choice of mine.

Feminists in the audience laughed and whispered — they would soon join other fans in the long line next door where Lessing was signing books. As I walked out, I heard someone arguing heatedly that Doris Lessing was

an autodidact, like so many other women writers. She wasn't a reactionary, but a witness to the times, and its changes — like Simone de Beauvoir.

I was struck by the comment, having been disturbed by Lessing's
untutored remarks about the women's movement, which amounted not so
much to a misunderstanding as a betrayal of the feminist cause.

Would Doris Lessing dismiss this charge? Decidedly. She is a creature,
a writer, a political and now religious thinker of such independence of
sensibility that she would probably — as she did toward the end of that
spring evening — have laughed cheerfully. For she added: "I hold some very
old-fashioned views, very different from what I thought any age up to
forty. I think that we are here for a purpose — to learn — and that there is a
God: I don't think that we are purposeless. Forgive me for that old-
fashioned and ridiculous view."

SELECTED
BIBLIOGRAPHY

PRIMARY SOURCES

Novels

The Grass Is Singing. London: Michael Joseph, 1950. New York: T. Y. Crowell, 1950.

Martha Quest. [Children of Violence, Vol 1.] London: Michael Joseph, 1952. New York: Simon & Schuster, 1964.

A Proper Marriage. [Children of Violence, Vol. 2.] London: Michael Joseph, 1954. New York: Simon & Schuster, 1964.

Retreat to Innocence. London: Michael Joseph, 1956.

A Ripple from the Storm. [Children of Violence, Vol. 3.] London: Michael Joseph, 1958. New York: Simon & Schuster, 1966.

The Golden Notebook. London: Michael Joseph, 1962. New York: Simon & Schuster, 1966.

Landlocked. [Children of Violence, Vol. 4.] London: MacGibbon & Kee, 1965. New York: Simon & Schuster, 1966.

The Four-Gated City. [Children of Violence, Vol. 5.] London: MacGibbon & Kee, 1969. New York: Knopf, 1969.

Briefing for a Descent into Hell. London: Jonathan Cape, 1971. New York: Knopf, 1975.

The Summer before the Dark. London: Jonathan Cape, 1973. New York: Knopf, 1973.

The Memoirs of a Survivor. London: Octagon Press, 1974. New York: Knopf, 1975.

Re: Colonised Planet 5, Shikasta. [Canopus in Argos: Archives, Vol. 1.] London: Cape; 1979; New York: Knopf, 1979.

The Marriages between Zones Three, Four, and Five. [Canopus in Argos: Archives, Vol. 2.] London: Jonathan Cape, 1970; New York: Knopf, 1980.

The Sirian Experiments. [Canopus in Argos: Archives, Vol. 3.] London: Jonathan Cape, 1981; New York: Knopf, 1981.

The Making of the Representative for Planet 8. [Canopus in Argos: Archives, Vol. 4.] London: Jonathan Cape, 1982. New York: Knopf, 1982.

Documents Relating to the Sentimental Agents in the Volyen Empire. [Canopus in Argos: Archives, Vol. 5.] London: Jonathan Cape, 1985. New York: Knopf, 1985.

The Diaries of Jane Somers. New York: Knopf, 1984. (Originally published in two volumes by Jane Somers as *The Diary of a Good Neighbour* and *If the Old Could . . .* [London: Michael Joseph, 1983–84; New York: Knopf, 1983–84].)

The Good Terrorist. London: Cape, 1985. New York: Knopf, 1985.

Other Major Works

This Was the Old Chief's Country. [Short Stories.] London: Michael Joseph, 1951. New York: Crowell, 1952.

Five: Short Novels. London: Michael Joseph, 1953.

Going Home. [Autobiographical essay.] London: Michael Joseph, 1957. London: Panther, 1968. New York: Ballantine, 1968.

The Habit of Loving. [Short Stories.] London: MacGibbon & Kee, 1957. New York: Crowell, 1957.

Each His Own Wilderness. In *New English Dramatists, Three Plays*, edited by E. Martin Browne. Harmondsworth, Middlesex: Penguin Books, 1959.

Fourteen Poems. Northwood, Middlesex: Scorpion Press, 1959.

In Pursuit of the English: A Documentary. London: MacGibbon & Kee, 1960. New York: Simon & Schuster, 1961.

Play with a Tiger: A Play in Three Acts. London: Michael Joseph, 1962. Also in *Plays by and About Women*, edited by Victoria Sullivan and James Hatch, 201–75. New York: Random House, 1973.

A Man and Two Women. [Short Stories.] London: MacGibbon & Kee, 1963. New York: Simon & Schuster, 1963.

African Stories. London: Michael Joseph, 1964. New York: Simon & Schuster, 1965.

Particularly Cats. [Autobiographical essay.] London: Michael Joseph, 1967. New York: Simon & Schuster, 1967.

The Temptation of Jack Orkney. [Short Stories.] London: Jonathan Cape, 1972. New York: Knopf, 1972.

A Small Personal Voice. [Essays.] Edited by Paul Schlueter. New York: Knopf, 1974.

SECONDARY SOURCES

Interviews

Interviews in anthologies or in the *Doris Lessing Newsletter* are not listed below.

Bannon, Barbara A. "Authors and Editors." *Publishers Weekly* 195 (2 June 1969):51–54.

Bigsby, Christopher. "Doris Lessing." In *The Radical Imagination and the Liberal Tradition. Interviews with English and American Novelists*, edited by Heide Ziegler and C. B., 188–208. London: Junction, 1981.

Bikman, Minda. "A Talk with Doris Lessing." *New York Times Book Review*, 30 March 1980, pp. 1, 24–27.

Driver, C. J. "Profile 8: Doris Lessing." *The New Review* 1 (November 1974):17–23.

Haas, Joseph. "Doris Lessing: Chronicler of the Cataclysm." *Chicago Sun Times (Panorama)*, 14 June 1969, p. 4ff.

Hazleton, Lesley. "Doris Lessing on Feminism, Communism and 'Space Fiction.' " *New York Times Magazine*, 25 July 1982, p. 20ff.

Oates, Joyce Carol. "A Visit with Doris Lessing." *The Southern Review* 9 (1973):873–82.

Wiseman, Thomas. "Mrs. Lessing's Kind of Life." *Time and Tide* 43 (12 April 1962):26.

Bibliographies

Burkom, Selma R., and Margaret Williams. *Doris Lessing: A Checklist of Primary and Secondary Sources*. Troy, N.Y.: Whitson, 1973.

Brueck, Eric T., ed. *Doris Lessing: A Bibliography of Her First Editions*. London: Metropolis (Antiquarian Books) Ltd., 1984.

Ipp, Catharina. *Doris Lessing: A Bibliography*. Johannesburg: University of Witwatersrand, 1967.

Pichanik, J., A. J. Chennells and L. B. Rix. *Rhodesian Literature in English: A Bibliography (1890–1975)*. Gwelo, Rhodesia; Mambo Press, 1977. Mambo Press, Senga Road, P. O. Box 779, Gwelo, Zimbabwe.

Seligman, Dee. *Doris Lessing: An Annotated Bibliography of Criticism*. Westport, Conn.: Greenwood Press, 1981.

Books and Monographs

Brewster, Dorothy. *Doris Lessing*. New York: Twayne, 1965.

Dahlhaus-Beilner, Barbara. *Wahnsinn: Symptom and Befreiung*. Amsterdam: B. Grüner, 1984.

Draine, Betsy. *Substance under Pressure: Artistic Coherence and Evolving Forms in the Novels of Doris Lessing*. Madison: University of Wisconsin, 1983.

Katherine Fishburn's *The Unexpected Universe of Doris Lessing* (Westport, Conn.: Greenwood Press, 1985) appeared too late to be considered in our introduction.

Holmquist, Ingrid. *From Society to Nature: A Study of Doris Lessing's Children of Violence*. Gothenburg Studies in English, vol. 47. Goteborg, Swedan: Acta Universitatis Gothoburgensis, 1980.

Knapp, Mona. *Doris Lessing*. New York: Frederick Ungar, 1984.

Rose, Ellen Cronan. *The Tree Outside the Window: Doris Lessing's Children of Violence*. Hanover, N.H.: University Press of New England, 1976.

Rubenstein, Roberta. *The Novelistic Vision of Doris Lessing: Breaking the Forms of Consciousness*. Urbana: University of Illinois, 1979.

Sage, Lorna. *Doris Lessing*. Contemporary Writers Series, no. 3783. New York: Methuen, 1983.

Schlueter, Paul, ed. *The Fiction of Doris Lessing*. Evansville: University of Evansville, 1971.

— — — . *The Novels of Doris Lessing*. Carbondale: Southern Illinois University, 1973.

Singleton, Mary Ann. *The City and the Veld: The Fiction of Doris Lessing*. Lewisburg: Bucknell University, 1977.

Spiegel, Rotraut. *Doris Lessing: The Problem of Alienation and the Form of the Novel*. Frankfurt, Bern, Cirenceser, U.K.: Peter D. Lang, 1980.

Taylor, Jenny, ed. *Notebooks/Memoirs/Archives: Reading and Rereading Doris Lessing*. Boston: Routledge & Kegan Paul, 1982.

Thorpe, Michael. *Doris Lessing's Africa*. London: Evans Brothers, Ltd., 1978.

— — — . *Doris Lessing: Writers and Their Work*, No. 230. Longman for British Council, 1974.

Special Numbers and Special Sections in Periodicals

Contemporary Literature 14 (1973), ed. Annis Pratt and L. S. Dembo.

World Literature Written in English 12 (1973):148–206.

Anonymous: A Journal for the Woman Writer 1 (1974):48–81, ed. Judy Rosenthal.

Modern Fiction Studies 26 (1980), ed. Margaret Church and William T. Stafford.

Selected Articles and Essays

Essays published in Doris Lessing Numbers (above) and in the *Doris Lessing Newsletter* (1976–) are not listed separately for reasons of space. Essays published in this collection are also not listed.

Bazin, Nancy Topping. "Androgyny or Catastrophe: The Vision of Doris Lessing's Later Novels." *Frontiers* 5 (1981):10–15.

— — — . "The Evolution of Doris Lessing's Art from a Mystical Moment to Space Fiction." In *The Transcendent Adventure: Studies in Religion in Science Fiction/Fantasy*, ed. Robert Reilly, 157–67. Westport, Conn.: Greenwood, 1985.

Brooks, Ellen W. "The Image of Woman in Lessing's *The Golden Notebook*." *Critique* 15 (1973):101–9.

Brown, Lloyd W. "The Shape of Things: Sexual Images and the Sense of Form in Doris Lessing's Fiction." *World Literature Written in English* 14 (1975):176–86.

Burkom, Selma R. "Only Connect: Form and Content in the Works of Doris Lessing." *Critique* 11 (1968):51–68.

Caracciolo, Peter. "Doris Lessing's 'Lights of Canopus': Oriental Sources of Space History." *Foundation*, no. 31 (1984):18–30.

Chaffee, Patricia. "Spatial Patterns and Closed Groups in Lessing's *African Stories*." *South Atlantic Bulletin* 43 (1978):42–52.

Fishburn, Katherine. "Anti-American Regionalism in the Fiction of Doris Lessing." *Regionalism and the Female Imagination* 4 (1978):19–25.

— — — . "The Nightmare Repetition: The Mother-Daughter Conflict in Doris Lessing's *The Children of Violence*." *The Lost Tradition: Mothers and*

Daughters in Literature, ed. Cathy N. Davidson and E. M. Broner, 207–16. New York: Ungar, 1980.

Foote, Timothy. "Portrait of a Lady." [Review of *The Summer before the Dark*.] *Time*, 21 May 1973, p. 99.

Gindin, James. *Postwar British Fiction: New Accents and Attitudes*, 65–86. Berkeley: Univ. of California, 1962.

Hynes, Joseph. "The Construction of *The Golden Notebook*." *Iowa Review* 4 (1973):100–13.

Hardin, Nancy Shields. "The Sufi Teaching Story and Doris Lessing." *Twentieth Century Literature* 23 (1977):314–25.

Howe, Florence. "Doris Lessing's Free Women." *Nation* 11 (1965):34–37.

Joyner, Nancy. "The Underside of the Butterfly: Lessing's Debt to Woolf." *Journal of Narrative Technique* 4 (1974):204–12.

Kaplan, Sydney Janet. *Feminist Consciousness in the Modern British Novel*, 136–72. Urbana: University of Illinois, 1975.

Karl, Frederick R. "Doris Lessing in the Sixties: The New Anatomy of Melancholy." *Contemporary Literature* 13 (1972):15–33.

— — —. "The Four-Gaited Beast of the Apocalypse: Doris Lessing's *The Four-Gated City*." *Old Lines, New Forces: Essays on the Contemporary British Novel*, ed. Robert K. Morris, 181–200. Rutherford, N.J.: Fairleigh Dickinson, 1976.

Krouse, Agate Nesaule. "Doris Lessing's Feminist Plays." *World Literature Written in English* 15 (1976):305–22.

Lardner, Susan. "An Angle on the Ordinary." *New Yorker* 19 (September 1983):140–54.

Lefcowitz, Barbara. "Dreams and Action in Lessing's *The Summer before the Dark*." *Critique* 17 (1975):107–20.

Leonard, Vivien. " 'Free Women' as Parody: Fun and Games in *The Golden Notebook*." *Perspectives on Contemporary Literature* 6 (1980):20–27.

Lifson, Martha. "Structural Patterns in *The Golden Notebook*." *Michigan Papers in Women's Studies* 2, no. 4 (1978):95–108.

Lightfoot, Marjorie J. " 'Fiction' vs. 'Reality': Clues and Conclusions in *The Golden Notebook*." *Modern British Literature* 2 (1977):182–88.

Magie, Michael L. "Doris Lessing and Romanticism." *College English* 38 (1977):531–52.

Marchino, Lois. "The Search for Self in the Novels of Doris Lessing." *Studies in the Novel* 4 (1972):252–61.

Mark, M. "Reports from the Front." *Village Voice*, 2 October 1978, 127–32.

Markow, Alice Bradley. "The Pathology of Feminine Failure in the Fiction of Doris Lessing." Critique 16 (1974):88–100.

Morris, Robert K. *Continuance and Change: The Contemporary British Novel Sequence*, 1–27. Carbondale: Southern Illinois University, 1972.

Mudrick, Marvin. "All That Prose!" [Review of Children of Violence and *The Golden Notebook*.] *Hudson Review* 18 (1965):110.

Mulkeen, Anne M. "Twentieth-Century Realism: The 'Grid' Structure of *The Golden Notebook.*" *Studies in the Novel* 4 (1972):262–74.

Parrinder, Patrick. "Descents into Hell: The Later Novels of Doris Lessing." *Critical Quarterly* 22 (1980):5–25.

Porter, Dennis. "Realism and Failure in *The Golden Notebook,*" *Modern Language Quarterly* 35 (1974):56–65.

Pratt, Annis. "Women and Nature in Modern Fiction." *Contemporary Literature* 13 (1972):476–90.

Rapping, Elayne Antler. "Unfree Women: Feminism in Doris Lessing's Novels." *Women's Studies* 3 (1975):29–44.

Rose, Ellen Cronan. "The End of the Game: New Directions in Doris Lessing's Fiction." *Journal of Narrative Technique* 6 (1976):66–75.

— — —. "The Eriksonian Bildungsroman: An Approach through Doris Lessing." *Hartford Studies in Literature* 7, no. 1 (1975):1–17.

Sarvan, Charles, and Sarvan, Liebetraut. "D. H. Lawrence and Doris Lessing's *The Grass Is Singing.*" *Modern Fiction Studies* 24 (1978/79):533–37.

Showalter, Elaine. *A Literature of Their Own*, 298–319. Princeton: Princeton University, 1977.

Spacks, Patricia Meyer. *The Female Imagination.* New York: Knopf, 1975.

Sprague, Claire. "Dialectic and Counter-Dialectic in the Martha Quest Novels." *Journal of Commonwealth Literature* 14 (1970):39–52.

— — —. The Politics of Sibling Incest in Doris Lessing's 'Each Other'." *San José Studies* 11:2 (1985): 42–49.

Steele, M. C., *"Children of Violence" and Rhodesia: A Study of Doris Lessing as Historical Observer.* Pamphlet #29. Salisbury: Central Africa Historical Association, 1974.

Stimpson, Catharine. "Doris Lessing and the Parables of Growth." In *The Voyage In: Fictions of Female Development*, edited by Elizabeth Abel, Marianne Hirsch and Elizabeth Langland, 176–90. Hanover and London: University Press of New England, 1983.

Stitzel, Judith. "Reading Doris Lessing." *College English* 40 (1979):498–504.

Swingewood, Alan. "Structure and Ideology in the Novels of Doris Lessing." In *The Sociology of Literature: Applied Studies*, edited by Diana Laurenson. Keele, England: University of Keele, 1978. *Sociological Review*, Monograph 26, pp. 38–54.

Tiger, Virginia. "Advertisements for Herself." *Columbia Forum* 3 (1974):15–20.

— — —. "The Female Novel of Education." *Dalhousie Review* 60 (1980): 472–86.

Weinhouse, Linda. "Incest and Repression in *The Grass Is Singing.*" *Revista Canaria de Estudios Ingleses* 8 (1984):99–117.

INDEX

Abel, Elizabeth, 9, 21, 101–7
Adalantaland, 16
adolescence, 6, 12
Africa, 4, 6, 9, 17, 20, 37–39, 40–43, 75, 78, 107–14, 142
alchemy, 19, 60–68
Al • Ith, 16, 60–68, 211
allegory, 19, 60–68
Ambien I, 17, 211
Ambien II, 17, 65
American Book Review, 209n
Amis, Kingsley, 22, 31, 167n, 174
amnesia, 89, 193
androgynous, 79, 205
Anna Karenina, 43
Annotated Alice, The (Carroll), 44
Antarctica, 205
Arithamea, 210–12
Arrow in the Blue (Koestler), 208
Ata, Ben, 16
Austen, Jane, 8, 70

Baader-Meinhof gang, 159
Balzac, Honore de, 1, 208
Barkham, John, 4
Barnouw, Dagmar, 21, 115–25
Barthes, Roland, 22, 154, 167n
Batts, Joseph, 12
Bazin, Nancy Topping, 95, 98, 100n
Bellow, Saul, 47
Bennett, Arnold, 189
Bertelsen, Eve, 20
Between the Acts (Woolf), 51
Biblical history, 157–68
bildungsroman, 5–6, 12, 10, 21, 24, 95, 117, 122–23, 174, 186
Birkin, Rupert, 69–74, 81–86
Blackenhurst, Paul, 10, 50–60
"Black Madonna, The," 108
"Black Notebook, The," 4, 69–86, 187–88

Blake, William, 41
Bleak House (Dickens), 11
"Blood on the Banana Leaves," 55
Bloom, Leopold, 10
Bloom, Molly, 93
Bloomsbury, 179
" Blue Notebook, The, " 10, 55, 57–58
Boehme, 2
Bostonians, The (James), 174
"braid of codes," 154
Brangwen, Gudrun, 69–86
Brangwen, Ursula, 69–86
Brewster, Dorothy, 19
Briefing for a Descent into Hell, 5, 13, 14, 15, 19, 22, 87–93, 98, 120, 127, 134, 136, 139, 149, *192–96*, 205–9
British Empire, 15
"Britishness," 41–42
Brontë, Charlotte, 8, 40, 56
Brontë, Emily, 56
Brown, Kate (Mrs. Michael Brown), 13, *86–93*, 139–40, 197–99, 207, 213–17
Brownmiller, Susan, 23, 218–221
Brown, Susan, 23
Bulkin, Elly, 181–82

Campanella, 22, 143–53
Canopean Necessity, 15
Canopus, 15, 23, 149, 154–68, 215
Canopus in Argos: Archives, 3, 5, 13–17, 19, 20, 60, 65, 99, 113, *154–68*, 200–204, 205–9, 209–12
Carroll, Lewis, 44
"Casebook on Doris Lessing" (Bertelsen), 20
Cassandra, 191
Catastrophe of the 1970s, 12, 128, 133, 190
chaos, 8, 115–25
Childhood's End (Clarke), 161

Children of Violence, 3, 5, 7, 8, 13, 19,
    21, 22, 38, 95, 99, 116–19, 126–27, 132,
    144, 173-74, *184–91*, 195–96, 209–12,
    218
Chronicler, the, 14
Churchill, Winston, 42
Church of Scientology, 204
Città Felice, 141, 152n
city, 16, 22
City and the Veld, The (Singleton), 19
City in the Desert, The, 95, 145
City of the Sun (Campanella), 22, 141–53
Cixious, Hélène, 102–3, 106–7n
Clarke, Arthur C., 161
clitoral orgasm, 82–86
"Cocktail Party, The" (Eliot), 35
codes, 153–54
Coldridge house, 11, 128
Coldridge, Lynda, 12, 95–97, 122–23,
    128–41, 189, 194
Coldridge, Mark, 128–41, 207–9
Coldridge, Phoebe, 12, 128–41
Cold War, 8, 11, 99
colonial, 4, 37, 40–41, 113, 195
communism, 2, 5, 8, 39, 127, 177
Communist party, 5, 40, 47, 103, 126–30,
    187
community of women, 5
Condition of England, 11
Connell, Evan, 87
Conrad, Joseph, 47
consciousness, 2, 5
Cosmic Clocks, The (Gauquelin), 201
cosmology, 135
"cracking up," 8, 198

Dalloway, Clarissa, 95
Deadeye Dick (Vonnegut), 216
de Beauvoir, Simone, 1, 223
deconstruction, 37
Dedalus, Stephen, 6, 7
Defoe, Daniel, 35, 36
Dermis Probe, The (Shah), 201
Derrida, Jacques, 39, 110, 113
De Silva, 10
Dianetics (Hubbard), 204
Diaries of Jane Somers, The, 113, 213–17
Diary of a Good Neighbor, The, 5, 17, 18
Dickens, Charles, 11, 126–27
Didion, Joan, 22, 192–96, 205
Dinnerstein, Dorothy, 99, 100n
Divided Self, The (Laing), 128–41
Doll's House, A (Ibsen), 89
doppelgänger, 50

Doris Lessing (Brewster), 19
Doris Lessing (Knapp), 20
Doris Lessing Hoax, 213–17
Doris Lessing (Sage), 19
Doris Lessing Newsletter, 20, 31n, 221n
Doris Lessing's Africa (Thorpe), 19
Doris Lessing Society, 20, 37n, 107n
doubles, 44–60
Drabble, Margaret, 2, 22, 72, 184–91
Draine, Betsy, 4, 15, 22, 153–68
dream, 38, 89
Dreiserian mold, 192
drugs, 96–100, 130–41

Earthsea trilogy (Le Guin), 203
écriture féminine, 101–2
Eliade, Mircea, 19, 142–53
Eliot, George, 8, 200
Eliot, T. S., 34–35, 37, 76
Ellis, Havelock, 6
Ellison, Ralph, 56, 199
Ellmann, Mary, 24, 190
Empire Puttiora, 15, 156–68, 202–4
England, 4, 5, 8
Everyman, 89
Everywoman, 13, 15, 89, 197–99
exile, 40, 107–14

"Fall of the House of Usher, The," 55
fantasy, 31
Fashion Changes, 18
Faulkner, William, 2, 9, 72
female, 5, 6
female space, 20, 21, 23, *69–86*
femininity, 77, 109
feminism, 12, 13, 21, 23, 80–81, 83, 87,
    199, 219
feminist criticism, 73, 101–7
First Men in the Moon, The (Wells), 155
Fishburn, Katherine, 97–98, 100n
Flaubert, Gustave, 189, 194
"Flavours of Exile," 108
formlessness, 45
Forster, E. M., 83
Foucault, Michel, 37
Four-Gated City, The, 5, 8, 11, 12, 22,
    40, 87, *95–100*, 115–25, 126–40,
    141–53, 174–76, 184–91, 197–99, 205,
    209–12, 218
Fowler, Maudie, 18
fragmentation, 2, 45, 87, *94–100*, 115
freedom, 219
Free Woman, 9, 10, *45–60*, 76, 105, 129,
    186–91, 218–19

Freud, Sigmund, 106, 185–87
From the Earth to the Moon (Verne), 155
Frontiers of War, 4
Frye, Northrop, 19

galactic, 15, 22, 209
Gauquelin, M., 201
Geller, Uri, 209
gender, 8, 39, 46, 67, *107–14*
Genly, Ai, 161
genre, 38
"Getting off the Altitude," 113
Gilbert, Sandra, 21, 94–95. See also Susan Gubar
Gissing, George, 69
God's Grace (Malamud), 216
Goffman, Erving, 19
going, 39–41
Going Home, 5, 21, *38–44*
Golden Notebook, The, 1, 3, 4, 5, 8, 9, 10, 11, 12, 18, 21, 22, 24, 34, 38, 40, *44–61*, 69–86, 88, 90, 96–99, *101–7*, 115–25, 126–41, 174–91, 192–96, 197, 209–12, 219
Golding, William, 2
Good as Gold (Heller), 216
Goodman, Ellen, 22, 213–14
Good Terrorist, The, 17, 23
Gottlieb, Robert, 216
Gracious Lady, The, 18
Gramsci, Antonio, 37
"Grass Is Singing, The," 171–72
Grass Is Singing, The, 4, 19, 38, 76, 126, 171–72, 184–91, 195–96. See also "Killing Heat"
Gray, Dorian, 47
Green, Martin, 14, 20, 31
Green, Saul, 10, 46, 126–41
Gubar, Susan, 21, 94–95. See also Sandra Gilbert

Hamilton, Edmond, 155–56
Hanson, Clare, 21, 107–14
Hearst, Patty, 159
Hearth and Home, 3
Heisenberg, Werner, 207
Heller, Joseph, 216
Hemingway, Ernest, 2, 216
Hesse, Anton, 7
heterosexual, 76–82
"Homage to Isaac Babel," 221
home, 39–42
homosexual, 76–82
Hounslow, George, 80–86

Howards End, 11
Howe, Irving, 10, 70–71, 74, 177–81, 205
Hubbard, L. Ron, 200–204
"Hunger," 153
Huxley, Aldous, 73

If the Old Could . . . , 17
Incent, 208–12
infidelity, 87
inner space, 20, 115
In Pursuit of the English, 5, 20, 41–42
Invisible Man (Ellison), 56, 199
Invisible Writing, The (Koestler), 208
Irigaray, Luce, 102–4, 106n

Jacobs, Molly, 10, 11, 45–60, 69–86
James, Henry, 40
James, William, 19
Jane Eyre (Brontë), 6, 56, 87, 95
Jason, 14, 88
Jesus, 208
Johor (George Sherban), 16, 156–68, 202–4, 209–12
Jones, Ernest, 171
Jong, Erica, 22, 197–99
Jouve, Nicole Ward, 8, 20
Joyce, James, 2, 9, 10, 40, 72–73, 110
Jung, Carl, 19, 23, 101, 185, 206
Jungian psychology, 143, 146–47, 184

Kaplan, Carey, 141
Karellan, 161
Karl, Frederick, 11, 98, 100n
Khrushchev, 40
"Killing Heat," 4. See also *The Grass Is Singing*
Kipling, Rudyard, 31, 34
Klad., 171–72
Klorathy, 17, 209–12
Knapp, Mona, 12, 20
Koestler, Arthur, 208–9
Kristeva, Julia, 102, 110
kunstlerroman, 95

Lady Chatterley's Lover (Lawrence), 78, 81–86
Laing, R. D., 2, 19, 22, 88, *126–41*, 190, 193
Landlocked, 8, 118–19, 189
Last and First Men (Stapledon), 156, 160–61
Last Man, 161
Law of Canopus, 16
Lawrence, D. H., 1, 21, 23, 69–86, 173,

179–80, 197
Leavis, F. R., 23, 36, 74, 101
Left Hand of Darkness, The (Le Guin), 161
Le Guin, Ursula, 161, 203
Leonard, John, 17, 204–9
Lessing, Doris, biographical data, 184; childhood experiences, 76; Communist, 39, 126–27; comparison to de Beauvoir, 1; emigration from Southern Rhodesia, 4; expatriate from Africa, 39; interview at Stony Brook, 115–16; manipulation of media by, 2; on marriage, 220; on women's movement, 221; sales of novels by, 213, 215; undergoes psychoanalysis, 5

WORKS:
"Black Madonna, The," 108
Briefing for a Descent into Hell, 5, 13, 14, 15, 19, 22, 87–93, 98, 120, 127, 134, 136, 139, 149, 192–96, 205–9
Diaries of Jane Somers, The, 113, 213–17
Diary of a Good Neighbor, The, 5, 17, 28
"Flavours of Exile," 108
Four-Gated City, The, 5, 8, 11, 12, 22, 40, 87, 95–100, *115–25*, 126–40, 141–53, 174–76, *184–91*, 197–99, 205, 209–12, 218
Going Home, 5, 21, 38–44
Golden Notebook, The, 1, 3, 4, 5, 8, 9, 10, 11, 12, 18, 21, 22, 24, 34, 38, 40, *44–61*, 69–86, 88, 90, 96–99, 101–7, 115–25, 126–41, *174–91*, 192–96, 197, 209–12, 219
Good Terrorist, The, 17, 23
Grass Is Singing, The, 4, 19, 38, 76, 126, 171–72, *184–91*, 195–96
"Homage to Isaac Babel," 221
"Hunger," 153
If the Old Could . . . , 17
In Pursuit of the English, 5, 20, 41–42
"Killing Heat," 4
Landlocked, 8, 118–19, 189
Making of the Representative from Planet 8, The, 3, 16, 151
"Man and Two Women, A," 87
Marriages between Zones Three, Four, and Five, The, 16, 21, *60–68*, 155, 163, 205–9, 212
Martha Quest, 6, 24, 74, *141–53*, 173, 186–91, 197–99

Memoirs of a Survivor, 5, 13, 19–21, 24, 31–37, 98, 141, 160, 200–204
"Old Chief Mshlanga, The," 111
"Old John's Place," 108, 110–14
"Old Woman and a Cat, An," 5
Particularly Cats, 24
"Pig, The," 109–14
Proper Marriage, A , 7, 174, 185
"Report on the Threatened City," 5
Retreat from Innocence, 5, 19, 52, 126, 153
Ripple from the Storm, A, 7, 8, 150, 185, 209
"Room, A," 5
Sentimental Agents, The, 17, 211
Shikasta, 15, 17, 19, 22, 60–68, 97, 99, 149, 153–68, 200–4, 205, 210
Sirian Experiments, The, 17, 18, 65, 151, 166, 205
"Small Personal Voice, The," 24, 37
"Story of a Non-marrying Man, The," 108
Summer before the Dark, The, 5, 13, 21, 72, 85, 86–93, 98, 139, 141, 197–99, 207–9, 213–24
Temptation of Jack Orkney, The, 5, 87, 89
"To Room Nineteen," 5, 87
"Trinket Box, The," 109–14
"Winter in July," 87, 111

Lilith, 3
"Literature of the Fantastic," 222
London, 11, 12, 13, 75, 78, 92, 118, 134, 176
Los Angeles Times, 3

McDarrah, Fred, 219–20
machismo, 78–79, 80–81
Madame Bovary (Flaubert), 194
madness, 22, 126–41
Madwoman in the Attic, The (Gilbert and Gubar), 21, 94–95
Mailer, Norman, 85
Making of the Representative from Planet 8, The, 3, 16, 151
Malamud, Bernard, 216
mandala, 88
Mann, Thomas, 73–74, 101, 185
Manuel, Frank and Fritzie, 143, 148, 153n
Man Who Died, The (Lawrence), 85
Man Without Qualities, The (Musil), 115–25
Marder, Herbert, 14
marriage, 7, 61–68, 171, 198, 220

Marriages between Zones Three, Four, and Five, The, 16, 21, *60–68*, 155, 163, 205–9, 212
Martha Quest, 6, 24, 74, *141–53*, 173, 186–91, 197–99
Marx, 106
Marxism, 23, 24, 101, 127, 177, 219
Massachusetts Review, 141, 152n
Masters and Johnson, 83
maternal, 92, 101
Memoirs of a Survivor, 5, 13, 19–21, 24, *31–37*, 98, 141, 160, 200–204
mercury, 63–65
Mermaid and the Minotaur, The (Dinnerstein), 99
Milliners of Marylebone, The, 18
Milton, John, 200–204
Möglichkeitssinn, 123
Moll Flanders (Defoe), 37
Morel, Paul, 6
Morris, William, 41
Mortimer, Penelope, 87
motherhood, 5, 198
Mother Sugar, 45, 69, 104, 130, 179
Mountbatten, Lord, 17, 222
Mrs. Bridge (Connell), 87
Mrs. Dalloway, 11
Mumford, Lewis, 151, 153n
Musil, Robert, 115–25
myth, 32, 83
Myth of the Eternal Return, The (Eliade), 152
mysticism, 154

naming, 49–50
narrative modes, 38
Nation, 4, 171n
New Left Review, 5
New Republic, 22, 70, 177n
New Statesman and Nation, 4, 5
Newton, Sir Isaac, 2
New Yorker, 4
New York Review of Books, 22, 125, 200n, 204n
New York Times, 2, 22, 192n
New York Times Book Review, 4, 204n
Nora, 89
Notebooks/Memoirs/Archives (Taylor), 19
Nott, Kathleen, 80–81, 84
"Novel and the Feelings, The," (Lawrence), 197
novel, the, 55
Novelistic Vision of Doris Lessing, The (Rubenstein), 19

Novels of Doris Lessing, The (Schlueter), 19, 76

Oates, Joyce Carol, 13, 22, 87, 174–76
Odysseus, 14, 88
"Of Mud and Other Matters: The Children of Violence" (Jouve), 20
Oh, Calcutta (Tynan), 220
"Old Chief Mshlanga, The," 111
"Old John's Place," 108, 110–14
Old Testament, 201–4
"Old Woman and a Cat, An," 5
orgasm, 49, 80–86, 103
Orwell, George, 126–27
Other, 61
outer space, 20–21, 115

parapsychology, 208
parody, 5, 9, 19, 78, 80
Particularly Cats, 24
Partisan Review, 197
patriarchal, 6, 12, 24, 94–100
Patten, Margaret, 12
Pickering, Jean, 21, 94–100
"Pig, The," 109–14
Plato, 142, 148
Plumed Serpent, The (Lawrence), 82–83
Poe, Edgar Allan, 55
politics, 20
Politics, The, 136–41
Portrait of Dorian Gray, The (Wilde), 44
Portrait of the Artist as a Young Man, A (Joyce), 95
possession, 107–14
Pound, Ezra, 108
Prison Notebooks (Gramsci), 37
prizes, literary, 2
Proper Marriage, A, 7, 174, 185
prophesy, 126
Proust, Marcel, 73
psychic, 132
psychoanalysis, 5, 102
Psychology of Sex (Ellis), 6
psychopolitics, 126
Pumpkin-Eater, The (Mortimer), 87

Quest, Martha, 4, 5, 6, 8, 12, 13, 14, 15, 18, 33–35, 50, 94–100, 117–25, 128–41, *141–53*, 173–76, 184–91, 205–9, 218–19

racial, 4, 171
racism, 4, 40, 43

radical, 37
Rainbow, The (Lawrence), 23, 71
Ramparts, 22
Rawlings, Susan, 87, 141
Real and Apparent Structures, 18, 24
realism, 31, 43
"Report on the Threatened City," 5
Retreat from Innocence, 5, 19, 52, 126, 153
Rich, Adrienne, 22, 88, 181–82
Ripple from the Storm, A, 7, 8, 150, 185, 209
Robinson Crusoe (Defoe), 35, 36
roman idéologique, 18
"Room, A," 5
Room of One's Own, A (Woolf), 70
Rose, Ellen Cronan, 5, 17, 19, 22, 141–53
Rubenstein, Roberta, 16, 19, 21, 60–68, 143
Rumi, Jalaluddin, 19

Sage, Lorna, 19, 20
St. John of the Cross, 192
St. Mawr (Lawrence), 78
Sand, George, 191
Saturday Review, 4
schizophrenia, 134–41, 190
Schlueter, Paul, 19, 76
Schorer, Mark, 72
science fiction, 155–68, 190
Scott, Robert Falcon, 205
Scrutiny, 23
Second Sex, The (de Beauvoir), 1
Sentimental Agents, The, 17, 211
sexual relations, 76–79
sexual stereotypes, 76–79
"Shadow of the Third, The," 49, 55, 105
Shah, Idries, 2, 19, 143, 147, 152n, 201–4
Shammat, 15, 156–63, 202–4, 211
Shelley, Percy Bysshe, 41
Sherban, George (Johor), 162–68, 202–4
Sherban, Rachel, 164
Shikasta, 15, 17, 19, 22, 60–68, 97, 99, 149, 153–68, 200–204, 205, 210
Short Stories and Short Fictions, 1880–1980 (Hanson), 107
Showalter, Elaine, 94
Sinbad the Sailor, 14, 88
Singleton, Mary, 19, 145, 153n
Sirian Experiments, The, 17, 18, 65, 151, 166, 205
Sirius, 15
Skinner, B. F., 203

"Small Personal Voice, The," 24, 37
Smith, Ian, 41, 42
Snow, C. P., 173
Somers, Jane (pseudonym of Doris Lessing), 2, 3, 4, 17, 18, 23, 24, 113, 213–14
Sons and Lovers (Lawrence), 95
South Africa, 74–76, 171
Southern Rhodesia (Zimbabwe), 4, 5, 6, 20, 39–41, 42–43, 195
SOWF, 158–68, 201–4
space fiction, 3
Spilka, Mark, 21, 23, 69–86
Sprague, Claire, 21, 44, 209–12
Stapledon, Olaf, 156, 160–61, 167n
Stendhal, 24
Stern, Thomas, 8, 52, 118
Stewart, Grace, 94, 100n
Stimpson, Catharine, 5
"Story of a Non-marrying Man, The," 108
Substance under Pressure (Draine), 19
Suez crisis, 40–41
Sufism, 2, 17, 143, 147, 152n, 162–64, 201–4, 205–9
suicide, 87
sulpher, 63–65
Summer before the Dark, The, 5, 13, 21, 72, 85, 86–93, 98, 139, 141, 197–99, 207–9, 213–14
Summerson, Esther, 11
"Sun between Their Feet, The," 110
symbolism, 62–65
Swedenborg, 2
S/Z (Barthes), 167n

Tass, 41
Tayler, Alfred Cook, (Michael) (Lessing's father), 15, 54
Tayler, Doris May (Doris Lessing), 15
Tayler, Emily Maude (McVeagh) (Lessing's mother), 15
Tayler, Harry (Lessing's brother), 15
Taylor, Jenny, 4, 19–21
Temptation of Jack Orkney, The, 5, 87, 89
Themba, Charlie, 10, 105
Thinking about Women (Ellman), 190
This Sex Which Isn't One (Irigaray), 102, 106n
Thorpe, Michael, 19
Tiger, Virginia, 21, 23, 86–93, 221–23
Time and Tide, 80
Times (London), 22, 173n
Times Literary Supplement, 4
Tolstoy, 1, 24

Tono-Bungay (Wells), 11
"To Room Nineteen," 5, 87
"Trinket Box, The," 109–14
Tulliver, Maggie, 6
Turgenev, 1
Turner, Mary, 171–72
Tynan, Kenneth, 220

Ulysses, 10
utopia, 12, 15, 38, 102, 117, 150–53
Utopian Thought in the Western World
   (Frank and Fritzie Manuel), 143, 153n

vaginal orgasm, 82–86
Vahshi, 16, 67
Van Gogh, Vincent, 10
veld (veldt), 17, 60, 132, 171, 173
Verne, Jules, 155
Vidal, Gore, 15, 22
Village Voice, 22, 218n
violence, 175–76
Vlastos, Marion, 21, 22, 126–41
Von Daniken, Erich, 207
Vonnegut, Kurt, 190, 201, 216

War of the Worlds, The (Wells), 155
Washington Post, 3, 213n, 215n

Watkins, Charles, 14, 135–41, 193–96, 207
Watkins, Jesse, 136–41
Waugh, Evelyn, 31
Wells, H. G., 155
West, Rebecca, 22, 191–92
Wilde, Oscar, 44
Wilder, Laura Ingalls, 142
Wilson, Angus, 189
"Winter in July," 87, 111
Women in Love (Lawrence), 21, 69–86
women's liberation, 22, 117, 188
Woolf, Virginia, 2, 9, 47, 51, 56, 72, 96
World War I (Great War), 8, 124
World War II, 124
World We Imagine, The (Schorer), 72
Wulf, Anna Freeman, 3, 4, 8, 10, 11,
   33–35, 45–60, 69–86, 101–7, 115–25,
   126–41, 177–81, 192–96, 197–99, 211–12

Yardley, Jonathan, 22, 215–217
Yeats, William Butler, 1
Yellow Notebook, 51–52

Zambia, 172
Zimbabwe (Southern Rhodesia), 4, 5, 39